D0535464

WAGNER IN PERFORMANCE

WAGNER IN PERFORMANCE

Edited by

Barry Millington and Stewart Spencer

YALE UNIVERSITY PRESS
NEW HAVEN AND LONDON · 1992

In memory of Sir Reginald Goodall

Set in Baskerville by Textflow Services Ltd., Belfast
and printed and bound by Biddles Ltd., Guildford and Kings Lynn

Library of Congress Cataloguing-in-Publication Data

Wagner in performance / edited by Barry Millington and Stewart Spencer.
  p.   cm.
  Includes bibliographical references and index.
  ISBN 0-300-05718-0
  1. Wagner, Richard, 1813–1883—Performances.2. Opera—Production and direction. 3. Performance practice (Music)—19th century.
4. Performance practice (Music)—20th century. I. Millington, Barry.
II. Spencer, Stewart.
  ML410.W19W12   1992
  782.1'092—dc20
  92-4964
                                                                              CIP
                                                                              MN

Contents

List of Illustrations

Introduction

Surprisingly little of the ever-increasing volume of Wagner literature
is devoted to the subject of Wagner in performance. Recent innovative productions — notably, the controversial *Ring* cycle presented at
the 1976 Bayreuth Festival — have sparked renewed interest in
Wagner's 'art-work of the future'. The present volume, addressed to
both specialists and the opera-going public, concentrates on particular aspects of the performance and reception of Wagner's works in
Europe and America. The essays by a group of leading scholars and
practitioners range widely, from the practical questions of staging
the operas to a consideration of the concept of 'fidelity' or 'authenticity' in performance. None the less, certain common themes emerge
which will, we hope, cast new light on the reception of Wagner's
works in the opera house.

The first theme concerns the revolutionary nature of Wagner's
demands on his interpreters, whether they be instrumentalists, singers,
or stage personnel. Combining a theatrical (as opposed to an operatic) background with a German Romantic's interest in the psychology of the characters he created, Wagner called for a new type of
singing actor who was required to give no less attention to the drama
than to the music. Dissatisfaction with existing conditions led him to
attempt to reform the system, first from within and latterly by found-
ing the Bayreuth Festival. Yet even in Bayreuth circumstances con-
spired to prevent him from realizing his ambition of 'model
performances'. It was an ambition which, as Mike Ashman points out
in his essay on changing production styles, Cosima and Siegfried
Wagner misguidedly sought to perpetuate, creating a monumental
performance style at odds with the 'mimic-musical improvisation'
(*GS* IX, 149–50; *PW* V, 150) that Wagner himself envisaged in his
later theoretical writings. Aspects of Bayreuth's fossilized style of
performance, and reactions to it, constitute a leitmotif of this volume.

Another common theme is the exponential increase in popularity of Wagner's music dramas — and this in spite of the fact that, at least for the first two decades or so of the twentieth century, the musical world, to quote Otto Klemperer, was 'in opposition to Wagner'. It is not entirely irrelevant to ask how Wagner himself might have reacted to this development. While its financial implications would no doubt have delighted him, the very idea of repertory performances of his works would almost certainly have filled him with horror. As Matthias Theodor Vogt reminds us, the *Ring* was conceived for a single run of performances, after which the theatre would have been torn down and the score — having served its revolutionary purpose — committed to the flames. Wagner's Young Hegelian cast of mind convinced him of the inevitability of historical change. Time and again he complained at performances of those of his works which he himself had outgrown; and, as Clive Brown recalls in his essay on nineteenth-century performing practices, the composer regarded Mozart's operas, for example, as quintessential products of the eighteenth century, which could not be made relevant to a later age by performing them in modern dress. In the case of his own Romantic operas and music dramas, however, it is precisely this ability to generate new interpretations and to assume new meanings for each successive generation that has given rise to the astonishingly multifarious approaches to the works seen on stage in recent decades. Indeed, there is some irony in the fact that a body of works once protected with almost religious awe and reverence should have become one of the chief beneficiaries of the post-war revolution in stagecraft — a revolution, moreover, initiated in, and constantly inspired by, Bayreuth itself. The changes documented by Patrick Carnegy and Mike Ashman, in their essays on stage design and production, raise profound aesthetic questions about the realization of opera on stage: questions about the 'authority' of the composer vis-à-vis the director and, indeed, the audience; about the sanctity of the text, score, and stage directions; and about the role of art itself in society. These issues are discussed in terms of their practical consequences by Carnegy and Ashman, and from a theoretical point of view by Jean-Jacques Nattiez, in his semiological approach to the subject. It is our hope that these three essays will raise the debate on opera production above the superficial level on which it is all too often conducted.

Not only are Wagner's works among the most popular pieces in the late twentieth-century stage repertory (exceeded only by Verdi and Mozart), they are also widely available on record, a development which, by dispensing with one of the essential elements of the total work of art, may well have inspired mixed feelings in the composer. Certainly, his Romantic attitude to modern technology prejudiced him against the new medium: 'Recently, when the phonograph was mentioned', Cosima Wagner noted in her diary, 'he spoke of the foolishness of expecting anything from such inventions — people were turning themselves into machines' (*CT*, 7 October 1882). None the less, the development is too important to be ignored and — as David Breckbill indicates — it provides us with important evidence in assessing changing vocal styles.

The third of the themes that recurs throughout the present collection of essays concerns what might be called the pluralism of approaches to Wagner in performance. Within years of the composer's death, arguments were already raging over the 'authenticity' of vocal and conducting styles, and the debate has continued throughout the twentieth century, as Christopher Fifield and Desmond Shawe-Taylor explain in their discussions of representative conductors and singers, respectively. It is a pluralism, too, which exists on an ideological level, as Amanda Glauert and Joseph Horowitz make clear in their microcosmic surveys of the musical life of late nineteenth-century Vienna and New York.

The death of Sir Reginald Goodall in May 1990 robbed the world of a leading Wagnerian performer. His merits as both coach and conductor are described elsewhere in these pages, and it is fitting that this volume should be dedicated to his memory.

The editors wish to thank all the contributors for their cheerful cooperation, and Robert Baldock and Harry Haskell of Yale University Press for their editorial suggestions and wholehearted support throughout the project.

Barry Millington
Stewart Spencer

Chapter 1

Conducting Wagner: The Search for Melos

Christopher Fifield

> The right comprehension of the *melos* is the sole guide to the right tempo; these two things are inseparable: the one implies and qualifies the other — Richard Wagner, *Über das Dirigieren*

Wagner defined *melos* as a singing style which shaped melodic phrases with rubato, tonal variation, and shifting accent, and its practice presented a problem for his interpreters, particularly conductors. Rather than survey all conductors from Wagner to Walter or Seidl to Solti, this essay focuses on several since his day who have accepted or rejected this Wagnerian ideal.

Until recently the opera conductor barely received a mention in reviews; when he did, it was invariably to report whether or not he had controlled his forces well. In 1882 Hans Richter's contribution to *Tannhäuser* was limited in the *Musical Times* to 'Herr Richter has not yet presented us with anything better', but in 1990 a reviewer of *Otello* conducted by Carlos Kleiber wrote in a British Sunday newspaper that what the maestro (a much devalued word since Verdi and Wagner) 'does better than anyone else I have ever seen is to combine fierce incisiveness of gesture with a supple, rounded touch, so that the loudest sounds never come out nasty or hard-edged. He strokes Verdi's gloomy orchestral pictures with his left hand, just edging the chords into place, and then thwacks the weight in with his right hand'.[1]

Wagner neither 'edged' nor 'thwacked' when he conducted at the 1877 Wagner festival in London. It would appear that he was a fine conductor in anybody else's music but not always in his own. Richter wrote in his diary of 'great uncertainties' in Act I of *Der fliegende Holländer*. 'The impression made upon me by the Master's conducting was of complete insecurity and, unbelievably, ignorance of, or even more, total obliviousness to his own works. Thereafter the Master handed the baton over to me, as he became aware of the friction amongst the performers. Half jokingly he said to the leader, August Wilhelmj, "It seems I have upset you nicely!"'[2] Shaw described Wagner's beat as 'nervous and abrupt'.[3]

It is not easy to make an English orchestra nervous, but Wagner's tense neuralgic glare at the players as they waited for the beat with their bows poised above the strings was hard upon the sympathetic men, whilst the intolerable length of the pause exasperated the tougher spirits. When all were effectually disconcerted, the composer's baton was suddenly jerked upwards, as if by a sharp twinge of gout in his elbow; and, after a moment of confusion, a scrambling start was made. During the performance Wagner's glare never relaxed: he never looked pleased. When he wanted more emphasis he stamped; when the division into bars was merely conventional he disdained counting, and looked daggers — spoke them too, sometimes — at innocent instrumentalists who were enjoying the last few bars of their rest without any suspicion that the impatient composer had just discounted half a stave or so and was angrily waiting for them. When he laid down the baton it was with the air of a man who hoped he might never be condemned to listen to such a performance again.[4]

Memoirs by two members of the opera orchestra in Vienna also report difficulties. The viola player Bachrich played in a concert in 1875 when Wagner conducted orchestral extracts from the *Ring*, ending with the final scene from *Götterdämmerung*.

Everything went very well. Then came the difficult place [twenty bars from the end] where the $\frac{6}{8}$ passage changes to $\frac{3}{2}$. I do not know why it happened; perhaps the Master was still excited by the events preceding it,[5] or perhaps he overlooked something in the score; in short there was a sudden crisis and things became very difficult for us, the more so as the Master's baton became very unclear, hung in the air, and finally functioned no longer. At such crucial moments the Vienna orchestra is unique. Each and every one knew how to put out their feelers and adjust, how to understand the energetic intervention by the leader and a loud life-saving drum roll; in short we all got back on the rails.[6]

At the end of 1875 Wagner returned to Vienna to prepare *Lohengrin*.[7] Joseph Sulzer wrote his impressions from the opera orchestra pit.

Wagner in no way handled a baton like a professional conductor. In some places the Master would conduct extremely precisely and rhythmically, at others, when either tired or wrapped in his own thoughts, nonchalantly or not at all; as a result an unholy confusion would sometimes have occurred were it not for a rescuing deus ex machina in the shape of Hans Richter who intervened at such moments. In fact Richter had foreseen such potential calamities, and in honour of the Master had undertaken the job of timpanist, from which seat he conducted with his sticks without Wagner noticing.[8]

There are few details of Wagner's rehearsal comments in *Lohengrin* beyond Sulzer's observation that in bar 54 of the Prelude the cymbals should not damp, that the tempo of the postlude to the third-act Bridal Chorus was markedly slower than usual, with the composer's explanation that if taken faster 'it would bear an unwelcome similarity to . . .' — and here, because Wagner's voice became 'an incomprehensible murmur', Sulzer speculates that he said one of Mendelssohn's *Songs without Words*.

Felix Mottl, once Wagner's personal assistant, kept diaries containing information which he later transcribed into the published vocal scores of *Lohengrin* and *Tannhäuser*.

7.11.1875 Richard Wagner stages his *Tannhäuser* at the Opera House. Venus aria very calm, steady quavers, then faster. Processional march very brisk alla breve.

2.3.1876 Richard Wagner personally conducted *Lohengrin* at the Opera. Richter and Sucher were afraid that, as the Master had not conducted operatic performances for such a long time, something might happen, so they placed themselves right and left in the orchestra in case they could help in the event of any faltering. However, they soon gave up any cause for concern as they saw how, as well as using the wonderfully suggestive power of his personality, he also directed the entire opera with the greatest perfection in technique. It was a wonderful evening . . . Prelude very, very slow and infinitely broad. Prelude in A♭ minor to 'Du trugest zu ihm meine Klage' very broad and expressive. Swan's Chorus trumpets began very *pianissimo*. Tempo began slowly, then much increased. At the end (*ff* A major) very fiery and brisk. No portamenti from the singers! Everything strictly in tempo! No recitative! 'Viel lieber tot als feig' not fast, orchestra muted *fp*; procession of the knights to the contest scene quite brisk. Herald, everything in tempo. Prayer in E♭ not too slow. Fight very fast. Final chorus of Act I not fast to begin with, only then gradually quickening.

Prelude to Act II, cor anglais [bars 18–19] first *mf*, the repeat almost inaudibly soft. After 'Gott' (Ortrud) a frighteningly long pause. The same before 'Du wilde Seherin'. The bass clarinet F♯ minor motif [a bar before 'Weißt du, wer dieser Held' (Ortrud)] very slow. Then the dialogue very flowing. 'In Liebe' B♭ major long, and joined to the A♭ and C♭ (oboe and muted horns). Oboes 'ins fernste Elend schickst' very strong crescendo. The figure ['Um Gott, was klagest du mich an?' . . . (Elsa)] very calm. The call to the gods very rapid and strong and without a pause before the triplets begin. 'Nur eine Kraft' really slow. Interlude [marked 'Schneller' five bars before 'Du Ärmste kannst wohl nie ermessen' (Elsa)] alternately fast [tremolando strings] and slow [winds]. Act III. Prelude. Not quick, but fiery! The Wedding Chorus 'Rauschen des Festes seid nun entronnen', a marked pulling-back of the tempo.

26.5.1876   Wagner says that the Prelude to *Die Meistersinger* is taken too slowly throughout. It should be a strong march tempo.[9]

Apart from the performance on 29 August 1882, during which he impulsively nudged Hermann Levi aside to conduct the last scene of *Parsifal*, Wagner did not conduct in Bayreuth. His concerns (and his son, Siegfried, eventually adopted the same priorities during his own Bayreuth career) were almost totally with the staging of his operas. Wagner had a poor opinion of the German Kapellmeister; what he had to say can be found in *Über das Dirigieren* (On conducting), but though his criticisms were directed at his predecessors, he had no time either for his contemporaries and predicted a gloomy future for his music. Not even the most devoted of his acolytes was immune from his complaint that no conductor fully understood either his tempi or the inner meaning of his music (he soon abandoned the metronome and used tempo markings instead), above all *melos*.

The one man who might have satisfied him was Hans von Bülow, but their working relationship was doomed from the moment Cosima left Bülow for Wagner. Apart from the composer himself and Liszt, who conducted the premiere of *Lohengrin*, Bülow was the first recognized interpreter of Wagner's music. After hearing *Rienzi* in Dresden in 1842, Bülow devoted himself to the composer and, as Hofkapellmeister in Munich, gave the premieres there of *Tristan und Isolde* (1865) and *Die Meistersinger von Nürnberg* (1868). In his meticulous preparation and rehearsals from memory (for five years he had been preparing a piano score of *Tristan*), Bülow virtually developed the system by which operas have since come to be staged everywhere, beginning with individual coaching of his répétiteurs so that they could prepare the singers to his satisfaction. He then rehearsed the singers both singly and in ensembles before the production rehearsals began. This schedule was also used for the orchestra with sectional and then full orchestral rehearsals before combining players and singers in *sitzproben* and stage rehearsals (there were eleven pre-dress rehearsals for *Tristan* before the final dress rehearsal).

Bülow was a consummate musician of formidable ability, absolute self-command, and acute intellectual power of interpretation, but he was quarrelsome, nervous, passionate, and given to extremes of mood. Felix Weingartner thought he lacked the necessary instinct for working in opera and that by devoting his entire attention to the orchestra, he ignored his singers. Bülow's search for Wagner's *melos* was dismissed by Weingartner as musical aberrations and excessive rubato. However, Richard Strauss, a Bülow protégé, had the highest regard for his intellect, his analysis of phrasing, and his grasp of the psychological content of Wagner's music.

Without Bülow, Wagner gathered assistants around him to form the so-called *Nibelungenkanzlei* (Nibelung Chancellery), first to copy and correct scores and parts, and then to assist in the two Festivals of 1876 and 1882. From 1892 this became a *Stilbildungsschule* (school for the development of style), and from now on devotion to the composer's ideals was paramount. A Bayreuth tradition was established, though until the survivors of the early years died out, leaving Cosima to define it alone, there were varying interpretations of just what that tradition was. Clearly, however, any deviation from the unwritten rules would lead to retribution, even a ban from the Master's theatre. There were those who were totally excluded (the Jews Mahler, Blech, Klemperer, and Walter), those who never advanced from rehearsal room to podium (Zumpe and Weingartner) and those, once favoured, who fell (Busch, Seidl, Strauss, who returned only after Cosima's and Siegfried's deaths in 1930; Mottl, whose musical activities outside Bayreuth were disapproved of; and even Cosima's own son-in-law, Franz Beidler, who sinned by demanding more than two performances of *Parsifal* in 1906).

Richter was impregnable to Cosima's artistic interference (the usual basis of the problem she had with her conductors). In October 1866 he came to Wagner at Tribschen to copy *Die Meistersinger* and assist as répétiteur and chorusmaster. He returned in 1870 to copy *Siegfried*. In 1875 he made a guest appearance in Vienna, whereupon he virtually took over all the major musical organizations there until the end of the century. His operatic repertory was dominated by Wagner; his last appearance was at Bayreuth in 1912 with his 141st *Meistersinger*.

The triumvirate of Richter, Mottl, and Levi excelled in *Die Meistersinger*, *Tristan*, and *Parsifal*, respectively. Shaw wrote:

Can we hope to replace the three great conductors? . . . Whoever has heard the *Tristan* prelude conducted by Richter on one of his fortunate evenings at St James's Hall, or the *Parsifal* prelude as he conducted it on one memorable occasion at the Albert Hall, knows more than Bayreuth can tell him about these works. Herr

Levi shows what invaluable results can be produced by unwearying care and exhaustive study. Herr Felix Mottl's strictness, refinement, and severe taste make the orchestra go with the precision and elegance of a chronometer. . . . To make an orchestra play the prelude to *Parsifal* as Herr Levi makes them play it is a question of taking as much pains and as much thought as he. To make them play the introduction to the third act of *Die Meistersinger* as they play it for Richter is a question of the gift of poetic creation in musical execution. The perfection attained by Herr Mottl is the perfection of photography. Richter's triumphs and imperfections are those of the artist's hand.[10]

Richter was not an intellectual conductor ('*Parsifal* is no work for today's rabble in their boxes; in today's theatres it will sound like an Ave Maria from the slanderous mouth of a rouged street-walker' [11]), but he was an intuitive musician and one for whom orchestral players had high regard. He saw the problems in finding successors to carry the Wagner torch, though when asked whether Wagner's works were difficult for a young conductor, he said: 'If I have to judge the abilities of a young Kapellmeister, I never give him a work by Wagner, for anyone can conduct them after a fashion; neither special gifts nor presence of mind are required. To such a young artist I give a score by Lortzing or Weber, or a little French opera by Auber or suchlike. Then I can see what's in the man'.[12] But Richter could not be so candid in his opinion of Siegfried Wagner as a conductor because he was too close to the younger generation of the Wagner family.

Mottl told us that Richter was summoned to Bayreuth by Cosima Wagner for his opinion of whether Siegfried Wagner, who hitherto was destined to be an architect, had it in him to be a musician. One morning they all sat down in the Festspielhaus and gave young Siegfried the prelude to *Das Rheingold* to conduct. After sixty or eighty bars Hans Richter took Frau Cosima's hand and, in a sobbing voice, whispered: 'He can do it, he can do it, the worthy son of a great father'. I, too, often experienced Siegfried Wagner's conducting. Once I was standing with a few acquaintances who belonged to the Villa Wahnfried's most intimate circle, and one of them, whose name makes no difference, said to me: 'You have had the good luck, Herr Schnitzler, to experience the most significant performance of the *Ring* that has ever been given in Bayreuth'. As answer all I could do was to point silently at the large marble plaque under which we were standing and upon which were engraved the names of the conductor and cast of the first performance of the *Ring* in Bayreuth.[13]

It was a certain detachment that set Richter apart, particularly from Mahler, with whom he was constantly compared in Vienna from 1897. Charles Villiers Stanford, who considered Richter and Bülow to be 'the archetypes from whom modern conducting has descended', contrasted the latter's spontaneity and instinctiveness with the former's 'straightforwardness'.[14] Yet despite this solidity, Richter was not without emotion. Even in his eighty-first performance of *Siegfried* (in 1909, thirty-three years after he first conducted it), 'there were certain passages that affected him deeply; for example the moment when Siegfried brings the Ring and Tarnhelm out of the cave after slaying the dragon. To him they are no more than pretty objects, but as the horns steal in with the Rheingold theme the orchestra beautifully tells us what they are and what they mean. To quote Richter's own words: "Tears run down my cheeks each time at this point".'[15] Photographs of Richter personify him as Hans Sachs; indeed, the breadth of the music of *Die Meistersinger* had its counterpart in his own nature. On the other hand, in *Tristan*, which has to live and breathe in a state of perpetual incandescence, he could be phlegmatic. In Adrian Boult's view, 'the mercurial Wagner of *Tristan* would be [Nikisch's], but the measured and solid *Meistersinger* was the property of Hans Richter'.[16] Richter's view was overall, seeing the architecture of the page rather than the inner life of a melodic line; in short he was no seeker of *melos*.

Felix Mottl, on the other hand, was. He had a passion for *Tristan* and on Christmas Day 1873 wrote, 'My study of *Tristan* begins now. I'm quite ill with longing for this work. I carry it around with me like the picture of a beloved . . .'.[17] This was a fateful work for him; it was the first and last opera he conducted in Bayreuth, and during his hundredth performance of it, on 21 June 1911 in Munich, he had a heart attack after which he died. At the time he was also working on a piano edition of the opera. Shaw described a performance of the Overture to *Der fliegende Holländer* which showed how Mottl's conducting style (a clue in the search for *melos*) owed much to Wagner's. '[His] treatment of those batteries of chords which lead up to the first *forte* in the quick movement reminded me of Wagner himself, whom I once saw stamping to them with his foot, and, I am afraid, swearing at the band between his teeth because they would not hit them out tremendously enough for him'.[18] The search for *melos*, then, did not preclude demonstrations of force. In the *Tannhäuser* Overture Shaw went on to praise Mottl's ability to vary his tempi, and to give his players space and time with great effect.

Have we not often shrunk from the coarse and unsatisfactory effect of the three trombones at the climax of the Pilgrims' March

in the first section of the overture? Richter . . . insists on the full
power of the *fortissimo*. Mottl effected a magical transformation.
The chant was as powerful as Richter could have desired; and yet it
was beautiful, broad, easy, with a *portamento* which an Italian singer
might have envied . . . . Instead of keeping strict Procrustean time
for the florid work of the violins, thus forcing the trombones to
chop their phrases so as to fit the accompaniment, Mottl gave the
trombones a free hand, allowing them to give the time to the
whole band, and making the violins wait, when necessary, between
the bars, so to speak, until the slow-speaking brass instruments had
turned their phrases with unembarrassed majesty. The effect was
magnificent . . . It is one of Mottl's salient characteristics as a
conductor that he seizes on the accents of the music with immense
energy . . . In short, though Mottl is a very forcible conductor, and,
in spite of all that has been said about his slowness, a very fast
conductor when the right tempo happens to be very fast, he is not
in the least an impetuous one: Mottl's face and gesture, entreat-
ing, imploring, remonstrating, deprecating, pleading, would have
softened hearts of stone.[19]

Arthur Nikisch was not a member of the *Nibelungenkanzlei*, but he
played the violin under Wagner in Beethoven's Ninth Symphony at
the ceremony of the laying of the foundation stone for the Bayreuth
Festspielhaus in 1872. He understood the *melos* theory and practised
it with a fluid baton technique. According to Boult, '*Tristan* . . . fitted
Nikisch like a glove. His impetuous irregularities of tempo . . . and
the glowing warmth of tone he drew from the orchestra must surely
have realized Wagner's deepest desires'.[20] Elsewhere Boult wrote, 'I
can conceive nothing more electric and memorable than two performances I heard him give in one week in Covent Garden in the
winter of 1906',[21] while his unpublished diary (15 January 1907)
describes Nikisch as 'magnificent. He is wonderful at the concerts
but in opera he is perfectly extraordinary'. Tchaikovsky compared
him to Bülow, the first practitioner of *melos*. 'In the same proportion
as [Bülow] is full of movement, restless, effective in the sometimes
very noticeable manner of his gestures, so is Nikisch quiet, sparing of
superfluous movements, and yet so extraordinarily commanding,
powerful, full of self-control'.[22]

In April 1912 Nikisch conducted a concert of Wagner orchestral
excerpts in New York. 'The Prelude to *Tristan* was played with a
wonderful surge of passion, an ebb and flow of emotional intensity, an
unerring marking of the melodic line. . . . The Prelude to *Meistersinger*
had imposing weight and a splendid stress of passionate utterance.
Where the three themes came together there was an extraordinarily

clear leading of their respective voices without a loss of the unity of the whole effect'.[23] Nikisch never conducted at Bayreuth, where concert conductors with international careers were thought unsuitable, though he would have done so in 1924 had he lived.

Another conductor at that time who (except on one occasion) was excluded from Bayreuth's podium was Anton Seidl. The reason was probably because his musical activities, like Nikisch's, were largely centred elsewhere, yet he had been an original member of the *Nibelungenkanzlei*, an assistant in 1876, Wagner's pianist until 1878, and conductor of Angelo Neumann's touring opera company, which performed only Wagner's operas. Wagner himself told Seidl to 'take more notice of the stage, follow my stage instructions, and you will then certainly encounter my music'.[24] Wagner repeatedly told his conductors that the roles of stage and musical director were one and the same; a conductor with no sense of drama had no insight into his music. The tenor Jean de Reszke said of Seidl, 'We feel that things can not go wrong when he is in his chair . . . . If I forget a line . . . I look at Seidl and read it on his lips'.[25] 'He never drowns out our voices with his huge orchestra', was another tribute paid Seidl.[26] Seidl could mould the tempi of Wagner's music to achieve maximum emotional effect.

August Spanuth, writing of Seidl's only Bayreuth appearance (*Parsifal* in 1897), insisted that 'none of the musicians — Levi, Richter and Mottl — were so intimately acquainted with the work or saw it in the process of creation as Anton Seidl did, for it was during the six years that Seidl lived with Wagner that *Parsifal* was composed. . . . All other *Parsifal* conductors allowed themselves to be influenced by Frau Wagner'.[27] This is not true, for Richter never conducted *Parsifal* and Levi (considered by Weingartner to be distinguished by 'the spiritual nature of his interpretation' in which he 'shed everything material and reduced technique to a minimum'[28]) was entrusted by Cosima with the opera for eight festivals until 1894 precisely because he had conducted its premiere in 1882 under Wagner's guidance (and produced a faster overall timing for the opera than most performances since). On the one occasion (1888) when Levi was replaced by Mottl, Cosima evidently interfered to such an extent that the poor man was utterly confused as to which tempi to take. With *Parsifal* it was not Mottl who received Levi's torch but Karl Muck, who was entrusted with the opera in all Bayreuth Festivals between 1901 and 1930.

Herbert Peyser described Muck as having an 'assured, concentrated but, withal, absolutely untheatrical domination', and considered his *Parsifal* as 'the only and the ultimate *Parsifal*; the *Parsifal* in which every phrase was charged with infinities; the *Parsifal* which was neither of this age nor that age but of all time'.[29] By the time Muck retired in 1933 he was a remnant of the previous century. Austere, dogmatic, and passionately devoted to the memory of Wagner, he was the genuine Bayreuthian. Frida Leider recalled his *Ring* in Berlin in 1926:

> Karl Muck took all the tempi much more slowly than those to which we were accustomed. This meant, for the singers, new breath distribution and a different handling of words and phrases . . . . His way of conducting *Parsifal* was a great revelation to me. The singers all feared his slow tempi, and before the first orchestral rehearsal I was somewhat apprehensive . . . . Gradually the unearthly music took possession of me. In the second act, when I began my big scene [as Kundry] with Parsifal, Muck's calmness and clarity enabled me to draw everything out of the role, as I had always previously tried to do. That *Parsifal* was one of my greatest artistic experiences.[30]

Gustav Mahler, one of the most important absentees from Bayreuth, understood *melos*. Like Strauss he was another composer/conductor, but the secret of his technique, like Wagner's, lay in conducting music by phrases, not by barlines. 'Conducting should be a continual elimination of the bar . . . . His baton strokes serve only to emphasise the significant melodic and rhythmic content at any one moment. Consequently he often glides completely over the first beat of a bar, and stresses instead the second or third beat, or wherever the principal emphasis should be placed'.[31] It was precisely this baton technique which had confused Wagner's London players in 1877.

Mahler was able to balance his orchestral forces, keep his singers clearly audible, and reveal the internal complexities of the instrumental accompaniment. His tempi were rapid, filled with dramatic life, and set him apart from the weighted performances which currently emanated from Bayreuth. He had a superb sense of proportion, a feel for dramatic pulse and timed climaxes that thrilled. 'He introduced startling accents and irregular melodic scansions'.[32] Strauss described Mahler to Bülow as 'one of the few modern conductors who knows about tempo modification; and he expressed splendid ideas in general, especially about Wagner's tempos (unlike certain presently accepted Wagner conductors)'.[33]

Mahler went to Vienna in 1897, and shortly thereafter was appointed music director. Richter had been a conductor there for nearly twenty-five years, and they became uneasy colleagues. Mahler heard *Die Meistersinger* under Richter. 'He conducted the first act, in which I enjoyed him enormously, like a master; the second like a schoolmaster; and the third act like a master cobbler'.[34] On the day

after his Vienna début with *Lohengrin* (12 May 1897), Mahler received a letter from an anonymous member of the orchestra:

> Your tempi, your nuances and accentuation — all these were
> Wagnerian in the true sense of the word. The Master himself
> conducted in this way; that is how it used to be played under his
> baton — no more alas! To start with, the Prelude was just as slow as
> it should be. The chorus after Lohengrin's farewell to the swan was
> wonderfully tender . . . . The climax of the prayer was magnificent.
> . . . Then in the second act, there was the passage 'In ferner
> Einsamkeit des Waldes', which nearly always drags . . . , then the
> Prelude to the third act, the wonderfully refined interpretation of
> the love-scene, and so much else besides. Nothing of this has been
> experienced here for years. Your conducting is truly Wagnerian,
> for you know how to modify the tempo with perfect fidelity to the
> Master's intentions. No detail is lost, yet nothing is out of propor-
> tion within the framework of the whole. A fine example was the
> almost imperceptible slowing-down in the opening chorus of the
> third act, in the passage 'Rauschen des Festes seid nun entronnen'.[35]

Felix Weingartner was an assistant at Bayreuth in 1886 and saw how
Cosima influenced Mottl's *Tristan* but later (1888) failed with Richter's *Meistersinger.* Never a tactful man, Weingartner made his views
known and so he never conducted in Bayreuth. In his pamphlet
Bayreuth (1876–96), he strongly attacked what he termed the 'Bayreuth rubato'. Though his target was Bülow and his admirers, he was
also incensed by Cosima's domination of Mottl, successor to Levi as
conductor of the 1888 *Parsifal*:

> They sought to make the clearest passages obscure by hunting out
> insignificant details. Now an inner part of minor importance would
> be given a significance that by no means belonged to it. Now an
> accent that should have been lightly stressed came out *sforzato.*
> Often a so-called 'breath-pause' would be inserted, particularly in
> the case of a crescendo immediately followed by a *piano,* as if the
> music were sprinkled with fermatas. These little tricks were helped
> out by continual alterations and dislocations of tempo. Where a
> gradual animation or a gentle and delicate slowing-up is required
> — often, however, without even that pretext — a violent, spas-
> modic accelerando or ritenuto was made.[36]

Weingartner rejected 'mere metronomic time beating or a senseless
mania for nuance'. The contemporary style which infuriated him was
the extreme and arbitrary deviation from the basic pulse of symphonic movements indulged by the 'tempo rubato conductors',
those on the search for *melos.* Wagner himself had warned against

'arbitrary nuances of tempo', but this warning was ignored by some of his successors. It was they whom Weingartner castigated, and not that unbroken line of conductors noted for their fidelity to the score and absence of mannerism. As he himself remarked in 1905, 'I need mention no names in order to point out that several conductors of importance have refused to have anything to do with these perversions of style'.[37] Richter and Muck would have been meant here. Weingartner identified two distinct styles of Wagner conducting which developed after the composer's death. One began with Bülow and continued through Mottl, Seidl, Nikisch, and Mahler to Furtwängler; the other, his own more purist style, was adopted by Muck, Strauss (a convert from his earlier, more Romantic days), Toscanini, and Knappertsbusch.

Weingartner had declared his approval of Furtwängler after a performance of *Tannhäuser* in Vienna. 'Now that's not bad at all. He keeps to his tempo, you see, and that I like'.[38] As a young man Furtwängler had heard unexceptional performances of the *Ring* in Munich, conducted by one of Wagner's original apprentices, Franz Fischer, and discounted any notion that performances in his day were necessarily superior to those which Wagner had attacked. He pointed out the danger of tradition (defined by Toscanini as the last bad performance) in German theatres, particularly Bayreuth, and urged a continual reappraisal of it against the work itself. 'Only a Wagnerian can end up despising Wagner. Let us ensure that we are not Wagnerians, but that we honour and love Wagner'.[39] His own baton technique suited the Wagnerian *melos*, emphasizing the preparatory or upbeat to indicate melody and orchestral sound, and not the downbeat which showed only rhythm and ensemble (Toscanini used to get furious at Furtwängler's ragged opening chords). Furtwängler had his detractors when it came to opera. Klemperer heard him conduct *Die Meistersinger* in Berlin. 'When there was a symphonic piece for the orchestra alone, it was very good. But when there were singers, it was not so good. He was no opera conductor'.[40] Frida Leider agreed. 'The great concert conductor was always anxious about his reputation in opera [and] in his concentration upon the music he was apt to forget the singers'.[41]

Furtwängler's great rivals in the Wagnerian arena were Toscanini and Knappertsbusch. Both had adopted a purist style, Knappertsbusch having a reputation for solid performances moulded by broad tempi, like his predecessor Karl Muck. Occasionally he would be galvanized into action. At Bayreuth in 1951, 'as if he had realised that the preceding parts of his *Ring* had been less than magnificent, Knappertsbusch suddenly came to life and conducted with colossal power and intensity. (The Funeral March in that performance was the talk of Bayreuth for the rest of the festival; I doubt if Knappertsbusch himself ever brought off such a shattering experience again)'.[42] Toscanini, with his reputation for speed, gave some surprisingly slow performances during his career. Friedelind Wagner was mystified that in Act I of *Parsifal*, Strauss (no young man in 1933) turned in a performance timed at 106 minutes, but Toscanini took 20 minutes longer! It was also a revelation to Ernest Newman when he heard Toscanini conducting *Tristan* in 1931 at Bayreuth. He thought he 'knew that work from end to end and from outside to inside; but I was amazed to find here and there a passage coming on me like a dagger stroke. I found that all, or practically all, he had done was to play the notes just as Wagner directs them to be played'.[43] In 1938 Lawrence Gilman described a performance of Act I of *Die Walküre*: 'What Toscanini gives us is the completeness of the music's truth . . . . Instinctively and always, in playing Wagner, he pursues the *melos*, the melodic principle, into every depth and height and extremity, every detail and ornament, of the tonal structure . . . . And always the beauty and sensibility of phrasing, the poetic penetration, the instant responsiveness to the shape and contour of the musical thought are final and consummate . . . . Toscanini reminds us that song and drama interpenetrate'.[44]

In 1929 Klemperer (who, early in life, had seen Cosima Wagner's stereotyped *Lohengrin* at Bayreuth and heard an over-romanticized *Tristan* under Nikisch in Hamburg) said of Toscanini's *Meistersinger* in Berlin that he 'had not heard a comparably complete performance of the work in any other theatre in the world', and marvelled at Toscanini's 'simple, natural and honest style'. The following year he described Toscanini's Bayreuth *Tristan* performances as 'more than beautiful, they are right'.[45] Early in 1929 Klemperer had been in charge of the Berlin Kroll Opera's production of *Der fliegende Holländer*, a milestone in twentieth-century Wagner productions. It was a fresh approach twenty years before Bayreuth rejuvenated its own ideas through Wieland Wagner. There were vitriolic attacks in the press: 'Tempi were ridiculously overdriven, finer dynamic shadings eliminated and all expression reduced to a minimum'.[46] In 1933 he again aroused fury with his pioneering staging of the original version of *Tannhäuser*, but Hitler's National Socialists soon banned it. On a personal note, the present writer attended the final rehearsal of a concert performance of Act I of *Die Walküre* at the Royal Festival Hall in London when Klemperer, barely able to move, seemed to spend more effort on turning the pages of his score than on conducting. His only comment after an uninterrupted run-through with the orchestra and singers, prepared by his assistant Reginald Goodall, was to the trumpets and trombones. In the passage immediately after

Siegmund extracts the sword from the ash tree and tells Sieglinde 'Siegmund, den Wälsung siehst du, Weib!' (Woman, you see [before you] Siegmund, the Volsung) there is a series of 'hairpins' (crescendi and diminuendi) in the brass parts, but no instruction from Wagner regarding how loudly they should peak. Klemperer wanted a much bigger crescendo, and the effect was shattering.

Today we are preoccupied by matters other than *melos* and even conductors are once again in danger of being eclipsed, in spite of 'edging' and 'thwacking'. It is no longer a case of Furtwängler's *Tristan*, Knappertsbusch's *Parsifal*, or Solti's *Ring*; conductors' names are now replaced by those of directors. The popularity of opera is rising and Wagner's audiences are worldwide; his music belongs to the people. Through recordings, we can all experience the Solti energy and the Karajan sound, the slow Knappertsbusch and the swift Böhm, the sentimental Walter and the majestic Goodall, and all those differences between Kleiber and Fricsay, or Kempe and Furtwängler. Today conductors no longer consider Wagner's theory and practice of *melos*; they are probably not even aware of its existence. They create a sound, they seek effect, and they do things in the recording studio which they could never do in the opera house in terms of balancing orchestra with singers, highlighting individual instruments, or choosing tempi (how much easier it is for a *heldentenor* to sing a Wagner opera such as *Siegfried* in twenty-minute takes than in its gruelling performance time of three and three-quarter hours.

In German opera houses life goes on much the same as in Wagner's own day and he would be just as vociferous in his condemnation of conducting practice today as he was in *On Conducting*. Operas are thrown on, productions revived (*stagione* fashion) with little or no rehearsal and without a glimpse or understanding by the participants of any interpretation a conductor might have. Mention has been made of Goodall; he alone has been a great seeker of *melos* — perhaps the last. His degree of preparation of the Wagner operas with his singers, orchestras and musical assistants in the Indian summer of his career (and mercifully the English and Welsh National Opera companies gave him the time and the necessary facilities to work the way he wanted to) was unique in modern times. We certainly still speak of Goodall's *Mastersingers* or his *Ring*, but the fruits of the labours of most contemporary conductors are more likely to be found buried beneath the piles of newsprint devoted to the stage directors and designers to whom Wagner now belongs. Conductors must resume the search for *melos* before the trail goes cold.

Chapter 2

Wagner and His Singers

Desmond Shawe-Taylor

Wagner is widely, and with good reason, regarded as the most revolutionary figure in the history of opera. In every sphere of that art — dramatic and musical structure, subject-matter, text, harmony, orchestration — his influence turned the world of opera upside-down; notwithstanding the still potent survival of Italian and French traditions, Wagnerian practice spread throughout the second half of the nineteenth century and has continued to dominate much of the twentieth. Similar comments might well be made about the host of fresh demands made on his singers; but in this field he was not to the same extent a revolutionary — or rather, in so far as he was so, it was less by intention than by the undeliberate and partly unforeseen consequences posed by his works in performance.

The artistic idol and inspiration of his early life, the soprano Wilhelmine Schröder-Devrient — unforgettable, for him, not only as Beethoven's Leonore[1] but as Bellini's Romeo — was an unfathomable (his word) dramatic and interpretative genius with (as he freely admitted) imperfect purely vocal powers; and he gladly welcomed her participation as Adriano, Senta, and Venus in the first performances of his early full-scale Romantic operas. Schröder-Devrient, however, was evidently a case apart; in general, what Wagner required of his singers was pretty much what most nineteenth- and even twentieth-century composers have usually demanded: beautiful tone, clear enunciation, a firm vocal line, and precision in musical detail. The famous notice which he placed in the wings of the Festspielhaus during the first *Ring* cycles — 'The big notes will take care of themselves; the little ones and the text are the chief things' — is essentially a plea for vocal and verbal precision: for accurate and careful execution of the many niceties scattered through the voice parts.

That he had strong and mainly traditional likes and affiliations in

15

the sphere of singing appears again and again from the internal evidence of his scores. It is not only the earlier operas — especially the widely admired *Lohengrin*, which rapidly conquered Italy, the land of song, after its Bologna premiere in 1871 — that display so clearly these traditional vocal affiliations; in the *Ring* itself the number of trills, mordents, appoggiaturas, and other such old-style ornaments, especially in the roles of Brünnhilde and her sister valkyries, is astonishing: even the villainous Hagen utters a whole-bar trill in the half-grim, half-humorous scene of his summoning of the vassals in the second act of *Götterdämmerung*. In the 1882 *Parsifal* performances nothing seems to have given the composer greater pleasure than the singing of the six solo Flowermaidens, chosen (as he proudly relates in his account of the performances)[2] from leading soloists in different German opera houses, singing together with complete artistic unanimity as well as 'matchless intonation', and without a trace of that 'passionate accent' and 'breaking of every melodic line' to which contemporary operatic music might well have accustomed them. During one of the performances (it was immediately after the words 'Kannst du uns nicht lieben und minnen, wir welken und sterben dahinnen') a hearty 'Bravo!' was heard one night from one of the boxes at the back of the theatre, and (it is said) indignantly shushed by members of the audience unaware that it proceeded from the composer.

Many such comments and incidents reinforce our notion of Wagner's relish for traditional vocal ornament and vocal beauty in general. Lotte Lehmann, who was a pupil of Mathilde Mallinger, the Eva of the first performance of *Die Meistersinger* at Munich in 1868, has passed on to us her teacher's story of how, during rehearsal, when a great many repetitions proved necessary for the scene of popular acclaim that follows Walther's Prize Song, she had introduced a small diversion by adding a trill to the long penultimate note of her soft final phrase 'Keiner wie du so hold zu werben weiß!' (No one but you knows how to woo so charmingly) and how Wagner had said, 'Let her have her fun. We'll keep the trill since Mallinger likes it so much'.[3] And there it stayed.

If, however, Wagner's musical instincts can be said to have predisposed him towards admiration for the traditional virtues of good singing, nevertheless his contemporaries and subsequent generations of musicians have complained, and not without reason, that the unprecedented demands made by his works in performance did much to strain and even ruin the very kind of singing — smooth, firm, accurate, agile — that he most admired. How can we reconcile the composer's own well-attested vocal preferences with the many bad vocal consequences that have actually come about and have seemed to derive from the practice of singing his works, and more especially his later works, in the theatre? Certainly he loved beautiful singing, and knew well what it was. But is it not equally clear that in the course of creation and composition, he constantly transgressed against what he must have known to be sound practical considerations? In his way he reminds us of Beethoven, who once replied to the complaints of Schuppanzigh about the difficulties posed by his violin-writing. 'Do you think I can consider your puny little fiddle when He [God Almighty] speaks to me?'

In the first place, there is the simple but crucial matter of length. From *Rienzi* onwards, Wagner had always inclined towards great length; if we discount the 'preliminary evening' of the tetralogy, *Das Rheingold, Der fliegende Holländer* is the sole exception. His leading roles, therefore — especially those for his dramatic or lyric tenors and sopranos — tended to provide a severe test of stamina to their exponents. Like Beethoven, again, at work on the colossal sonata that we call the *Hammerklavier*, Wagner must surely have known that he was posing a great strain on his interpreters; but in the course of actual composition he shut his eyes to this obvious truth.

In the second place, there are the more difficult and complex questions of the volume of orchestras and the size and capacity of opera houses, then and since — and more especially now. Here, perhaps, we find another instance of Wagner's contriving to ignore practical considerations. On the one hand, we find him in 1865 proposing to reorganize the Music School in Munich with the intention of cultivating voices suited to the heavier roles of his music dramas; on the other hand, there is the curious case of his plans for the first performance of *Tristan und Isolde* in the same year.

For at least several weeks during 1865 he contemplated (and even persuaded his conductor, Hans von Bülow, and King Ludwig II to agree to) the use of the Residenztheater. To those who know this famous and beautiful little theatre (though destroyed in the last war, it is not essentially changed today, the original rococo interior having been preserved and inserted within a new identically sized 'outer case'), it seems absolutely astounding that the composer and Bülow could have considered for a moment the performance of *Tristan* in this house, rather than in the nearby Hoftheater (now Nationaltheater), where it was eventually given. How, we ask ourselves, was the *Tristan* orchestra — even though the number of its strings was not so precisely specified as those of the *Ring* — to have been physically accommodated in the Residenz orchestral space; and how was its sound, however carefully controlled by the conductor, to have had sufficient space for expansion in that fine and delicate auditorium? Have we not here another instance of a kind of self-deception, by which this most practical of artists could for a while persuade himself of a manifest impossibility? At all events, the experience — it only reached the rehearsal stage before Wagner abandoned the idea — played its part in his decision to provide a covered and invisible orchestra at Bayreuth.

During Wagner's lifetime, and still more during the century since his death, opera houses — and concert halls too — have increased remorselessly in size, so that by now capacities of more than three thousand are quite frequently encountered. The article on 'singing' in *The New Grove Dictionary of Music and Musicians* notes in this connection the nineteenth-century use of new vocal categories such as *tenore robusto, tenore di forza, heldentenor,* etc. (there are female equivalents) as indicating already 'a taste for weightier timbres, more brilliant upper registers, more sonorous low notes and greater volume in general'; and the twentieth century with its increasingly large houses has certainly not diminished these demands, however feebly they may have been met, and with whatever consequent damage to promising young voices.

At this point we may pause for a moment to look back and consider who, after Schröder-Devrient, were the singers of whom Wagner seems to have thought most highly in performances of his own works. Tenors being, for him even more than for Verdi, the crux of the problem, we may consider them first. During the period when Schröder-Devrient was creating the roles of the early Wagnerian heroines, the Bohemian tenor Joseph Tichatschek, likewise a member of the Dresden Opera, was entrusted with Wagner's leading tenor parts: he was the first Rienzi and Tannhäuser, and also an admired Lohengrin. He evidently had a beautiful and well-trained voice, excelled in Mozart and Weber roles, and charmed all his associates by his lively good-humour; but he seems to have been a singer pure and simple, without much dramatic perception.

Wagner's other outstanding tenor of the pre-Bayreuth years, a very different character, was the extraordinary Ludwig Schnorr von Carolsfeld, son of the well-known painter Julius, and husband of the ten-years-older Malvina, *née* Garrigues, who was, though of European ancestry, the daughter of the Brazilian consul in Copenhagen. Schnorr was a man of wide general cultivation and a highly precocious singer, who was appointed principal tenor of the Karlsruhe company at the age of twenty-two; only six years later, and now married, he settled in Dresden and soon became famous in the roles of Tannhäuser and Lohengrin, having already begun to study the role of Tristan to his wife's Isolde. The composer knew of the young tenor's reputation and hopes, but at first — as he admits in his memoir of the singer — had avoided an encounter because he had heard reports of his corpulence, surprising in so young a man and especially inappropriate to a Tristan.

Such were Schnorr's qualities, however — his charm, goodness of heart, general culture and sheer musicianship — that the composer soon succumbed, and was absolutely amazed at the poetic insight and beauty of tone and phrasing shown by the young tenor during the few performances that he was able to give of *Tristan* in 1865. After only four performances (or five, counting the very public dress rehearsal) the tenor fell victim to some kind of fever, described as a species of 'rampant gout', and possibly caused by exposure to icy stage draughts during the prolonged immobility of the third act, and died shortly after his twenty-ninth birthday. Wagner's long memoir is one of the most moving and emotional pieces among his prose works, and leaves us in no doubt of the tenor's artistic and poetic powers; its only fault is that it almost ignores the evidently admirable contribution of Malvina — whom Wagner had also much admired during the performances, but who became unbalanced and exceedingly tiresome after the shock of her husband's death, and was unable to continue her professional career.

It is not altogether clear whether these initial *Tristan* performances, unlike most of their successors until relatively recent times, were uncut; at all events, many people in the musical world freely attributed Schnorr's sudden collapse and death to the excessive strain of rehearsals and performances on so young a singer. The sole touch of criticism which the composer allows himself is to admit that Schnorr's voice was not quite so fine an instrument as Tichatschek's (it was said by other admirers to have been somewhat baritonal and veiled in timbre); for his intelligence and for the subtlety and beauty of his whole interpretation, no praise could be too high. There are few nineteenth-century singers about whom we feel so intense a curiosity — and so keen a regret that the phonograph should have come too late to permit us the merest glimpse of his tone and style.

As we have seen, Wagner had from the first been fortunate in having several of the outstanding German singers of the day among his admirers and interpreters; and during his later years it is hardly too much to say that he was free to pick and choose those whom he regarded as the best and most suitable to his requirements. Evidently, by the time of the Bayreuth Festivals and of the concurrent European Wagner tours organized by Angelo Neumann, a very high level of talent was available both to the composer and to Neumann. Wagner himself writes in lyrical praise of his first Bayreuth Wotan, Franz Betz (he had also been the first Hans Sachs, in Munich); of the Bayreuth Siegmund, Albert Niemann; and of his Alberich, Karl Hill;

and we understand, from a mass of contemporary testimony, that
Amalie Materna, the first Kundry and first Bayreuth Brünnhilde,
Emil Scaria, the first Gurnemanz, and many others of the first casts
were also artists of superlative achievement.

Of all these once famous names, unfortunately, only two —
Hermann Winkelmann, the first *Parsifal,* and Marianne Brandt, one
of the three original Kundrys — made, late in life, a few primitive
recordings; one might add to these the more significant and more
easily accessible records of Lilli Lehmann, but Wagner did not live to
witness her Bayreuth Brünnhilde of 1896, and admired her only
(very warmly, it must be said) as the 1876 Woglinde, Helmwige and
Wood Bird, regretting her inability, for personal reasons, to return in
1882 as leader of the *Parsifal* Flowermaidens.

Enough has been said to indicate how high a vocal level, in the
estimation of the composer and of many good musicians, had been
attained in the premieres and early performances of Wagner's works.
After his death, however, we begin to encounter complaints of 'the
Bayreuth bark' and other such unfavourable comments on a new
style that had begun to pervade Wagner singing. A species of unlovely
declamation, at its worst akin to shouting, had — it was said — begun
to supplant the smooth and lyrical style that the composer evidently
preferred, and indeed demanded. To generalize in such matters is
difficult, even rash; but students of singing have become aware that,
especially in Germany, a more forceful and declamatory style began
to spread and take root during the period between Wagner's death
and the First World War — and is by no means extinct at the present
day.

Qualification of any such sweeping statement is always necessary.
Some splendid singers, certainly, appeared at Bayreuth towards and
around the turn of the century: among them the English-born mezzo-
soprano and occasional soprano Marie Brema; Anton Van Rooy, the
superlative Wotan, Hans Sachs and Flying Dutchman (himself a
Dutchman and a Bayreuth discovery, whose career there lasted,
however, for only five years because of his participation in the un-
authorized New York *Parsifal* performances of 1903); and the Czech
soprano Emmy Destinn, who sang Senta to Van Rooy's Dutchman in
Bayreuth's first *Fliegender Holländer* in 1901. In 1904 the Gramophone
Company despatched a recording team to Bayreuth, and made seventeen Wagnerian excerpts, of which eight are included in a recently
issued compact disc (The Harold Wayne Collection, volume 5: Symposium 1081) together with most of the somewhat later Winkelmann
recordings. The results achieved in 1904 are vivid, especially the
lively and lyrical contributions of the Loge (Otto Briesemeister), the
Mime (Hans Breuer), the Siegmund (Alfred von Bary), and the

Wolfram (the then little-known Clarence Whitehill). During the 1890s and the first two decades of this century, however, there were also plenty of Bayreuth declamatory 'barkers' (as we can gather, for instance, from Bernard Shaw's account of various festival visits during this period); and the Bayreuth management began to acquire a name for the toleration and even encouragement of this unlyrical style.

Throughout those early years it was often observed, with good reason, that the casts assembled by Maurice Grau during his eleven-year reign at the New York Metropolitan Opera (1891–1903: there were two 'missing' years in the sequence of seasons) and his four concurrent Covent Garden seasons (1897–1900) were by far the finest to be heard anywhere in the world. It was further noticed that only a small proportion of Grau's best singers (who included Ternina, Nordica, Fremstad, Gadski, Eames, Schumann-Heink, Brema, the two de Reszke brothers, Lassalle, Bispham, and Van Rooy) were of German birth.

A feature of these early New York casts that now strikes us as surprising is that so many of the singers, especially the sopranos, were equally distinguished in the lighter French and Italian roles, and continued to excel in these parts alongside their Brünnhildes and Isoldes, Siegfrieds and Tristans. Not only did Jean de Reszke continue to perform his famous Gounod roles after the triumph of his Tristan and Siegfried; Nordica did not relinquish her Susanna (*The Marriage of Figaro*) or her Violetta (*La Traviata*) at the approach of her Wagner heroines, and even tackled the wholly florid role of Philine (*Mignon*) during the same period; and Lilli Lehmann was another soprano whose Philine surprisingly coexisted with her Brünnhilde and Isolde, not to mention her Norma and *Fidelio* Leonore. Nobody was surprised when Nellie Melba presented (though in Italian) both Elisabeth and Elsa during her first season at the Met, receiving good notices in both parts which encouraged her to tackle — only a few days after her first Violetta at that house — the role of Brünnhilde in *Siegfried*, with both de Reszkes in the cast, and this time in German. Her Brünnhilde was a never repeated fiasco, and even threatened to endanger her voice; but can we not learn something from the mere fact that so good a vocal judge as Maurice Grau, with Nordica and Litvinne at hand, should have given Melba exclusive rights in the role (in *Siegfried* only, of course)?

The general picture of these early New York performances of late Wagner, and of their closely similar counterparts at Covent Garden — performances by which many good judges were much impressed — suggests that the prevailing orchestral style of the period was far less massive and forceful than that to which our ears have grown accustomed in the course of the past hundred years. Then, as now, many people thought that Wagner was, in general, a noisy and over-emphatic composer; but these are relative terms, and depend for their meaning on the norm to which, consciously or unconsciously, the composer was being compared. Only gradually, it seems, was the dubious idea accepted of the Wagnerian singer as a distinct species, capable of standing up for himself or herself against fearful odds. Furthermore, the singers' tasks were until quite recent times frequently lightened by the widespread practice of making substantial cuts, especially in *Tristan*. We may feel virtually certain that Jean de Reszke invariably benefited from the huge, then standard cut in the first part of the long scene between the lovers in Act II and in the scene of Tristan's delirium in Act III: and it is even doubtful whether the stalwart Melchior was ever expected to sing the complete versions of these scenes either at Covent Garden or at the Metropolitan — although he must surely have done so at Bayreuth in 1930 (under Toscanini) and 1931.

During the period leading up to the First World War — and to a lesser extent during the inter-war decades — it was customary for each country, especially those with established national operatic traditions such as France, Italy, Russia, the Scandinavian countries, and Hungary to perform the Wagner operas in its own language and with native singers; among these casts were to be found several notable Wagnerians, such as the French sopranos Rose Caron, Suzanne Balguerie, Germaine Lubin, and the Russian/French soprano Félia Litvinne, the Flemish tenor Ernst van Dyck, the French bass-baritone Jean-François Delmas, the Italian tenor Giuseppe Borgatti, and the Italianate (originally Spanish) tenor Francesco Vignas (Viñas).

Under the inspiring and determined guidance of Hans Richter, Covent Garden launched its first English-language *Ring* (two cycles, without cuts) in 1908, with three further cycles in early 1909, and introduced such notable singers as the soprano Agnes Nicholls (Sieglinde and the *Siegfried* Brünnhilde), the tenor Walter Hyde (Siegmund), the American baritone Clarence Whitehill (Wotan) and the bass Robert Radford (Hunding).

That year of sombre memory, 1914, began in England with an unprecedented quantity of Wagner performances, largely prompted by the emergence of *Parsifal* from the embargo that had previously prevented its legal stage performance outside Bayreuth. At a special February/March German opera season at Covent Garden no fewer than fourteen *Parsifal* performances, together with twelve of other mature Wagner works, were given at Covent Garden; and in the usual Grand Season which followed from April to July there were five more *Parsifals*, together with two complete *Ring* cycles. New singers of consequence heard during these seasons, under conductors who included Arthur Nikisch, Albert Coates, and the naturalized American Artur Bodanzky, were the tenors Carl Burrian and Jacques Urlus, the basses Paul Bender and Friedrich Plaschke, the sopranos Claire Dux and Gertrude Kappel, and the mezzo-soprano Kirkby Lunn.

The period following the First World War was, for British operagoers, the time of the artistically fruitful but short-lived British National Opera Company — which built on the strong foundations laid during the war by the Beecham company, and included such fine artists as the tenor Frank Mullings and the bass Norman Allin. There was some indignation and much controversy in 1924, when the BNOC found itself denied its by then customary lease of Covent Garden for the summer season. Whatever the abstract rights and wrongs of that now distant debate, so rich were the German casts assembled at short notice with the help of the principal conductor, Bruno Walter, and so high the general level of both singing and acting during the German parts of those inter-war seasons, that the fortunate generation which began its Wagnerian opera-going about that time was amazed and delighted by the beauty and brilliance of performances such as they had never imagined.

Now it becomes possible — instead of relying on mere assertion — to produce some concrete evidence of the singing regularly heard at that time. In 1925, the year after the German operatic invasion, the new electrical method of recording began to supersede the old acoustical method with singers crowded around a horn and a small orchestra doing its best in the background. Within a few years, substantial extracts began to appear from the Wagner operas (and, to a lesser extent, from those of Richard Strauss, especially his *Rosenkavalier*) which did something like justice to the dramas and their music, and justice, too, to that remarkable generation of their interpreters. Opportunities were missed, of course, in those still early days of large-scale recording; but at last it had become possible to acquaint a wide public with large portions of the music dramas and with an outstanding generation of singers.

As it happened, a surprisingly large number of them (including Frida Leider, the supreme Brünnhilde and Isolde of that time; Lotte Lehmann, the uniquely warm and impassioned Sieglinde and impulsive Eva; Elisabeth Schumann (a Mozart rather than a Wagner singer, who nevertheless shared with Lehmann the role of Eva), and Friedrich Schorr, who increasingly seems to stand on a pedestal of his own in the roles of Wotan, Hans Sachs and the Dutchman) were born in 1888, so that during those vital years they were in their prime: in their late thirties and forties. Only two years younger, the ebullient and indefatigable Danish heldentenor Lauritz Melchior came likewise to dominate the leading Wagner roles, Siegmund, Siegfried, Tristan, and Parsifal; his evident faults — a certain vagueness in the matter of rhythm and note values — were freely censured at the time, but his heroic timbre, splendid declamation, and tireless energy have made it increasingly clear, as the years pass, that he was the outstanding heldentenor of the century.

To the already mentioned names from those inter-war Wagner casts many more hardly less distinguished must be added: the lyrical and radiant Florence Austral as a much appreciated Brünnhilde and Isolde; the delicate soprano Tiana Lemnitz as a beautiful Eva; the warm-voiced Herbert Janssen, renowned for his great partnership with Melchior as Kurwenal in the last act of *Tristan*, as well as for his touching Wolfram and ripely humorous Kothner; the versatile mezzo Maria Olszewska and the more statuesque contralto Sigrid Onegin, who for one season grandly deployed her noble voice as Fricka and Brangäne, but surprisingly did not return. Another fine Wagnerian bass-baritone, second only to Schorr in his achievements, was Rudolf Bockelmann; the Viennese bass Ludwig Weber began a long association with Covent Garden; and fine singers who returned soon after the war from the pre-1914 seasons included the dramatic soprano Gertrude Kappel, the tenor Jacques Urlus, and the bass Paul Bender. The Nibelung brothers of those years included Albert Reiß and later Heinrich Tessmer as Mime, and Eduard Habich as Alberich. By and large, it was an era of vocal richness.

Throughout the casts, and from top to bottom of the scale, we were indeed royally served in those lavish days; and when in 1936 the beloved Frida Leider began to contemplate retirement from the roles of Brünnhilde and Isolde, the fresh-voiced Kirsten Flagstad — not so much younger, indeed, but with her great soprano only recently subjected to the strain of those roles — was at hand to carry the heroic torch. Very naturally, ardent supporters of these two superb Wagnerian sopranos contested their merits fervently. In truth, their great virtues were in striking contrast: Leider darkly impassioned of tone, with tremendous dramatic impulse and a wonderful grip on the declamation of the text, while Flagstad seemed then and throughout her career the embodiment of pure, radiant, heroic singing. That acute critic Richard Capell summed up the matter by saying of Flagstad that 'her Isolde was a stately Nordic princess, more proud than passionate. No other Brünnhilde in her time has seemed so much a Valkyrie born'.[5] Opera-goers of the 1930s counted themselves fortunate to have two such Wagnerian sopranos, profoundly different yet both irreplaceable, to choose between.

So rich was the Wagnerian vocal talent of those inter-war years that any attempt to summarize it is sure to result in omissions — and in comparisons that are unusually difficult to sustain. Nor is it easy to attempt an explanation — other than that of mere chance — for such an explosion of talent. We can readily account for a more recent decline of standards by those well-worn but largely valid explanations with which we have become sadly familiar: the continual mobility of singers in the age of jet travel, their lack of a secure and at first reasonably obscure base in which to set down their artistic roots, their over-heavy and over-diversified work-load, the ever-present temptation to tackle unsuitable roles because of the shortage of more appropriate exponents, the constant pull of recording and of broadcasting and television engagements. There is simply (we are obliged to conclude) too much afoot, too many conflicting temptations, to permit the steady maturing of voice and style in some quiet but artistically not negligible backwater. Is it conceivable that a Flagstad of the 1990s or the 2000s could spend the first half of her artistic career singing a general repertory in a small and distant theatre, and then, approaching the age of forty, find herself equipped with a voice in flawless condition when the heavy Wagner parts in major houses at last come her way and offers begin to pour in from all the operatic centres of the world?

As in so many other fields, the Second World War created a far more serious disruption of civilized life than did the First; and it is not surprising that the performance of Wagner's large-scale, demanding, and now also ideologically suspect works should have suffered, both in their native Germany and in the rest of Europe. When Covent Garden staggered to its feet during the winter of 1946–47, Wagner was at first felt to pose too heavy a problem; moreover, for idealistic reasons, the newly formed company attempted during its early years to adhere to a policy (fairly soon abandoned) of performing everything in English; and it is a remarkable tribute to the cooperative spirit of several international stars, and perhaps also to their old affection for the historic house, that for some years they attempted to learn and perform in translation works which they knew intimately in the original German.

Already in January 1948 one of the new generation of leading Wagner singers, the bass-baritone Hans Hotter (recognized in Germany before the war as an outstanding Wotan, but hampered in the development of his career by the war) learned and performed the role of Hans Sachs in English. Considering the great length of the part, this was indeed a noble, not to say quixotic, undertaking; and it was not surprising that he should have seemed bothered by having to sing familiar notes to unfamiliar English words. When, in the follow-

ing month, *Tristan* was revived, English was not attempted, and
Kirsten Flagstad's still radiant Isolde was heard with the original text;
but for some years to come foreign artists of distinction, even Flagstad,
occasionally had to struggle with an unfamiliar and inferior text.
During this period Ludwig Weber renewed his pre-war association
with Covent Garden, dominating the 1950 *Ring* cycle to such an
extent that one reviewer described it as 'Hagen's *Ring*'; Elisabeth
Grümmer, a tender-voiced soprano in the Tiana Lemnitz tradition,
became a Covent Garden favourite; and so did Set Svanholm in the
heldentenor parts, to which he was found to be well fitted by his
physique and virile declamation, though wanting in sensuous beauty
of tone. By this time the notion of Wagner in English had been
quietly abandoned.

All in all, this was not a great Wagner period at Covent Garden,
and several of its best features, most notably the continued radiance
of Flagstad's heroic soprano, were more in the nature of an 'after-
glow' from the inter-war seasons than a post-war dawn; from her 1957
début onwards, however, Birgit Nilsson — a genuine successor to
Flagstad and Leider — became an indispensable Brünnhilde and
Isolde. Other good singers, such as the soprano Astrid Varnay and
the tenor Ramon Vinay, proved welcome visitors, but did not put
down roots at Covent Garden. During the 1950s some admirable
conductors and sound Wagnerians were active at Covent Garden,
including Rudolf Kempe, Erich Kleiber and Clemens Krauß and
Georg Solti's decade (1961–71) at the house not only included, as
might have been expected, a full quota of well-organized Wagner
revivals, but raised the general standard of performance, especially
in respect of the orchestral playing.

During all this time, there was on the Covent Garden staff an
ardent and extremely capable Wagnerian conductor in the person of
Reginald Goodall; but too little use was made of his great talents,
either as a coach (in which capacity his skill was outstanding) or as a
conductor, and his naturally self-effacing temperament allowed this
situation to continue. He functioned for many years as a 'house
conductor' of proved ability, rather than as an expert of outstanding
gifts. Gradually the word spread of his remarkable talents, especially
in the Wagner repertory; and the turning-point for their recognition
came, not at Covent Garden, but at Sadler's Wells during the last year
before that company's move to the London Coliseum, and more
especially at the Coliseum itself.

Early in 1968, Goodall conducted an outstandingly spacious and
serene performance of *The Mastersingers* (in English) at Sadler's
Wells, which proved hugely successful with the public. When, later in
the year, the company made its bold and eventually very successful

move to the Coliseum in St Martin's Lane, it was natural that one of the earliest productions there should be of this splendid *Mastersingers* — and now without the cuts that had still been thought necessary at Sadler's Wells. It was a triumphant evening, and the first of many Wagner performances at that house which led to enormous enthusiasm among both professional musicians and the general public. It was generally agreed that the outstanding features of Goodall's Wagner were his prolonged and patient tuition of the cast, his lyrical approach to the scores, his spacious handling and care for detail, and a more general quality which derived from his profound love and knowledge of the score and from a remarkable capacity to convey this informed enthusiasm to singers and orchestra alike. If he was a very fine Wagner conductor, he was a still finer Wagner coach; and it is, of course, this aspect of his work that particularly concerns us here.

It was characteristic of Goodall's approach that he should choose and maintain very broad tempi, and this quality of his readings was the only point in which they proved at all controversial. His deep knowledge of every nook and cranny of score and text resulted in a quiet determination that nothing should be scamped or lost. In Wagner performances tempi have always varied widely — not least at Bayreuth, where a systematic and (one hopes) accurate system of timing each act in performance under the long succession of conductors has been in operation for over a hundred years: in fact, since the opening of the festival in 1876. Some of these printed timings are certainly strange, the supposedly tempestuous and dynamic Toscanini, for example, registering some of the slowest performances ever heard in the house, in *Tristan* and *Parsifal.* At Covent Garden, where cuts in the *Ring* and *Tristan* and *Die Meistersinger* used to be frequent, no such system of timings prevailed; and habitués formed a general impression that Walter, Furtwängler, and Kempe represented a kind of normality, in which adequate space for detail and lyrical expansion, and for the full communication of the singer's art and human feeling, coexisted with drive and overall momentum. Beecham, another outstanding Wagner conductor, was likewise a man to cherish orchestral detail, but he was also impetuous and fiery, sometimes racing ahead through lyrical or humorous scenes in a way that scarcely allowed their flavour to be fully felt or conveyed.

Lotte Lehmann, not usually regarded as a 'difficult' singer, used to confess that she found some of Beecham's Wagner tempi hard to adjust to; perhaps she wondered whether his detailed knowledge of the score included an equally detailed knowledge of the text. When he led *Die Meistersinger,* that little episode in the first act — so dear to the seasoned Wagnerian — in which one of the Masters fails to answer to his name in Kothner's rollcall, and is declared by his apprentice to be absent owing to sickness, used to flash past unnoticed and apparently uncherished; and I have harboured my doubts whether Beecham, intent on the flowing orchestral polyphony, really knew just what was going on. With Goodall, there could never be even a passing doubt on such a matter; during his performance a kind of security reigned which in no way diminished the drive and continuity of the whole effect.

During the three years from 1970 to 1973 the Sadler's Wells Company (as it was still called in its new home, the Coliseum, until it became the English National Opera in 1974) mounted and completed, under Goodall, its enormously successful complete *Ring* in Andrew Porter's new and strikingly clear translation. A worthy group of principals had been found and lovingly coached for this great venture, headed by Rita Hunter as Brünnhilde, Alberto Remedios in the leading tenor roles, and Norman Bailey as Wotan.

Only an uncritical patriot could aver that these fine singers and their colleagues — and I must not forget the Beckmesser and Alberich of Derek Hammond-Stroud — were on the same level as the group of outstanding German singers heard in these roles at Covent Garden between the wars; but under the conductor's guidance and with the benefit of his tireless and detailed preparation they were able to rise to the level of their great chance. This was — and for some while remained — a *Ring* to live in the memories of its fortunate audiences. In the middle of its unfolding, the unflagging conductor returned to Covent Garden (in 1971) to lead a remarkably fine *Parsifal*, with Jon Vickers as the hero, Norman Bailey as an intensely human and moving Amfortas, Amy Shuard as an uncommonly musical Kundry, and the veteran Gottlob Frick, a favourite post-war Covent Garden bass, emerging from semi-retirement to give us, as Gurnemanz, a performance of rare solidity and nobility of tone and utterance.

The cycle of Goodall's mature Wagner interpretations was rounded off by his 1979 performance of *Tristan* with the Welsh National Opera at Cardiff, his 1981 ENO *Tristan*, his 1983 WNO *Parsifal*, and his 1986 ENO *Parsifal*. Although we live in an ever-increasingly international world of music, with big occasions freely available to us on disc or by radio from Bayreuth and other leading Wagner centres, Goodall's English cycle during the period from 1968 to 1986, with its lovingly coached group of singers as well as its mastery of flow and orchestral detail, continues to occupy a central place in the experience of its English listeners. It is felt to have set a standard.

Chapter 3

Producing Wagner

Mike Ashman

Richard Wagner grew up, worked and died in an age where there were no specialist opera directors.[1] For much of the nineteenth century, production was a two-dimensional service medium for getting a work on stage, lacking the central creative role it was to play in the twentieth century. A *mise-en-scène* was achieved by a haphazard combination of stage-manager, ballet-master, composer, librettist, conductor, singer, and (sometimes) the occupant of a post which the Dresden Court Theatre (where Wagner was Kapellmeister from 1843 to 1849) called variously *Literator* or *Oberregisseur für Schauspiel und Oper* — a kind of Dramaturg *avant la lettre*.[2] Sets and costumes (especially for premieres of works by not yet established composers) were mostly assembled from repertory stock, rather than being newly designed. Wagner himself drily noted this trend in a review of *Der Freischütz* at the Paris Opéra in 1841. Ottokar wore 'Turkish dress', his court 'Chinese costumes', and the remainder 'the costume of Bohemia', so 'one was bound to assume that the mighty sultan had also extended his territories north-westwards to Prague and Teplitz'.[3]

It was not a question of production being considered of secondary importance to the musical result; it was quite simply a case of production — in the sense of an organized, dramaturgically related, rehearsed staging — scarcely existing. This approach died hard. As late as 1855 so theatrical a composer as Verdi could write with naive delight about a newly published book of *disposizioni sceniche* for *Les Vêpres siciliennes* that now 'any child could do the staging'.[4] Even Wagner had to be involved twice with seriously compromised stagings of *Der fliegende Holländer* (the Dresden premiere in 1843 and his improvised Zurich 'festival' of 1852) before confessing to Liszt that he had finally learned 'with much trouble and toil, how important to this opera the décor is'.[5]

Wagner's experiences with what he once termed 'the vulgar theatrical career' of his works took him from a conductor 'shouting drastic directions concerning the necessary movement'[6] — at the hastily assembled Magdeburg premiere of *Das Liebesverbot* in 1836 — to producer of the premieres of the complete *Ring* and *Parsifal*. From the early 1840s he began a lifelong campaign for detailed musico-dramatic preparation of opera for the stage. A letter to Liszt (September 1850) — concerning Eduard Genast, stage-manager for the Weimar Court Theatre's recent premiere of *Lohengrin* — pinned down obvious gaps in contemporary practice:

> [Genast] remained entirely on the proper standpoint of the stage-manager, who arranges things in a general way, and justly leaves it to the individual actors to find out for themselves what concerns them only. . . . I ask him now to interfere even there . . . let him be the trustee of infant actors. Call the whole *personnel* to a *reading rehearsal* ; . . . take the score and from the remarks therein inserted explain to the singers the meaning of the situations and their connection with the music bar by bar.[7]

Realization of this plea for specialist production rehearsal would be, Wagner believed, 'a revolution which will lift our theatrical routine out of its grooves'.[8] He repeated it in his essay about staging *Tannhäuser* and added more theoretical support in *Eine Mitteilung an meine Freunde* (A communication to my friends): 'I required the actor in the forefront, and the singer only as the actor's aid' — a neat reordering of Hegel's hierarchy of text, then music, then perform-ance.[9] Later, after two seminal confrontations with supposed centres of operatic excellence — the *Tannhäuser* scandal in Paris in 1860–61, and the aborted Vienna premiere of *Tristan* in 1862–63 — he called for continuous working collaboration in production between chief musical coach, conductor, and producer — the latter to be ap-pointed with 'a care entirely unknown as yet' to be 'an official of equal standing with the two other directors'.[10]

From a methodological point of view, Wagner's legacy to opera production was important. In time his seemingly idealistic rehearsal conditions became something like the norm for many European opera houses. It is harder to assess the significance of both his own work as producer and his writing on the interpretation of individual works. Much of this — at least before King Ludwig II invited him to Munich in 1864 — was governed by the battle to establish an appre-ciation by performers of the novel dramatic demands of his operas. The specific examples cited in the essays on staging *Holländer* and *Tannhäuser* evidently relate to frustrations encountered during early performances in Dresden and Berlin. The bar-by-bar description of the Dutchman's entrance, the painstaking explanation of Tannhäuser's mental state at 'Zum Heil den Sündigen zu führen'

('to lead the sinner to salvation') and the admonition to Senta not to
be dreamy certainly indicate Wagner's (at that time) radical desire
for 'naturalistic' acting. But they must also be read as attempts to
stimulate contemporary singers and their stage directors to think in
terms of more than stand-and-deliver performances of set-piece arias.
For that reason it is surely misleading to take them as gospel *Modellbuch*
instructions which should be applied to any production of the work
concerned; like many of Wagner's actual stage directions, they should
be seen more as visions, or atmospheric guidelines. More far-reaching were his attempts to extend the dramatic participation of the
chorus beyond the naive A to B moves shown in early Paris Opéra
production books — the Wartburg guests are instructed *not* to take
'possession of the wings like two regiments of well-drilled troops, in
wait for further operatic business'[11] — and the type of psychological
character detail which he attempted to feed to Albert Niemann, his
Paris Tannhäuser:

> There is too much physical strength in your rendering of the
> narration up to your arrival in Rome: that is not how a man would
> speak who had just been roused from madness to a few minutes'
> lucidity, a being from whom others shy away when they meet him,
> who for months has gone almost entirely without food, and whose
> life is sustained only by the glimmer of an insane desire. . . . Even if
> Tannhäuser were to be somewhat hoarse in the 3rd act, this would
> be no great misfortune.[12]

Although for the Munich *Holländer* of 1864 — the first in the soon
interrupted sequence of 'model productions' promised to Ludwig —
Wagner felt compelled to take over the conducting from Franz
Lachner, the frustrations he experienced at watching what was hap-
pening on stage subsequently persuaded him to lay down the baton
for major new productions of his works.[13] Even then he did not
assume full stage control of the premieres of *Tristan* and *Die
Meistersinger*, preferring instead to work via hints and suggestions
following careful individual preparation at private music rehearsal.
He lionized Ludwig Schnorr, the creator of Tristan, because the
singer had 'derived an ideal understanding of my work from within
the piece itself, and . . . made it truly his own'[14] and noted, with a hint
of self-mockery, how Schnorr attended to 'the highly pedantic perti-
nacity of my directions'.[15] Wagner would have us believe that he
hardly had to direct Act III of *Tristan* at all. The success of that
production encouraged his greater involvement in the complex
ensemble work of *Die Meistersinger* and even an initial feeling that the
Court Theatre's quite novel decision to appoint an outside stage-
manager (Reinhard Hallwachs from Stuttgart) for the production

was a waste of money when he himself was present.[16] The Munich
Meistersinger — the best-received Wagner premiere since *Rienzi* —
initiated the team production work that was to be a feature of the
first Bayreuth Festivals — the composer himself as arbiter and supreme demonstrator, a 'stage-manager' to look after the fine details,
and an adventurously used choreographer (here Lucile Grahn, who
effectively staged the Riot Scene).

Accounts of Wagner's passion and skill for demonstrating movement and atmosphere in rehearsal become more numerous from
this period on — annoyingly replacing precise descriptions of what
Wagner actually did:

> How well he understood the art of spurring on his men, . . .of
> making every gesture, each expression tell! . . . Then in the great
> final scene of the first act how he dominated, moved, and inspired
> his company — assigning places, prescribing gestures, and arrang-
> ing expressions, till the tableau was perfect and the whole cortège,
> Landgrave, knights, chorus, horses, and dogs took their places
> with the utmost artistic precision.[17]

Angelo Neumann's description of Wagner rehearsing *Tannhäuser* in
Vienna in 1875 is typical, although this comment — and a more
detailed one about the procession to the minster in *Lohengrin* — do
show that Wagner's work as producer was far from limited to coaching solo roles. The least reverential (hence the best) account of the
composer at rehearsal comes from Richard Fricke, the Dessau ballet-
master appointed Wagner's production assistant for the 1876 Bayreuth *Ring*. 'He just has to sweat out all over again what he has been
through composing the piece; . . . in this frame of mind he is compelled to block a scene and then do it all differently another day'.[18]
These much remarked changes of mind suggest less the excitable,
absent-minded genius than the improvisatory director more interested in the psychological *gestalt* of a scene than bread-and-butter
exits and entrances. Fricke often demurred when Wagner attempted
literal matches of rhythm and movement (the giants' entrance, many
of Hunding's actions, or the first Gibichung scene in *Götterdämmerung*),
suggested doubles for movements of complex action (like the first
scene of *Das Rheingold*) and hinted at more symbolic solutions to
Siegfried's dragon fight or the Norns' scene. Wagner rejected Fricke's
suggestions only when he felt they were selling his detailed
scenography short — although the point about reduction of movement obviously stuck when it came to *Parsifal* six years later.

The purely technical demands of Wagner's operas (especially the
Ring and the open transformations required in *Tannhäuser* and
Parsifal) were as great — and as much discussed — as their dramatic

and musical ones.[19] Contemporary accounts and reviews (including Wagner's own retrospective) often expressed disappointment at what was achieved in the first *Ring* production.[20] Wagner's long-term involvement in scenography began at first hand with problems experienced during the initial run of *Tannhäuser*, and started to become obsessive (including many detailed lighting notes) in rehearsal for the Munich *Holländer*. His choice of collaborators for Bayreuth was daring — artists, and even academics, working in tandem with an experienced scenic studio[21] – and he demanded a rare degree of close collaboration between them and himself as producer. The results — in comparison with, say, the productions currently being toured by the Saxe-Meiningen theatre company — often appeared bound to a dated historical realism. Although Wagner's writings sometimes attempted to lend academic credibility to his mythological reworkings by clothing them with an assumed historical context, he never intended to do this on stage. He was critical of Botho von Hülsen's setting of Act II of *Tannhäuser* (in the work's belated Berlin premiere) in designs (by Carl Wilhelm Gropius) copied from the actual Wartburg, and insisted in Paris on a more freely invented set. He wanted Josef Hoffmann to dissociate the Gibichung hall from 'medieval chivalry' and 'show *man* without all these conventional attributes'.[22] Nor did he want a stage full of naturalistic detail. Hoffmann was chided for 'neglect of the dramatic intentions in favour of his regard for arbitrary details of landscape scenery', and Paul von Joukowsky was bullied until he designed flowers for Klingsor's magic garden so enormous 'that the maidens might seem to grow out of them'.[23]

Wagner's famous comment about 'inventing the invisible theatre' — made in a fit of despair in 1878 during work on *Parsifal* — is as open to enthusiastic misinterpretation as his exhortation to 'do something new', or his wish to 'do everything differently' in the 1877 Bayreuth *Ring* that never was. But such remarks suggest strongly that he had no belief that he was handing down a tradition of production for his works. While his passion for fine detail and a then unheard-of naturalism in operatic acting made important new demands on his singing actors, the visionary nature of his stage directions frequently outstripped the imaginative and technical facilities available to contemporary theatre practice. Wagner's attempts in the latter part of his life to break away from the court theatre painters' tableaux which dominated grand opera for much of the nineteenth century were not really successful. This factor, combined with a natural desire to attempt, in his own productions, as many of his scenic instructions as possible, unwittingly contributed to the visual paralysis that overtook Bayreuth (and the many opera houses it influenced) until the 1930s.

And, while the *Ring* production widely toured by Angelo Neumann's company between 1882 and 1889 was undoubtedly important in terms of breaking a lance for the accessibility of the newly composed tetralogy, it remained essentially a copy of the 1876 Bayreuth staging, and thus became a further retarding influence on European Wagner production.[24]

'The creator of dramas from the spirit of music has left us with everything for the performance of his works in the most precise detail. Even the lighting of individual figures or groups at various dramatic moments is quite fixed. . . . The Master himself staged all his works and informed us what worked in these performances and what did not. It is not a question of discovering new things, merely of perfecting individual details.'[25] Under this banner Cosima, then to a lesser extent Siegfried, took over the dual role of intendant/producer at Bayreuth, attempting to strangle the infant prodigy of Wagner production at birth and, as Wieland Wagner later hinted, 'turning the virtue of fidelity into the sin of fossilization'. Cosima completed a Bayreuth canon of Wagner's mature works by preserving the work of the first two festivals — for her 1896 *Ring* she instructed Porges, Mottl, and Levi to collect together all the rehearsal notes taken in 1876 — or by cloning existing productions from Munich and Vienna. Cosima's management of Bayreuth was successful: she established the Festival as a regular event and built up and maintained an impressive and influential roster of artists. But she remained largely closed to the growing phenomenon of interpretative production.

One of the positive aspects of this negative was to accelerate an inevitable reaction of freeing Wagner from Wagner. Commentators both theoretical and practical took their starting-points from what they failed to see at Bayreuth. Romain Rolland could not find the 'second *Iliad*' he had expected to see in the 1896 *Ring* staging. Stanislavsky noted prophetically that 'even a Wagnerian god can be made plausible by virtue of a psychological grasp of his innermost nature and thus be transformed into an extremely effective stage figure whom we see related to us on a human level'.[26] Bernard Shaw's eloquently reported frustrations led him to seek parallels between the *Ring* and the social history of Wagner's own times that were to be avidly studied by twentieth-century producers. And the visit the Swiss scenographer Adolphe Appia made to *Tristan* in 1886 (Cosima's first 'new' festival production) convinced him that Wagner's 'vision issuing from the womb of music' could best be realized by wholly jettisoning nineteenth-century pictorialism: 'Up to now the actor has always been an independent unit within a scenic environment, with which he could in no way interrelate; . . . one even subordinated the action to all imaginable scenic possibilities; . . . the means to achieve a fusion between actor and scenic environment did not exist before the advent of Wagnerian drama'.[27] This conclusion was to prove a watershed for European production ideas and lit a slow-burning fuse underneath received ideas about the role of scenery and lighting in all theatre. Appia's belief that Wagner's music contained 'the drama's *original* life' was not to be successfully realized on a stage until Wieland Wagner's productions in 1950s' Bayreuth. But his proposed reforms — a hugely developed role for lighting, reduction of scenery to symbols of physical and psychological action, simplification and stylization of costume, and a style of movement based more on choreography — started to influence production styles at the turn of the century towards a non-realistic direction.

At St Petersburg's Mariinsky Theatre in 1909 no less a figure than Vsevolod Meyerhold made his operatic début with *Tristan*. He pointed out that 'metal helmets and shields glinting like samovars' constituted a 'historicism without secrets' and that 'the artist who designs costumes and props according to his own imagination creates a more convincing and credible stage picture than the set designer who plunders museums for the costumes and props which he then proceeds to use on stage'.[28] Meyerhold and his designer, Alexander Konstantinovich Chervachidze, reduced their sets to a single sail, castle walls, rocks, and the all-important new cyclorama — a striking anticipation of Wieland Wagner's 1962 Bayreuth production. In Vienna, the partnership of Gustav Mahler and the Secessionist designer Alfred Roller (with August Stoll as nominal stage director) adapted a partially stylized, pared-down approach to *Tristan* and the first two *Ring* dramas, with expressive use of coloured lighting, a novel placing of Isolde's tent on a lower level of the Act I ship and the cutting of realistic appearances by Grane and flying valkyries. Other Appia-influenced work came from Hans Wildermann (Cologne 1911–12) and the team of Franz Ludwig Hörth and Ludwig Sievert (Freiburg 1913), whose *Ring* placed the (conventionally costumed) singers on a bare rake, or segments thereof, with a cyclorama and much use of a revolve. Their *Parsifal* incorporated Appia's suggestion that a cathedral was au fond a petrified forest, making for a theoretically smooth (and symbolic) transformation from Grail domain to Grail temple.

The astonishingly advanced nature of Wagner's dramaturgy has received far too little critical attention. His narrative methods and dramatic dialogues parallel Ibsen's and Flaubert's and anticipate Proust's. It was thus no surprise that Wagner's aesthetics (at least) were rapidly absorbed into the intellectual coin of pre-1914 Europe — see, for example, the obsessive interest of Proust, Joyce, and D. H. Lawrence. But the cultural world after 1918, especially musically, was

1 Ludwig Sievert's sketch for Act II of *Die Walküre* (Frankfurt am Main, 1925) follows the geometric approach developed by Appia.

potentially 'in opposition to Wagner'. The phrase is that of the conductor/composer Otto Klemperer, whose challenging music directorship of Berlin's Kroll Opera in the late 1920s saw some of the earliest, and most famous, attempts to interpret repertory operas along literally deconstructionist lines. For his *Fliegender Holländer* Klemperer chose a noted theatre director, Jürgen Fehling, who had never worked in opera before, and a designer, Ewald Dülberg, whose costume sketches for *Parsifal* had once been rejected as too bold. The production set an important precedent for later twentieth-century producers (Wieland Wagner, Harry Kupfer, Herbert Wernicke) by opting, on largely dramaturgical grounds for the 'original' version of the score — the social side of the drama was thrown into high relief by the lack of a 'redemption' ending.[29] It was staged in modern dress on a luridly coloured Bauhaus-influenced set shorn of any atmospheric illusion. Fehling directed his cast in the expressionist style of Fritz Lang's *Metropolis*, an idea supported by Ernst Bloch's important publicity essay *Rettung Wagners durch surrealistische*

2   At the Berlin Kroll Oper, between 1927 and 1931, Otto Klemperer sought to reinvigorate operatic staging by drawing on Bauhaus modernism. Ewald Dülberg's designs for *Der fliegende Holländer* (1929) banished all traces of Norwegian maritime folk culture and, as in Act III, presented only the symbolic essence of the ships.

Kolportage (literally, 'Saving Wagner by hawking him around in a surrealist manner'). The right-wing (increasingly Nazi-dominated) press attacked the Kroll for 'cultural Bolshevism' — perhaps the first of many times that experimental Wagner producers have been branded as left-wing crazies — but the philosopher/musicologist T. W. Adorno prophetically noted that the production 'mobilized a reserve of actuality in Wagner ... which will explode today or tomorrow.'[30]

Other important experimental *Ring* stagings of the 1920s were created by Franz Ludwig Hörth and the designer Emil Pirchan (Berlin 1928–29) — in expressionist style and using film (in the mixed-media style of the experimental Berlin theatre director Erwin Piscator) for the entry of the gods into Valhalla — and Saladin Schmitt and Johannes Schröder (Duisburg 1922–23), whose 'expressionist coloured light music' was intensely disliked by Siegfried Wagner. With the Nazi accession to power, experiments in German Wagner staging were rapidly terminated — literally in the case of the next Fehling/ Klemperer collaboration. Invited by the maverick Heinz Tietjen[31] to stage an anniversary *Tannhäuser* at the Berlin State Opera in 1933, Fehling produced the opera as a battle between the Apollonian and Dionysian in the soul of the protagonist, representing this on stage by large symbolic props of a harp and a leopard skin. He also showed the Venusberg as a place of terror and emphasized the latent violence in the Wartburg knights when Tannhäuser hymns Venus. Most of the by now traditional medieval picture clutter — including the menagerie that accompanied the Landgrave in Act I — was dispensed with, although the production played in historical costumes of carefully linked colour scheme. Like the *Holländer* before it, Fehling's *Tannhäuser* was an important marker for subsequent productions, especially that of Götz Friedrich in Bayreuth (1972). The Nazi *Kampfbund* removed it from the Berlin stage after just four performances.

The National Socialist view of Wagner was represented by such horrors as the crude Nuremberg *Meistersinger* of 1935 with a flag-lined festival meadow designed by Benno von Arent, the *Reichsarchitekt*. Ironically, Bayreuth itself, following the deaths of Cosima and Siegfried in 1930, entered a period of conservative experimentation under the artistic directorship of the Berlin team of Heinz Tietjen (producer and often conductor) and Emil Preetorius (designer). Rehearsal footage of a 1938 *Götterdämmerung* shows acting and blocking of antique, monumental gestures, but Preetorius's stage shapes (notably the Dutchman's ship, the Valkyrie Rock, and Valhalla) reveal a constructive awareness of Appia's geometry and more recent expressionist trends. Until the Wieland Wagner revolution of the 1950s, the Preetorius look — gentle abstraction/simplification of basically naturalistic scenery — had much influence on world Wagner staging. A more radical, one-off experiment of the period took place in Russia, where the film director Sergey Eisenstein was commanded to stage *Die Walküre* in tribute to Stalin's new ally, Hitler. The director's quest for 'audio-visual unity' and his study of Wagner's mythic source material led him to stage most of the work's textual narrations with the aid of 'mime choruses' of actors — Wotan and guests appeared during Sieglinde's 'Der Männer Sippe', for example, — to give Hunding a large retinue of followers and dogs, and to play Act II in three distinct locations. Most of this illustrative epic detail was to be forgotten until the 1970s.

Wieland Wagner had already designed (largely traditional) sets for *Die Meistersinger* and *Parsifal* in 1930s' Bayreuth[32] and commenced a career as producer/designer in smaller theatres. There were clear antecedents for the style which he initiated at the reopening of the

3   The film director Sergey Eisenstein's staging of *Die Walküre* in Moscow, 1940, animated the myth behind the music, as here by mime groups during Sieglinde's story in Act I.

Festival in 1951 — most notably the work of Appia and Edward Gordon Craig, and the bare mechanics of classical Greek theatre (much discussed in Wagner's own writings). But Wieland's work in Bayreuth (and in Stuttgart) until his death in 1966 must be accounted a major landmark in the history of Wagner production.

In *Parsifal* (premiered in 1951), a comprehensive spiritual confrontation with the work produced scenery motivated entirely by the 'expression of *Parsifal*'s changing spiritual states'.[33] The Grail domain was essentially a lit space with cyclorama and projections; the Grail temple a raised plinth with the knights grouped around it in an almost complete circle, its architecture suggested by the red-gold outline of four pillars. Within this framework the singers' movement was either monumental, slow, or non-existent, with great use being made of the space between people — Wieland's dramatic confrontations took place either a long way apart or nose to nose. There is a certain irony in the fact that his handling of large ensembles gave the chorus that function of 'a scenic machine made to walk and sing'[34] to which Wagner himself had so objected. But few nineteenth-century choruses can have moved with the precision and concentrated ecstasy that Wieland drew from such moments as the departure of Daland's sailors in Act I of the *Holländer*, the arrival of Lohengrin, the summoning of the Gibichung vassals, or the entry of the knights into the Grail temple.

Wieland's interpretations were quintessentially selective: aspects of a work were put into high focus to throw light on the whole. About the controversial 1956 *Meistersinger* — dubbed *'ohne* [without] Nürnberg' because of the lack (in its first year) of any indication of the town in Act II or of the festival meadow in Act III — he wrote: 'I have centred the individual acts on their high points. I decided these were . . . the congregation's opening chorale . . . , the spirit of St John's night . . . , the "blessed" Quintet and the great "Wach' auf" chorale. There should be neither too much nor too little "milieu' in the production . . . so that . . . above all the element of common humanity . . . can shine strongly through.'[35]

Wieland was also a great developer of productions after their first appearance. By 1963, after twelve years in the repertory, the *Parsifal* production was barely recognizable from its 1951 opening: there remained only the definition of the central oval area where (Greek-style) most of the action was placed and the plinth in the Grail temple. Wieland's first *Ring* (1951–58) began in essence as a highly simplified version of Preetorius's pre-war setting. Taking Act I of *Die Walküre* as an example, by 1953 the naturalistic tree, doorway, and bric-à-brac had vanished in favour of a back-lit rectangle and a rootless central pillar; and by 1957 just that pillar and a triangular beam construct remained in a lit circle, the whole placed on the famous *Scheibe* — the circular (ring-shaped) disc that Wieland found as a unifying device for the whole cycle. Likewise, the Valkyrie Rock in 1951 showed an Appiaesque platform (indicating cliff) and an abstract tree; from 1953 on it became simply a domed empty space at the top of the world, fronting an apparently endless cyclorama sky.

Performance recordings bear witness to Wieland's fanatical work on text and meaning — clarity of enunciation, dramatic shading of phrases, and dynamic use of pauses or added expressive sound such as the knights' cry of pain as Titurel's coffin is opened in Act III of *Parsifal*, Sieglinde's orgasmic scream as Siegmund draws Nothung from the tree, or the terror of the Rhinemaidens as Alberich nears the gold. All had a firm grounding in the speaking-through-singing demanded by Wagner himself at preliminary rehearsals for the first *Ring*.

In 1961, while often lifeless imitations of his work were starting to spring up in most European opera houses, Wieland almost literally began again. 'There can of course be no talk of anything being completed', he had written in 1951. In letters to his collaborators and in interviews he sought continually to widen the net of influences on his productions — citing Brecht (for the 1963 *Meistersinger*), Picasso and Jackson Pollock (for the ever-developing *Parsifal*), Henry Moore (for the symbolic shapes in the 1962 *Tristan*) and 'primitive' artists (for the 1965 *Ring*). While the *Ring, Tristan,* and *Tannhäuser* became more hieratic and abstract in their settings and more statu-

4   Fricka (Margarete Ast) and Wotan (Edgar Keenon) in the first scene of *Die Walküre*, Act II, at Kassel, 1974. Ulrich Melchinger's production, with designs by Thomas Richter-Forgách, incorporated modern high-tech fantasies.

esque in their movement and blocking, *Die Meistersinger* was placed in an Elizabethan-style theatre with more broadly comic characterization and Renaissance comic-strip costumes. Wieland did not live to complete this new direction (especially in the *Ring* production).

In 1970, when Wolfgang Wagner's second new Bayreuth *Ring* was still ringing some last changes on Wieland's *Scheibe* and timeless, mythical production style, Ulrich Melchinger and Thomas Richter-Forgách began a Wagner cycle in Kassel whose anarchic approach harked back to the 1920s but whose characters inhabited a decidedly 1960s' futuristic world of sci-fi and Pop Art. Melchinger's approach put the works back on trial: his *Ring* was definitely four dramas rather than one, and he was not afraid (in *Götterdämmerung*) to confront the opera's stained performing history by showing the Gibichung hall as a pseudo-vision of Benno von Arent. Characters appeared (such as the Wood Bird) and actions were staged (such as the Volsung twins making love before the curtain fell on Act I of *Die Walküre*) that Wielandism had banished to an imaginary distance. Pantomime and comic aspects — and sexual ones — were stressed, especially in *Siegfried*. Melchinger's *Ring* had been preceded by a *Parsifal* in similar vein and was followed by a *Holländer* — the first of three 1970s' productions of this last-named work in which events took place in one of the characters' dreams. Its protagonist was a bogus black magician, a Dracula-like trickster luring credulous young girls to a fate worse than death. Melchinger's important and still underestimated work of (literally) deconstruction peeled another layer off the onion of Wagner production as illusionist fantasy. The anti-Appian revolution had begun.

In Leipzig and Berlin, Joachim Herz, one of Walter Felsenstein's two principal disciples, had already anticipated many trends of Wieland Wagner's post-Appia phase. His 1960 *Meistersinger* (Leipzig) must have been a major influence on Bayreuth in 1963 — a Renaissance comedy played in an Elizabethan stage world devoid of romanticized medieval pomp. His 1962 *Holländer* (later filmed) went further than Wieland in placing the production at the time of the work's conception. His *Ring* cycle (Leipzig 1973–76) had, like Melchinger's, definite built settings (by Rudolf Heinrich) — a kind of anachronistic nineteenth century — and used more locations and scenes than Wagner's stage directions literally prescribe. Act II of *Die Walküre* began inside Valhalla (this became a norm for stagings of the 1970s and 1980s), Act III of *Siegfried* had at least three settings, Siegfried's Rhine Journey and Funeral March were staged and interpreted (the latter as Wotan mourning Siegfried) and action was incorporated from early drafts of the libretto — many Nibelungs were present with Alberich outside Fafner's cave. Herz's production went far towards opening up the social levels of the *Ring* as mirrored in its own historical context and anticipated key directions in Bayreuth's centenary *Ring*. Relatively isolated from world critical attention in the old-style East Germany, Herz's pioneering work has not always received its due in contemporary chronicling.

Felsenstein's other main disciple was Götz Friedrich. His Bayreuth *Tannhäuser* of 1972 restored much of the experimental fire lacking there since the death of Wieland Wagner. It showed Tannhäuser as the artist-outsider in a predominantly hostile (and militaristic) Wartburg society, had the roles of Venus and Elisabeth doubled, and (at least at the first performances) had the final chorus performed in contemporary dress. Like Wieland's Bayreuth *Tannhäuser* productions, it took a similar starting-point to Fehling's Berlin staging of 1933 (there was even a prominent prop harp) with overtones of the isolated German artist in history — Goethe's Tasso, or Heinrich von Kleist. As in all Friedrich's major Wagner productions to date, there was a Wieland-like use of a simple performing area as the basic set unit. But his direction of the singers returned to a realism that was by turns brutal and expressionistic — at the end of her Act III aria, the heartbroken Elisabeth literally crawled offstage. This *Tannhäuser* paved the way for the *new* 'New Bayreuth' of Chéreau, Kupfer, and Friedrich himself, and was instrumental in writing 'finis' to two

5 The final scene of *Das Rheingold* at the Royal Opera House, Covent Garden, 1974–76. Josef Svoboda's designs for Götz Friedrich's production used a hydraulic platform whose motion was 'a symbol of constantly changing and self-generating energy'.

decades of imitation Wielandism worldwide. Friedrich's subsequent London *Ring* (1974–76) played on the 'theatrum mundi' of Josef Svoboda's mobile hydraulic platform. He ably combined the twin influences of Felsenstein's realistic handling of actors with Wieland Wagner's use of a bare stage, coupling this with effective open scene transformations. Ingrid Rosell's costumes were cunning reworkings of mythical models with limited contemporary reference until *Götterdämmerung.* The production essayed a more heroic dramatic style than had been seen in the *Ring* for decades and made a considerable impact on a then rather dormant British opera scene.

The Bayreuth centenary *Ring* production of French theatre director Patrice Chéreau (working with his regular design team of Richard Peduzzi and Jacques Schmidt) proved another landmark in Wagner production. The filmically realistic acting style — which set new standards for opera production — , the major exploration of sub-text to point up dramatic motivation, and the deliberately anachronistic settings, props, and costumes that used elements from the 1850s to the 1970s had all been pioneered in Chéreau's work with the Théâtre

National Populaire in Lyons and Paris. His iconoclasm was matched
by the extreme visual beauty of Peduzzi's settings — influenced by
the neo-Romantic work of Giorgio Strehler and Ezio Frigerio in
Milan — and an unswervingly clear exposition of personal relationships, often of radically new tenderness (the Volsung twins, Wotan's
embracing the dead Siegmund) or violence (the deaths of Siegmund
and Siegfried, the treatment of Alberich in *Das Rheingold*). Chéreau
also gave the clearest exposition to date of several new trends of
thought about characters suggested by Herz, Friedrich, and Jean-
Pierre Ponnelle — the handling of Wotan as a bad loser, the strong
paralleling of Wotan and Alberich in *Siegfried*, and the highly ambivalent treatment of the 'innocence' of the Rhinemaidens.

The effects of Chéreau's 1976 *Ring* — televised widely in the early
1980s and issued on video disc in 1988 — are still being felt. The two
directions it suggested — a return to neo-Romantic pictorialism and
an 'updating' of the action of the cycle — have both been widely
explored. If the neo-Romantic way has often led to a misplaced
conservative intention to rediscover the presumed literalness of
Wagner's stage directions in the spirit of *his* times (for example, the
brave but ultimately confused Peter Hall/William Dudley *Ring* in
Bayreuth in 1983 or the museum creations of Otto Schenk and
Günther Schneider-Siemssen for the New York Metropolitan Opera
Ring in the late 1980s) it has also provided the occasional true
inspiration (Ponnelle's genuinely Romantic, medieval *Tristan* in Bayreuth in 1981). The 'updating' of the cycle, with particular reference
to the theme identified by Chéreau of man destroying Nature through
misuse of mechanical energy, was the mainspring idea behind
Friedrich's second completed *Ring* (Berlin 1984–85) and Kupfer's in
Bayreuth (1988). Friedrich and his designer, Peter Sykora, set the
action in a massive 'time-tunnel', a kind of nuclear shelter where the
survivors reenact the play of the *Nibelung's Ring* in an attempt to
understand man's downfall. Once again the costumes were modern-
ized mythical and Friedrich's direction incorporated the newer, sharper,
less realistic acting style 'pioneered' by Hans Neuenfels, Ruth Berghaus,
and other contemporary German directors that is in many ways a
throwback to Russian and German experimentation of the 1920s.

Kupfer made a strong Bayreuth début in 1978 with a *Holländer* set
firmly in the 1840s and seen as Senta's dream; there were even *two*
Dutchmen — a suitor introduced by Daland and the more lurid
figure of his daughter's imagining. At the end a deluded Senta
committed suicide by jumping from a window into the street.[36]
Kupfer's *Ring*, also post-holocaust, was set by designer Hans
Schavernoch on a 'road of history,' another ingenious unit setting
for the cycle. Kupfer directed many of the roles in a realistic, human

6 *Siegfried*, Act II, in Otto Schenk's production of the *Ring* at the Met, 1989. Günther Schneider-Siemssen's designs sought to use modern technology to fulfil Wagner's original scenic intentions.

way (especially the gods and the Wotan/Fricka relationship), providing more valuable insights into the text through demythologizing. In Brussels (1991) Herbert Wernicke staged a less political *Ring* in a unit setting which retained geographical elements from all four works during the cycle. Costumes were part-modern, part-folkloric. Many of Wernicke's ideas — including an omnipresent grand piano with Erda seated at it — were theatrical rather than sub-textually interpretative. He had previously staged a *Holländer* played entirely in Daland's rich bourgeois living room — a potent image for the Dutchman as outsider — and a modern-dress *Meistersinger*.

Even the most experimental of later twentieth-century Wagner productions have maintained a referential narrative visual framework, using either present-day or nineteenth-century equivalents for necessary symbols and scenery — that is, until Berghaus brought her 'writing degree zero' approach to bear on *Parsifal*, the *Ring* (Frankfurt 1982 and 1985–87) and *Tristan* (Hamburg 1990). Berghaus (and her designer, Axel Manthey) work by finding 'signs' in set and costumes to delineate the essential points of the drama; their stage geography is mostly emotional and symbolic rather than showing naturalistic time and place. Narrative or melodramatic tension is almost completely banished; facts about the work are presented in

7   The gods enter Valhalla in Ruth Berghaus's production of *Das Rheingold* at Frankfurt (1985), with designs by Axel Manthey, one of the adventure playground sets in this bafflingly brilliant *Ring*.

isolation from naturalistic chronology. Psychological character states are often shown physically — for example, the gods in *Das Rheingold* are hampered in their dealings with the other characters by having to walk on small, square platforms. Berghaus's productions call into question the whole premise of conveying information in the staging of a work, and seem certain to leave a mark on end-of-the-century Wagner production — the Richard Jones/Nigel Lowery Scottish Opera *Ring* cycle begun in 1989 being a case in point.

The complexity of the dramaturgical and scenographical demands of Wagner's operas made their creation and establishment in the repertory a key factor in the growth of the role of the producer. The first Bayreuth Festivals probably created most interest because of the sheer scale of the works being presented; since that time key productions there have become benchmarks for production worldwide, and the stagings of Wagner himself, of Wieland Wagner, Friedrich, Chéreau and Kupfer have had far-reaching influence on the entire operatic repertory on stage. The history of Wagner interpretation *per se* became something of a testing ground for the state of opera production in general. Despite Cosima's well-intended narrow-mindedness it rapidly became clear that the attempt to confine the music dramas to the pictorial world of nineteenth-century grand opera meant merely imprisoning them. So the first work to be done — heralded by Appia's discoveries — was in the area of the performing space: the chance to establish dramas of the mind, rather than dramas of scenic location. The 'attacking' productions of the post-1918 period demonstrated beyond doubt that Wagner's dramaturgy was universal. Interplay between characters and the subject-matter of their dramatic dialogues — as with the Greeks, Shakespeare, and Goethe whom Wagner idolized — could function in different times and spaces. Producers, like conductors and singers before them, came out from behind the works, starting to choose and direct rather than merely illustrate. To Wieland Wagner was given the platform to make a wide-ranging and continuous statement about the whole Wagner canon. The timeless, mythical direction he chose is still provoking a reaction today. In the 1970s a flood of newly available background material — *Cosima Wagner's Diaries*, the *Brown Book*, a complete edition of Wagner's autobiography, *Mein Leben* — added more fuel to the dramaturgical interest in the works. The focus shifted to exploring the works in the context of their contemporary history, both Wagner's and that of the world around him. This, combined with increased study of the musicological problems and history of Wagner's scores, has resulted in both more aspects of a work being staged than ever before and a growing feeling that no one production need attempt to be all-embracing.

Chapter 4

Designing Wagner:
Deeds of Music Made Visible?

Patrick Carnegy

If it might be going too far to hold Wagner responsible for the arts of stage production and design as we understand them today, he nevertheless played a central role at their birth. Eduard Hanslick called Wagner 'the world's first *Regisseur* [director]',[1] and in 1885 that was already a two-edged compliment. For could not all this directorial virtuosity be no more than a marketing front for operas of suspect musical value? What Hanslick stumbles on here is not a value judgement of any significance but rather the realization that in Wagner's works stage production assumes a wholly new importance. With the possible exception of the spectacular shows at the Paris Opéra earlier in the century, not since the engineered stage marvels of Inigo Jones and Bibiena had stage marvels *per se* absorbed so much thought, money, and invention and sought so large a share of the public's interest and attention.

It was Wagner's gift for coaxing totally committed vocal and physical performances from his singers that earned him Hanslick's description. Wagner was less successful in pursuit of stage settings of equivalent power. On the one hand he was tempted to emulate the grandiose marvels of the Paris Opéra, while on the other he strove none too confidently for something that would be more than sumptuous stage dressing and would be the faithful servant of the inner life of the music and drama.

Towards the end of his life he spoke of his works as 'deeds of music made visible' ('ersichtlich gewordene Taten der Musik'),[2] without being over-explicit about what that 'visibility' was, or how it was to be achieved. Although it is often suggested that Wagner's visual taste in stage décor was limited to epic realism and Romantic naturalism, this is a partial and misleading truth. Resisting the historical and mythological conjurations of King Ludwig's scenic artists (who had been responsible for the Munich performances of *Holländer*, *Tristan*, *Lohengrin*, *Tannhäuser*, *Die Meistersinger*, *Das Rheingold*, *Die Walküre*,

and *Rienzi*), for the first complete performances of the *Ring* at
Bayreuth Wagner took the highly unusual step of commissioning *not*
an established scene-painter but a landscape artist. This was Josef
Hoffmann of Vienna, whose designs were handed over to a scenic
supply studio (that run by the brothers Max and Gotthold Brückner
of Coburg) for practical realization. (His first idea had been the
gloomily symbolic artist Arnold Böcklin, to whom, as an inspirational
source, Cosima Wagner later returned for Bayreuth's 1896 *Ring*
production.) When it came to *Parsifal*, Wagner again turned to an
artist rather than a scene-painter — this time a young Russian, Paul
von Joukowsky.

The fruit of both these initiatives disappointed Wagner's expectations, though without exposing the true source of the problem. He
did, however, get as far as concluding that his stage directions 'must
remain puzzles for aesthetic criticism until they have fulfilled their
purpose as technically fixed points in a complete dramatic representation, as hints for acting, as stimuli for the creative imagination'.[3]

The importance of this statement lies in its admittance of a *plural-
ity* of interpretative possibility, in its acknowledgement that the operas were not dependent on the saving grace of a single, definitive,
set of stage pictures. It was in the same spirit that, very much earlier
(23 August 1856), Wagner had told August Röckel that the artist was
not wholly master of his creations and need not be ashamed to stand
before them like an outsider, discovering in them more than he had
consciously put there.

The reason why the modern art of *Inszenierung* (staging) comes
into being with Wagner is that his works make unprecedented demands in this area. It is not just the scale of the scenic demands
(often scarcely less great than those made by, say, Meyerbeer or
Verdi), but a palpable, articulate demand that more than stage
decoration and scenic spectacle were required. Wagner wanted the
staging to be an organic whole with the musical drama — something
that would be beyond decoration and scene-setting and serve the
inner life of the drama and not just its external aspect. The Festspielhaus was designed to create a total illusion for the spectator. The
invisible orchestra, the totally dark auditorium, the double proscenium arch were all part of a conspiracy to merge the spectator's
sensory world with that of the stage. It was the apotheosis of the
theatre of illusion, seducing the spectator into believing that he or
she was part of a timeless mythic world. What unfortunately de-
tracted from this goal was that the aesthetic and technical problems
of constructing credible journeyings through the bed of the Rhine,
from open mountain tops down into the bowels of the earth and
back, and then across a rainbow bridge into Valhalla, were beyond

8   An artist's impression of the Bayreuth Festspielhaus in 1875. Modelled on a Greek amphitheatre, the auditorium employed un-Greek devices (sunken orchestra, darkened auditorium) to maximize the spectators' sense of immersion in the mythic world of gods, Nibelungs and heroic humans.

nineteenth-century scenic technology. At crucial points the illusion faltered. Strenuous mechanical efforts to bolster it up left little room for the cultivation of a visual world sympathetic to the inner life of the drama. Advisers like Carl Brandt and Richard Fricke counselled Wagner unsuccessfully against certain scenic literalisms (the dragon, chariot with rams, and so on) which, as experienced theatre men, they recognized were doomed to fail both as credible stage effects and as symbolic markers.[4] They vainly argued that an unseen dragon would make a far more powerful impression on the imagination than a pantomime prop — and history, as in Wieland Wagner's 1965 Bayreuth *Ring*, has proved them correct.

All in all, Wagner the *régisseur* succeeded in securing from his performers a level of exceptional mimetic characterization in tune with the expressive potential of the words and vocal line, but without being able to match this with any equally imaginative visual world.

Questions of faithful rendition, of stylization, of symbolism, of critical and interpretative staging are posed and concentrated as never before in Wagner's works. The composer's Schopenhauerian recognition that music was preeminent in the hierarchy of the constituent elements in the *Gesamtkunstwerk* (or total work of art) was responsible for his abandonment of the 'equality of all elements' position he had advocated in *Oper und Drama*. It created more problems than Wagner knew how to solve, but it was with his intuition that staging must seek its validation in the score as well as the text that the story of modern staging begins.

No photographic documentation of either the 1876 *Ring* or the 1882 *Parsifal* at Bayreuth survives. This is unfortunate in that neither Hoffmann's sketches for the *Ring*, nor Joukowsky's for *Parsifal*, nor the subsequent magazine illustrators and engravers give a reliable impression of what the settings actually looked like and how they worked in practice. There is, however, a photographic record of Angelo Neumann's touring version of the *Ring*—itself an impresarial achievement scarcely less remarkable than Wagner's feat in staging his works in the Festspielhaus. Under the flag of 'as performed at Bayreuth' Neumann improved many of the creakier parts of Wagner's staging. He became a virtuoso in the deployment of coloured-steam technology, but the photographic and eye-witness records give the impression that the scenic contribution was little more than a picturesque backdrop for the musical and histrionic virtuosity of the singers.

It was not until 1896 that the *Ring* returned to the Bayreuth stage. In the twenty years since the premiere no new thought about scenic design had impinged on general consciousness. Nothing changed because it was neither expected nor desired that anything should change. Cosima Wagner herself showed a certain genius in the coaching of the principal singers, though her only goal was scrupulous observation of Wagner's own direction as she and her assistants remembered it.

Cosima commissioned the scenic artist Max Brückner to follow Wagner's staging rubrics to the letter. He and his brother Gotthold were perhaps the best-known suppliers of theatrical scenery and effects in Europe. They were expert at furnishing a stage with flats and drops painted down to the last leaf and stone, and with virtuoso handling of every trompe-l'oeil device, including false perspective and in-built shadows. Cosima praised Brückner for the 'conscientious, affectionate regard for every detail of the poem', but her son-in-law, Houston Stewart Chamberlain, disparaged them as 'sufficiently well-known Brückneresque window dressing without a trace of inventiveness or genius'.[5] The most interesting thing about this comment is the highly unusual expectation that design might make a *creative* contribution to a production.

The conservative, nationalistic tenor of Chamberlain's copious historical and literary studies should not allow credit to be withheld from him as the first among the Bayreuth circle to recognize and

9, 10 For the world premiere of the *Ring* at Bayreuth, 1876, Wagner's chosen designer was the Viennese landscape painter Josef Hoffmann. His designs, as for Hunding's hut in Act I of *Die Walküre* (*above*), were translated into painted scenery by the Brückners' scenic studio in Coburg, and bore little relation to what the scenery actually looked like on stage. No photographic record of the 1876 Bayreuth *Ring* survives: a photograph of the same scene (*below*) taken in Leipzig, 1878, of the impresario Angelo Neumann's touring version of the *Ring*, provides some idea.

fight, unsuccessfully, for an approach to stage design utterly different from the composer's. This approach was that of his protégé
Adolphe Appia (1862–1928), a young Swiss theatrical visionary who,
as a nineteen-year-old music student, had attended one of the first
performances of *Parsifal* at Bayreuth in 1882.[6] Deeply moved by the
music, he felt that its transcendental impression was betrayed by
luxuriant settings which vainly strove to create illusions of picturesque grandeur.

The essence of Appia's critique was that the music embodied a
drama that was always developing, infinitely supple and rich in eerie
gradation of light and shade. But Wagner's Bayreuth settings were a
succession of illustrative, static tableaux, and once a scene had been
set the lighting hardly varied. The purpose of stage lighting, as then
understood by Wagner and the most advanced stage-managers, was
simply to illuminate a painted picture and as much as possible of the
actors. Appia especially hated footlights — the epitome of unnatural
lighting (the sun, he remarked, was not generally observed to do its
work from below).

Appia was a wholehearted Schopenhauerian in that he believed
that the primary force in opera was music, and that whatever the
prescription of the stage instructions it alone held the clues to the
staging, whose business it was to be the 'opened eye of the score' —
an idea wholly consonant with Wagner's 'deeds of music made
visible'. Scenery painted on flats had to be abolished. The settings
needed to be vaguely suggestive, or even coldly abstract, in order that
they should be capable of changing with time even as the music does.
The principal agent of change was to be the recently invented
electric lighting console with its ability to orchestrate a play of light
upon the stage in exact sympathy with the music. For Appia, there
was a powerful affinity between music and light in that both expressed what Schopenhauer called the inner essence of phenomena.
But light could also imitate phenomena, that is, suggest fire, clouds,
water, and so on — just as music could. The goal of these reforms was
to clear the stage space so that attention would be focused principally
on the singing actor. Just as the space around him was to be determined by the music, so were also his movements, gestures, and vocal
expression, though it was not until Appia's eurhythmic work with
Emile Jaques-Dalcroze (from 1906) that he began to see how this
might be done.

Appia worked out detailed staging scenarios which carefully distinguished between the realistic and transcendental content of each
work. In *Parsifal* the action was to be determined solely by the
psychological development of the hero. The *Ring* could not be
staged without some compromise between realism and abstraction to

point up the contrast between action-dominated passages when 'Wotan's creatures act of their own volition' and those of 'pure musical expression' when they act as puppets responding to Wotan's own will. He considered that *Die Meistersinger* needed a definitive, even historically specific, setting, whereas in the introverted world of *Tristan* the scene on board ship in the first act is 'the last glimpse of the material and tangible world'.

What Appia wanted, above all, was to interiorize the drama, and nothing suited this aim better than *Tristan*. The main principle for staging it, he said, consisted in 'making the audience see the drama through the eyes of the hero and heroine'. When Isolde enters at the beginning of the second act, 'she sees only two things: the absence of Tristan and the torch; the reason for his absence'. The stage is thus to be dominated by 'a large bright torch in the *centre* of the picture . . . . When Isolde extinguishes the torch, the setting takes on a uniform chiaroscuro in which the eye loses itself, unarrested by any line or object. Isolde rushing to meet Tristan is plunged into a mysterious darkness increasing the impression of depth which the setting gives to the right half of the stage.' This way of thinking may not seem so strange today, but in the 1890s it was wholly new.

The first practical trial of Appia's ideas did not come until 1903 in the private theatre in Paris of the comtesse de Béarn, when scenes not from Wagner but from Byron's *Manfred* with Schumann's music, and from the second act of *Carmen*, were given with the help of a lighting system devised by Mariano Fortuny. Appia's work with Jaques-Dalcroze at a festival theatre at Hellerau, outside Dresden, impressed a wider audience. Max Reinhardt and George Bernard Shaw were among those who attended performances in 1912 and 1913 of Gluck's *Orfeo* which epitomized the classical austerity of Appia's ideas. Knowledge of these had spread among cognoscenti, but there was to be no limelight trial of his lifetime's work on Wagner until Toscanini invited him to design *Tristan* for La Scala in 1923. For this Appia turned his back on the geometric, abstract severity he had developed with Jaques-Dalcroze and returned to the visionary scenario from the 1890s which was quoted above. Appia's friend Jean Mercier came in as technical director and injected *some* colour, such as a dark-blue cyclorama for Act I, into Appia's characteristically monochromatic scheme. The public's response to Appia's scenic contribution was far from enthusiastic, but Toscanini was warmly supportive and one favourable critic compared the scenic style with Caravaggio's paintings, and likened the effect achieved in Act III to that of Rembrandt's etchings.

For *Das Rheingold* and *Die Walküre* at Basel (1924–25) Appia made new designs which bore no trace of the mystic Romanticism and

11, 12   The Swiss artist Adolphe Appia produced non-representational settings in contrast to the Romantic archaeology of Wagner's stage instructions. Appia's sketch (*above*) (early 1890s) for the end of Act II of *Die Walküre*, and the same scene (*below*) when finally staged at the Stadttheater Basel, 1925, revealed the gap between design and realization.

symbolism of the designs, all rejected by Cosima Wagner, he had prepared for Bayreuth in the 1890s. The settings, in Hellerau '*Espaces rhythmiques*' style (that is, 'rhythmic spaces' in abstract, minimalist vein), were combinations of platforms, stairs, ramps, and a few pillars, with curtains masking the wings, a plain blue-grey backdrop, and the occasional use of a traveller curtain to cut off the upstage area for more intimate foreground scenes. Although the public response was more sympathetic than in Milan, hostile reaction triumphed and the *Ring* was not completed. Appia continued to dream and to design — for Gluck, Ibsen, Goethe's *Faust, Lohengrin, Die Meistersinger,* and a magnificent *Lear* project — but had only secured the merest handful of actual stagings before his death at the age of sixty-five in 1928. But such was his reputation, which his writing helped to spread, that by the time he died many European and Russian directors had adopted or adapted his ideas. Appia's friends Oskar Wälterlin and Jacques Copeau spread the gospel in France and Switzerland, while Jean Mercier took it to America. Vsevolod Meyerhold's *Tristan* at St Petersburg in 1909 showed clear signs of Appian influence, but this was not to touch Bayreuth until Emil Preetorius began the work of replacing the settings hallowed by tradition but which could not be patched up for much longer. The wind of change was not blowing exclusively from Appia's direction, but it was his designs and theories which were the decisive break with Romantic naturalism and which first suggested how electric lighting could revolutionize theatre history. This, however, was not to be widely apparent until Wieland Wagner's Bayreuth productions of the 1950s fulfilled the promise of Appia's dreams.

Since then, forty years of unprecedented theatrical innovation have put Appia's work into critical perspective. Appia was in pursuit of definitively perfect stage realizations, of the discovery of 'ideal' stagings deduced primarily from the music. He could not bear it that any element in the drama should be undetermined. Appia allowed no sense of latitude, nor even of limits within which such alternatives and variations would be tolerable or desirable. In this sense he is strangely aligned with Cosima Wagner — both were in pursuit of idealistic stagings, if from totally different angles: hers that of refining and perpetuating the whole book of the composer's intentions, his that of liberating the scenic potential he heard in the music. If Appia had had more opportunity to see his ideas developing on the stage rather than on the drawing-board, he might have become more flexible in his demands. But it was to be many years before the goal of a 'perfect performance' was seriously questioned, and the notion that 'great works were greater than they could ever be performed' gathered momentum with its corollary that different approaches to the same work are both possible and hugely desirable.

In 1903, the year in which Appia had seen the first trial of his ideas in the comtesse de Béarn's private theatre, *Tristan* was staged at the Vienna Hofoper in commemoration of the twentieth anniversary of Wagner's death. This was probably the first major professional production which quite deliberately sought to break away from Bayreuth orthodoxy. It was conducted by Mahler, who chose as designer the artist Alfred Roller, president of the Viennese Secession and friend of Gustav Klimt. Just as the Secession had come into being through dissatisfaction with the monumental style of late nineteenth-century academy art, so now the same principle challenged, if less radically than Appia, the illustrative world of traditional staging. This was partly a matter of getting a cleaner stage picture in which the expressive power of colour and light could begin to play a more prominent role.

Mike Ashman, in chapter 3, has referred to Mahler and Roller splitting the deck level in *Tristan* to separate Isolde's quarters from those of the crew (the ship also sported a defiant red sail); other radical amendments included allowing the play of light on the waves to be seen, a starry night sky for Act II instead of the canonical leafy canopy, and the use of fluctuating light to mirror the lovers' moods and feelings. Here, as in Roller's subsequent *Ring* and other designs for Vienna, there was a radical departure from leaf-and-branch invocation of Nature in favour of suggestion (a projection of scudding clouds but no horses for the valkyries' ride), and stylization of almost expressionistic intensity (a 1903 study for Scene 2 of *Das Rheingold*, in the Theatersammlung of the Österreichische Nationalbibliothek, shows soft mauvy-pink clouds against a greeny sky). None of this would have been possible without the relatively novel use of a cyclorama, solid scenery, and a rapidly developing lighting technology.

The Secessionist delight in exuberantly decorative effects is seen in the costumes and furnishing detail which make not the least pretence at archaeological exactitude. A photograph of Act I of *Tristan* shows a wealth of *Jugendstil* detailing in Isolde's couch and ample medicine chest.[7] The 'modernism' of Roller's approach was not enthusiastically received by the Viennese. Radical though it seemed — and was — at the time, the aesthetically decorative qualities of his work absorbed him too swiftly into the new mainstream of extravagant, impeccably detailed theatre design (for example, Roller's décor for the world premiere of *Der Rosenkavalier* in 1911). His *Jugendstil* initiative was widely copied. As an escape route from nineteenth-century historicism it played an important part, but it too quickly became divorced from Roller's original reforming intentions (seen also in superbly structural designs for *Don Giovanni*, which used a pair of double-level adaptable box-towers — a characteristic feature of his work) so that the sheerly decorative impulse triumphed over the more severely organic needs of the Wagnerian music drama as Appia would have seen them. Roller's Secession style scarcely changed between 1914 and 1933, by which time he was sufficiently safe and venerable for Bayreuth to entrust him with the first changes to *Parsifal* settings since the work's premiere a half-century before (1882). In the Grail Temple massive green-tinged pillars contrasted with the red costumes of the knights, while the almost *pointilliste* colour effects of classical *Jugendstil* flickered in the Good Friday meadows. The Bayreuth traditionalists were, of course, outraged by these innovations.

Roller paved the way for important theatre work by, or inspired by, other major figures in the history of twentieth-century art. The consensus conservatism of most opera houses and the turbulent radicalism of cubism, expressionism, abstraction, constructivism, and Bauhaus structuralism could not have been further apart. Artists like Kandinsky and Kokoschka were irresistibly drawn to the theatre, often because they saw it as a highly desirable extension of their work as painters. Kandinsky's own non-figurative development had been crucially influenced by Wagner's music, which had helped suggest the possibility (and validity) of painting as a free interplay of colour, form, and line without having to 'represent' anything in particular.

Modern artists, however, were to have little impact on Wagnerian staging until Otto Klemperer's directorship of Berlin's Kroll Opera (1927–31). This brief period of ceaselessly innovative theatre work (terminated by the Nazis) brought the brave new horizons of modern art into the opera house. The Kroll designers included such names as László Moholy-Nagy and Oskar Schlemmer, and prominent among them was Ewald Dülberg, whose proposed Gauguinesque treatment of the Flowermaidens as Tahitian beauties had been rejected by Hamburg in 1914. (A cult of seeing an exotic tribal primitivism in Wagner doubtless owed much to the immense impact of the visual vocabulary of Diaghilev's Ballets Russes, 1909–29.)

By the late 1920s the mood for Tahitian exoticism had long since passed. Dülberg's designs for *Der fliegende Holländer* in 1929 were conceived with its producer Jürgen Fehling, a pupil of Leopold Jessner, whose Berlin productions (1919–25) had, probably independently of Appia, developed starkly simplified stagings relying on the effects of light on steps, ramps, and block-built scenery.

The chastening winds of 1920s' *Neue Sachlichkeit* (New Objectivity; perhaps best translated, by John Willett, as 'The New Sobriety') filled the sails of Dülberg's *Holländer*. The ships were reduced to the barest schematic symbols — three red squares for the Dutchman's, a single orange-framed rectangle for Daland's. There was no attempt to move the ships, no Romantic evocation of the sea's moods by projections, no rocky coast. Against a predominantly dark-blue background, functional lighting disclosed the diagrammatic seas and ships by making the apparently solid rear wall of Daland's house temporarily transparent. All traces of Norwegian maritime folk culture had vanished. The Dutchman was stripped of his beard and hat, while Senta was a simple peasant girl who 'looked as though she might have stepped out of a drawing by Käthe Kollwitz'.[8]

This production had flung down the gauntlet of modernism and was excoriated by the many factions who felt that Germany's cultural heritage was at risk. It was, but from National Socialism, which was so shortly to put a stop to all such decadent experimentalism. Fehling's and Dülberg's *Holländer* was no isolated phenomenon at the Kroll. Other operatic classics like *Fidelio* received equally revolutionary treatment. The shock of radical reappraisal of staging's contribution to opera was one which managements and public alike were not prepared to begin to digest for another quarter of a century.

Appia's ideas had sprung from the music: his rationale of staging was that it should free the stage space from every decorative, illustrative irrelevance so that the singing-actor could most directly communicate and release the subterranean power of the music. The Kroll's aesthetic was that scenic invention could make a new and legitimate contribution to perception, altering for the better the way we responded to familiar works. The scene designer sought not only to give an 'honest' presentation (in *Neue Sachlichkeit* spirit) of the necessary visual symbols, but also to invite the audience to look at theatre in a different way, just as impressionism, cubism, expressionism, and other movements in art had done for perception of the world around us.

Nazi cultural policy effectively curtailed both the avant-garde adventurousness exemplified by the Kroll and the evolution elsewhere of a more stylized approach to scenic design. But despite the Führer's fondness for Bayreuth, Wagner's own theatre enjoyed a measure of independence and, with an ironical sense of timing, began to make changes in another direction than the monumental, neo-Germanic naturalism favoured by state policy. Emil Preetorius's *Ring* designs of 1933–42 were a resourceful compromise between the imperatives of Bayreuth's canonical literalism and the freer, consciously symbolic shapes and spaces advocated by Appia in the 1890s. Preetorius, a Jungian at heart, saw the *Ring* as embodying 'archetypes of eternal events'[9] and sought to avoid any historical sense of time and place. His answer to Wagner's mimetic evocations of Nature in the music (which he recognized as perhaps the major scenic problem to be

13 Emil Preetorius's design for *Die Walküre*, Act III, at Bayreuth, 1933-42, was a skilled compromise between Bayreuth conservatism and the concentration on essentials advocated by Appia since the 1890s.

solved) was to complement these with theatrical suggestion rather than pictorial illusion.

For the great film director Sergey Eisenstein, the *Ring* told of mythic times when man and Nature were indivisible. He regarded Wagner as a precursor of 'the audio-visual polyphony of contemporary montage', and in his sole opera production — of *Die Walküre* in 1940 at the Moscow Bolshoy — his visual imagery had no other purpose than to illustrate the myth behind the music. Hunding's hut was dominated by an immense ash tree with a vast tangle of branches which Eisenstein had vainly hoped would be allowed to reach into the auditorium, thus welding audience and performers as co-celebrants of a primitive ritual drama. No opportunity was lost to demonstrate the integration of man and Nature: Fricka's rams were human/animal cross-breeds who pleaded with her for Siegmund's life, while at the end of Act II (also presided over by the ash tree) the rocky cliffs heaved up and down with the music during Siegmund's fight with Hunding. Nothing was referred to in music or text without Eisenstein trying to show it visually — thus the use of the mime extras described by Mike Ashman (see chapter 3), and not only the valkyries but Wotan himself taking to the air on wires. Eisenstein's hope of using film to depict the events of Siegmund's Act I narration did not materialize, and it is hard to know how successful was his attempt (perhaps not dissimilar from the introduction of colour into his last film) to find a fluctuating coloured-light equivalent for the music of Wotan's Farewell.

This extraordinary attempt to put the filmmaker's eye to work on Wagner had been commissioned by Stalin in celebration of the Nazi-Soviet pact signed in 1939. By 1941 Hitler had invaded the USSR, and *Die Walküre*, no longer the myth of the moment, was never revived. It was time for Eisenstein's anti-German film *Alexander Nevsky* (1938) to be shown again. It may not be over-fanciful to imagine that reports of Eisenstein's obsession with illustrative techniques in *Die Walküre* may have influenced Walter Felsenstein's strategy of *Realistisches Musiktheater* (realistic music theatre) at the East Berlin Komische Oper from 1947.[10]

But it was not until the Wagner grandsons, Wieland and Wolfgang, took control at Bayreuth from 1951 that the long overdue revolution in design and production could begin in earnest. The war had created a climate in which it was imperative, and most of all in the new Germany, that Wagner's works should be seen to have a better, truer life apart from the emblematic nationalism that had been thrust upon them. Yet whatever the considerable background political pressures, there can be no question that the view of Wagner manifest in the productions of New Bayreuth was first and foremost a response to the intrinsic content of the works themselves. Not that there was anything 'aesthetical' about it. Rather did it spring from passionate conviction that the values of myth and archetype were preeminent, and that the *Ring* was an incomparably potent map of the human psyche.

This was the true import of the insights of Adolphe Appia and the pioneer scenic reformers. It was high time that they were honoured in Wagner's own theatre, although it can well be imagined what resistance they encountered from the surviving members of the Fafner fraternity, whose sole expectation of Bayreuth was that it should be the faithful guardian of the Grail. 'Cosima's ban and curse on Appia's book *Musik und Inszenierung*,' wrote Wieland Wagner, 'was responsible for stuffing Bayreuth with moth-ridden conceptions for decades, so that its original revolutionary function changed into its opposite'. He argued that it was 'an insult to Wagner the composer to identify his mythological conceptions with the notorious mediocrity of nineteenth-century impotent and pseudo-naturalistic painters, who sought, without making any original contribution to the process, to adapt the achievements of Classicism and Romanticism to the taste of the *nouveau riche*'. Only in Germany and Switzerland, claimed Wieland, 'have any courageous attempts been made to break free from this slavish attitude by placing the conceptions of twentieth-century cubism, expressionism, and abstract painting at the service of Wagnerian opera'.[11]

Wieland had studied with the Munich artist Ferdinand Staeger and had always interested himself at least as much in design as in production. It is hardly possible to imagine a more daunting assignment, and under a harsher spotlight, than the thirty-four-year-old Wieland's first Bayreuth *Ring* of 1951. This should perhaps best be seen as a logical extension of Preetorius's tactful progress towards a stronger, cleaner look within traditionalist guidelines. From 1953 those guidelines were questioned ever more radically by Wieland in his quest for the innermost life of the drama. In essence this goal was identical with that of Appia, but Wieland had the authority and superb technical support that Appia had lacked. Wieland was particularly fortunate in his lighting designer, Paul Eberhardt, with whose help he orchestrated an endlessly inventive play of light upon the stage and cyclorama.

Apart from abstract patterning and stylized textural effects, there was soon not a pictorial drop or flat to be seen in the *Ring, Tristan,* and *Parsifal.* Everything was achieved by the effects of light penetrating and interfusing a stage space in which simple, elemental shapes and objects predominated. It was a theatre of depth-illusion: darkness enveloping and uniting stage and audience. The singers emerged from near total gloom. Specific visual imagery was kept to minimal points of reference. It was left to the imagination, to the spectator's 'theatre of the mind', to complete the picture. Thus was solved the problem of dragons, bears, horses, rams, and other impossibilities alluded to in the text — they had not so much been 'left out' as consigned to a life of their own in the murkier margins of the stage.

Wieland showed himself unfailingly resourceful in the invention of visual symbols complementary to the archetypal truths and patterns he discerned in the music. He had hoped that Henry Moore might have helped him flesh out his archetypal view of the *Ring,* but the sculptor declined and Wieland had perforce to do the job himself. In *Tannhäuser* (1961) there was no wayside shrine for Elisabeth's prayers but only a huge black cross towering out of sight behind the proscenium. In *Tristan* (1962), each act was dominated by a phallic representation — whether the prow of the ship, the all-seeing totem of the second act, or the sharp, pierced segment which presided over Tristan's delirious death-throes. The curve of the stage floor suggested the surface of some mysterious, alien planet. In her Transfiguration, Isolde, in yellow, rose up like a new sun while the light behind her was that of the moon's final eclipse into eternal night.

Wieland's second and last *Ring* (1965) was extraordinarily successful in its evocation of a shadowy, subliminal world. A disc, or *Scheibe,* raised about 1.8 metres above stage level, was the unifying central

14 Wieland and Wolfgang Wagner's post-war Bayreuth (from 1951) owed a great deal to Appia's vision and found the lighting technology to do justice to it. In Act I of Wieland Wagner's *Tristan* (1962) all that remains of the ship is its towering, stylized prow.

feature and principal arena of action, with a curved cyclorama behind (Wieland's earlier *Ring* had also used a *Scheibe*, but in a rather different way). The lower part of the cyclorama, immediately behind the *Scheibe*, was kept dark so that the action seemed to be floating in space and even disembodied at times, an effect often accentuated by using a narrow follow spot to illuminate only a singer's head and shoulders. The impression was of a dream half-recalled, with archetypal images and patterns, sometimes indeterminate, sometimes quite explicit, as in *Das Rheingold* where the gilded blocks of the hoard, when completely piled, showed a primitive icon of the female form. In *Siegfried*, two glints of light and a little smoke sufficed to suggest that the opening of Mime's cave had transformed itself into Fafner's mouth when the dwarf first tells Siegfried of the dragon. With the ex-

15   In Scene 4 of Wieland Wagner's *Das Rheingold* (1965) the golden ransom piled in front of Freia built a primitive icon of female fertility.

ception of Brünnhilde's awakening, the stage never seemed much more than twilight bright. The eye was never tempted to stray into the distance of a Romantic Rhine perspective but always concentrated firmly on the *Scheibe*. Such constructional scenery as there was resembled subterranean rock formations. When Hagen summoned the vassals, the circle of light on the *Scheibe* expanded to reveal that they were already there, surrounding the space. They, like everyone and everything else, were omnipresent and only awaiting their cue to appear.

Wieland's stagings were a brilliant solution to those contradictions and inconsistencies which undermine the very notion of music drama. If they refused to echo the more mimetic musical effects, they magnificently served the more abstract, Schopenhauerian qualities of Wagner's scores. In the dim light, the mysteries of *Urwelt* and archetype were invited to make themselves manifest.

Myth and psychology apart, Wieland always sought to cut through accumulated cliché and to revitalize the living heart of the operas. This was very evident in two productions of *Die Meistersinger*, the first

(1956) rejecting specific evocation of sixteenth-century Nuremberg in favour of the bare minimum of visual reference — for example, in Act II a huge floral sphere suspended above Sachs's head on a largely bare stage instead of the expected representation of a half-timbered street scene and elder tree. The second production (1963) was located in and around an Elizabethan Globe-style theatre.

Wieland Wagner's work at Bayreuth and at Stuttgart (which he liked to call his 'Winter Bayreuth', and where he staged sixteen productions) was cut short tragically early by his death in 1966. This was all too soon after he had, at long last, discovered in Pierre Boulez a conductor (in the first place for *Parsifal*) whose philosophy of ceaseless change and radical reappraisal matched his own. Possibly out of dissatisfaction with the conservatism of many of the conductors with whom he worked (sometimes, as in the case of Hans Knappertsbusch, a conservative of genius), Wieland adopted a progressively robust attitude to his grandfather's scores, confident in the belief that 'with all the great composers who wrote for the theatre the initial impulse was not the music but the theatrical idea'.[12] This led to cuts (such as the episode of Gutrune's anxiety in the Gibichung hall before Siegfried's body is brought in) and undermined the tenability of the hypothetical notion (admittedly Appia's rather than Wieland's) that the staging was to be 'the opened eye of the score', the faithful servant of the *music* rather than anything else. It was, however, Wieland's great achievement to have put irretrievably out of court the idea, to which Bayreuth had previously been dedicated, that there was any vitality in *Werktreue* as the goal of performance. 'A naturalistic set today', he argued in 1966, 'would simply destroy an illusion, not create one'.[13]

The *new* illusion that Wieland created had one important thing in common with the old one which had been Wagner's goal in 1876: namely, that both presupposed that the *Ring* was a coherent unity that had to be demonstrated in performance. This was to provide a toe-hold on a slippery cliff face for those who were looking for what could be done after Wieland, whose production strategy (very much against his own attitude) became an orthodoxy that was widely copied, just as Cosima's old one had been. Another creative provocation was that Wieland's preoccupation with finding visual equivalents for the psychology of the music drama rather than serving its external narrative action had led to a rather static, impersonal kind of acting which by some was dubbed Wieland's 'oratorio style'. His visual concepts tended to be more memorable than his *Personenregie* (or direction of the principal singers — that of the chorus was on a far higher, innovative plane). There, at the very least, lay the hope of a new direction.

16 The final scene of *Das Rheingold* in Rudolf Heinrich's design for Joachim Herz's *Ring* in Leipzig (1973-76): the proletarian workers who have built Valhalla watch the gods moving in to take possession. This production established the *Ring* as an allegory of the evils of nineteenth-century capitalism.

The stage interpretation of Wagner's works as myths of the human psyche found its apotheosis in Wieland Wagner. But one element that had been overlooked was the social and political concerns which had fired Wagner and which for commentators like Bernard Shaw were the key to the meaning of the *Ring*. Wagner had turned to myth not solely because he wanted to revive the ethos of Greek theatre, and not primarily because he consciously sought to dramatize neuroses, but because myth was a most powerful explanatory paradigm of social and political evil. Götz Friedrich's *Tannhäuser* production at Bayreuth in 1972 created a huge stir by resurrecting this emphasis. But the first major production to set the *Ring* in Wagner's own time and to stage it as an allegory of the injustices of nineteenth-century capitalism was that of Joachim Herz in Leipzig (1973–76). Rudolf Heinrich's designs were images of bourgeois triumphalism and proletarian degradation. The Valhalla revealed at the end of *Das*

Rheingold was an industrialist's mansion, and the gods took possession of it watched by the workers who had built it for them. Photo
blow-ups were used not to create an illusion of Wagner's age but, in
Brechtian spirit, to quote it. The effect was that of turning the pages
of a photograph album where one responds to the images without
needing to be deceived by them.

Herz and Heinrich demythologized in order to reconnect modern
audiences with the real-life historical context which had been the
point of departure for Wagner's explanatory myths. Variations on
this theme became widespread in the 1970s, as in Pier Luigi Pizzi's
designs for Luca Ronconi's production of *Die Walküre* (La Scala
1974) where Act II, Scene 1 was a Bavarian palace decorated with
murals of scenes from the *Ring*, and with Wotan as Wagner, Fricka as
Cosima, and Brünnhilde as Florence Nightingale. The dominant
principle was of visual quotation, 'The Ride of the Valkyries' being an
equestrian monument in a museum gallery, burlesqued in the antics
of a visiting party of schoolgirl valkyries.

Critical production and design strategy became best known through
the Bayreuth *Ring* of 1976. Everything about this was provocative,
beginning with Wolfgang Wagner's choice of the French team of
Pierre Boulez, Patrice Chéreau (producer), and Richard Peduzzi
(designer) to mark the centenary of the *Ring*'s first production. This
was an immensely intelligent critique of the theatre of illusion, using
a striking succession of purely theatrical images to build a diachronic
bridge between Wagner's world and that of today. Wotan, in Wagner's
brocade dressing-gown, was a manic-depressive inventor keeping
himself in touch with the earth's gyrations by means of a huge
Foucault pendulum, while Siegfried grew up to assume, in *Götterdämmerung*, the dinner-jacket of a society operagoer. Armed revolu-
tionaries witnessed the rites of his funeral bier. Wagner himself was
in retreat from the Industrial Revolution; what better irony than to
call his mountain landscapes to order with Satanic mills? How other
than for Nothung to be forged with the help of a drop-forge conveniently left for Siegfried by the Wanderer?

To symbolize the exploitation and rape of Nature, the Rhine had
become a hydroelectric dam, its daughters toting for riverside custom in a froth of scarlet petticoat. The Wood Bird was a caged
instrument of Wotan's will, while real horses were back for the
'burials in a country churchyard' with which the valkyrie undertakers
were concerning themselves. The Valkyrie Rock became first (1976)
a mini-Matterhorn surrounded by gas jets, and from 1977 the ruin of
a castle-keep or chapel on a hill. The design carried a palpable echo
of Böcklin's famous painting *The Isle of the Dead*, marking an ironically
late Bayreuth début for an artist favoured by Wagner himself. The

17   In the first scene of *Götterdämmerung*, Act III, the Rhinemaidens plead with Siegfried for his help to restore the flow of the dammed and polluted Rhine: Patrice Chéreau's Bayreuth centenary production of the *Ring* (1976), with designs by Richard Peduzzi.

Gibichung hall was an industrial baron's villa on the Rhine, the architecture of power manifest in soaring neo-Classical pilasters. The final cataclysm and flood was enacted on a harbour sea-front with a people's revolution poised to erupt.

There was no attempt to impose a unifying design concept, each particular setting being designed to maximize its potential as an acting space for that particular scene. Suffused with predominantly dull, greyish light, the stage picture was often surreal and dreamlike. But what Chéreau demanded of the singing actors was flesh-and-blood behaviour. For Chéreau there was no privileged divinity in the Wotan family, who were simply people engaged in power struggles with other people. This was a human, all-too-human drama presented as straight theatre without any special recourse to myth or psychology. It posited no unity other than whatever might be the sum of its own contradictions. The *Ring* had been unmasked as a Brechtian epic.

Inevitably, this 'revenge of the French' had a very rough ride in its first year, but its totally uninhibited approach to a work carrying such an immense burden of performing tradition was a liberation, open-

ing up the *Ring* to millions when shown on television, when unpreju-
diced neophyte viewers discovered in it an almost *Dallas*-like appeal.
Above all it showed that the *Ring* was wide open for reinterpretation,
and that the time had come when any serious production would have
to engage with the span of over a century between the work that
Wagner imagined and the world of its modern audience.

The high-tech fantasies of our own day impinged on the *Ring* in
producer Ulrich Melchinger and designer Thomas Richter-Forgách's
exploratory production in Kassel (1970–74). This was another venture deliberately contesting the sense of visual coherence achieved at
Wieland Wagner's Bayreuth. Quotations from a plethora of sources,
from nineteenth-century salon painting to Pop Art and Star Wars
technology, and a surrealistic juxtaposition of images from past,
present, and future deconstructed any sense of unity or specific
background; Hunding's hut had for its household deities two huge
seated figures like Egyptian gods. In the Ride of the Valkyries robot-
like figures that might have been designed by Oskar Schlemmer
exercised in an arena surrounded by totemic figures, possibly representing horses. The Magic Fire was a huge neon halo hovering over
the sleeping Brünnhilde. This scenic adventure-playground may have
strained in its determination that the public should see their world
reflected and refracted in Wagner's, a strategy that was to be developed and refined by producers like Ruth Berghaus, Götz Friedrich,
and Harry Kupfer.

The scenography designed by Axel Manthey for Berghaus's Frankfurt *Ring* (1985–87) provided a box of brightly coloured toys on a
revolve — an experimental kit for use by the characters in their task
of discovering who they are and reading their own riddles. The
method in its very serious madness was to deal as lightly as possible,
yet as purposefully as a forensic scientist analysing a stain or a
psychoanalyst a verbal slip, with the textual imagery and its quiddities.
The auto-destructive behaviour of the gods was cleverly manifest in
the way they stalked awkwardly about in their palpably built-up boots
— the source of their superior stature being also that of their clumsi-
ness. Fricka stripped Wotan of the plastic mac and trilby he had
taken refuge in as disguise, and humiliated him by hanging his
power-boots by their laces round his neck. At the opening of the hut
door in *Die Walküre*, the whole hut rose up into the flies, leaving
Siegmund and Sieglinde not so much exultantly free as vulnerably
alone — the scenic environment played against the actual situation.
Much play was made with fetishistic objects (especially with chairs)
and the set presented the performers with artificial physical chal-
lenges like narrow ledges complementary to the mental and behav-
ioural ones imposed by Wagner's text and music. No identification

or empathy with the characters was invited, one of the objects being to offer maximal resistance to Wagner's dramaturgy in the hope of drawing maximal energy from it. In such an intellectualized approach, the design assumes an almost quodlibet function, valuable in proportion to its subversive effect.

The obstinately oblique angle to the original adopted by Berghaus and Manthey could not have been more different from the passionately *engagé* readings of Götz Friedrich with designer Peter Sykora, and of Harry Kupfer with Hans Schavernoch. Friedrich's Covent Garden *Ring* of 1974–76 had taken an 'honest-to-technology' approach consistent with Friedrich's view that Wagner's alienation from the nineteenth century was manifest in his preference for mythopoeic rather than, with the exceptions of *Rienzi* and *Die Meistersinger*, historical or contemporary subject matter. Josef Svoboda's designs addressed Friedrich's hypothesis that four time-frames were posited in staging the *Ring*: Nordic myth, Wagner's life, the world of today, and a Utopian vision representing some kind of resolution of the relationship between the three preceding time-frames. The stage need therefore make no attempt to evoke legendary Iceland, northern Sweden, nineteenth-century Germany, or a space-fiction (which was what Ralph Koltai did in his designs for the English National Opera's *Ring* [1970–73], which Reginald Goodall conducted without being excessively concerned with the production one way or another).[14]

For Friedrich, it was enough to accept that the arena *was* the Covent Garden stage, the *Ring*'s world embodied in a gigantic square hydraulic platform whose motion was 'a symbol of constantly changing and self-generating energy'; the stage picture thus consisted largely of abstract imagery, avoiding all specific sense of time and place. But over the next decade Friedrich was by no means alone in believing that the *Ring* could also be seen as a potent expression of contemporary problems, and particularly those of man's exploitation of the environment.

The rape of Nature is, after all, a central topic in the *Ring*, as Wagner conceived it, and one did not need overmuch imagination to see in it intimations of ecological catastrophe. Chéreau's and Peduzzi's dam on the Rhine and caged Wood Bird were a response from this angle, which was to be taken further by Friedrich's Berlin *Ring* of 1984–85. The latter picked up on Chéreau's argument that to connect fully with a modern audience, the production must engage what is, or should be, that audience's concern with the threat of nuclear immolation, of ecological and cosmic catastrophe. The locale, as in Friedrich's earlier London production, was the stage itself,

18 *Siegfried*, Act II, from the silvery space-age *Ring* designed by Ralph Koltai for Glen Byam Shaw's and John Blatchley's production at the English National Opera, 1970-73.

but the action became a series of linked events, connecting through the time-tunnel with any moment in history (past or future) when Wotan-like behaviour would precipitate similar consequences.

Gods and Nibelungs were confined to a defensive underground time-tunnel (initially modelled on the Washington, D.C., subway and on Henry Moore's drawings of the London Underground as a war-time refuge) where, as in a play within a play, they were condemned to re-enact the events which had brought them to their incarceration. Designed by Peter Sykora, this *Ring* was an 'endgame' showing, in Friedrich's words, 'what human beings had done to their history and natural surroundings'. The time-tunnel was a visual metaphor for 'the encapsulation of personages who have themselves shot up the heavens'. Its purpose was to create a purgatorial space with associations 'reaching from the early Christian catacombs to an atomic waste-storage area'.[15] The time-tunnel concept was first designed for the considerable stage-depth of the Deutsche Oper Berlin, and its suggestiveness was diminished in the subsequent reworking necessitated by the shallower stages in Japan (Deutsche Oper on

19 Brünnhilde guarded by a cube of lasers in Harry Kupfer's Bayreuth *Ring* production of 1988, with designs by Hans Schavernoch.

tour) and at Covent Garden, where Friedrich's revised production was first seen as a cycle in 1991.

The idea of a perspective vanishing into infinity was also used in 1988 on the immensely deep Bayreuth stage by Harry Kupfer's designer Hans Schavernoch, who built a *Weltstraße*, or street of world history, vanishing into past and future some fifty metres behind the proscenium. Laser effects darted out to map it as the bed of the Rhine, or rain down fiery arrows to conjure Brünnhilde's rock. Valhalla was New York's Trump Tower, the rainbow bridge a vertical ribbon of lasers as the gangster-like gods ascended in their private elevator. Not for the first time the America of Manhattan found itself on stage in Wagner as a symbol of power-crazed folly. Hunding's hut afforded a chill Nordic hospitality indebted to Ibsen: it folded up from the floor to offer Siegmund shelter, sinking back out of sight again when the lovers escaped to begin their adventures on the *Weltstraße*. Mime and Siegfried made their home in the rusted remnant of an industrial boiler, while Fafner's cave was sheer Jabberwocky, the monster itself a coil of stainless-steel flue-liner.

The Norns wove the world's fate in a rooftop forest of radio antennae, the Gibichung hall became a penthouse in the ultimate skyscraper. Robbed of their gold, the Rhinemaidens teased Siegfried from the safety of a wrecked space module. Schavernoch's images evoked the nightmare of man battling to find a future in a world where all that remained of Nature was the Wanderer's pathetic mechanical yo-yo that stood in for the Wood Bird. High-tech and low-tech are impotent to help without the redeeming fire of love. Brünnhilde's sacrifice was cheapened to impotence by being 'quoted' as a spectacle staged for groups watching it on television sets. Un-noticed, two children with flashlights slipped away, seeking escape from under the slow descent of a guillotine curtain.

Kupfer's production set up a taut dialogue between Wagner's vision and fragmented modern consciousness. Chéreau had focused his *Ring* on Wagner's equivocal relationship to industrialized man. For Kupfer and Schavernoch the *Ring* had now turned on its darkest side. They sought to show us that it cannot be located either in Wagner's world or in our own, but only through theatrical images of future shock.

If too few artists (David Hockney's *Tristan* for Los Angeles in 1987 is an important exception) have shown interest in Wagnerian stage design (or managers in inviting them?), then it should be said that the dynamic stage pictures created by Wieland Wagner, Richard Peduzzi, or Hans Schavernoch are surely in the very front rank of artistic achievements in any sphere since the Second World War.

Where, then, do we now stand? The dominant strategy for staging Wagner is still essentially analytic and 'critical', and it is one in which design is playing a major role. Its rationale is that the distance between ourselves and Wagner is now so great that any attempt to capture or recreate a unifying vision that Wagner might have recognized is impossible. Indeed, the aim is to put nothing on stage unquestioned; rather to set up an inquisitorial dialogue between our horizon, one hundred years of performance practice, and Wagner's world. Wagner's works are prized both for what they are and as a perennial catalyst for theatrical change and renewal, as oracles whose answers echo our own enigmatic questions.

This approach, which has gathered force since the early 1970s, has given great offence and been found puzzling and hard to come to terms with by many otherwise open-minded Wagner lovers, who have often felt that vandals have been let loose in the shrine. Others, excited by the long-overdue arrival in opera of interpretative freedoms long taken for granted in spoken theatre and film, have responded with recognition and enthusiasm to production and design concepts across a bewilderingly wide spectrum: Brechtian assaults on Wagner's theatre of illusion, overtly political interpretations, surrealistic fanta-sizing, deconstructions with extensive use of 'quotation' techniques, multiple framing (play within a play), time-travelling between different periods, suspensions of belief, suspensions of disbelief, all-out critical fragmentation, antiheroic and deflationary presentations, the pursuit of unity, the pursuit of disunity, science-fiction fantasies, productions attacking, denouncing, debunking Wagner, and productions handing the burden of sense-making entirely over to the audience.

It is a measure of the enduring vitality and capacity of Wagner's works that they can elicit such a wealth of often enthralling and provocative responses. As most, though certainly not all, of these responses would claim that the music and singing are indisputably prime, attempts at evaluation have to begin and end with assessment of their relationship with the music and singing. Here, huge aesthetic and hermeneutic imponderables obtrude. How, for instance, to decide whether such criteria as 'deeds of music made visible', or the staging as 'the opened eye of the score', have been satisfied? And how can one talk about — let alone assess — design apart from the production and musical performances that it serves? Appia's basic tenet that design and production have no other function than to create the most potent space for the singing-actor's performance is surely still the starting-point from which evaluation has to begin.

Chapter 5

'Fidelity' to Wagner: Reflections on the Centenary *Ring*

Jean-Jacques Nattiez

In 1977, a year after the scandal sparked by the Patrice Chéreau/ Pierre Boulez centenary *Ring*, the Bayreuth Festival published an anthology of invective inspired by one hundred years of Bayreuth productions. At a time when a 'conservative' *Ring* has been broadcast on television in a production from the Metropolitan Opera and when the debate on authenticity has never been livelier,[1] it is legitimate to ask, once again: What is 'fidelity to Wagner'? It is a question we may conveniently approach by reflecting in some detail on the historic production of the *Ring* that was seen at the Bayreuth Festival from 1976 to 1980. The following extracts from the aforementioned anthology will provide a context.

1925 (prompted by the use of follow spots in *Parsifal*): 'Even if a sense of piety could not persuade the heirs of Bayreuth to respect the Master's will, common sense ought to have told them that, being Romantic in essence, the Wagnerian music drama needs to be staged in a Romantic manner'.

1928: 'The description of the setting and actions on stage at the beginning of Act I of *Die Walküre* is just as eternally valid as the notes in the score and the words of the poem'.

1933: 'Whatever approach one adopts to this production [of the *Ring*], it remains a blot on the history of the festival. . . . Wagner explicitly demands the theatre of naturalistic illusion'.

1935: 'Should it not be the supreme law, especially in Bayreuth, to obey the Master's will?'

1951–52: 'Should one stick to tradition, in other words, stick to what Wagner wanted and specified in his scores and writings, or should one strike out in new directions, directions ostensibly more in keeping with the spirit of the age?'

1953 (inspired by the 1953 revival of Wieland Wagner's 1951 production of the *Ring*): 'What does "the spirit of the age" have in common with the universal and eternally human ideas implicit in Wagner's dramas?'

1976: 'We need a new Wieland to cleanse these Augean stables and guide us back to the imperishable values inherent in the *Ring*'.[2]

Although Chéreau and Boulez, like their supporters, have explicitly insisted that the interpreter should have a free hand, they, too, have not failed to appeal to the concept of fidelity to Wagner, as if, ultimately, failure to respect the composer's intentions was in itself a fault. It is in this sense that we must interpret Carlo Schmid's remark: 'Monsieur Chéreau, you have been more than a mere producer, you have been the literal and faithful interpreter of the philosophy which Wagner turned into music, and elevated to the level of myth'.[3] Or take Numa Sadoul's assessment of Chéreau's production: 'Rarely has Wagner been as "present" in his work, rarely has a *Ring* been able to do him justice or to pay him homage and treat him as lovingly as has this particular *Ring*. There is constant fidelity to the libretto, the stage directions, the music, and the composer's intentions'.[4] Alain Satgé has written that 'ignorance or ill will begins when the audience [hostile to Chéreau] invokes some vague idea of "fidelity" to Wagner, since it seems difficult nowadays to stage a production of the *Ring* which conforms more profoundly to the stimulating Wagnerian Utopia of "musical theatre" '.[5] Chéreau himself insists: 'I follow Wagner's intentions, I follow his indications or, rather, I always take at least something from . . . Wagner's instructions as a producer. . . . I try to follow the text totally, to feed on what is said there, including the contradictions'.[6] Of the final scene of *Das Rheingold* he has said that the gods 'now know that the rot has already set in. And this is one of the premises on which the text is built . . . , a theme that is written into the music. . . . Indeed, Loge says as much.'[7] For his part, Boulez insists: 'This "declamation" reflects Wagner's own intention, especially in the scenes involving dialogue'.[8] 'The Wagnerian orchestra is really an accompanying orchestra, Wagner said as much in 1876!'[9]

In the following study, my primary objective will be to present a theoretical framework which, advanced in the form of a series of principles, is based on my concept of semiology. This framework will then allow us to define those criteria which play a part in formulating the 'judgement of fidelity'. I shall then attempt a broad characterization of the attitude of both Chéreau and Boulez towards the premises on which Wagner's texts are based in order to discover whether it is possible to speak of fidelity or treachery towards the composer.[10]

The Principles of Semiology

1 All forms of human production are *symbolic* forms to the extent that

(a) they result from some *poietic* activity, in other words, they involve a process of creation;
(b) they reveal themselves in the form of a material *trace*, which is both the result of the poietic activity and the point of departure of the esthesic activity;
(c) they give rise to *esthesic* activity, in other words, they involve perception.

2 A symbolic form is a form because it reveals itself as a material trace which can be preserved (as a score or libretto) or recorded (musical execution or stage presentation).

3 If there is no poietic activity, there will be no trace. But we have only indirect evidence of these poietic processes. This evidence falls into two types:

(a) *external* to the trace — letters, remarks, sketches. It will be noted that these examples of poietic evidence are also traces, hence symbolic forms, and hence the object of further interpretations.
(b) *inferred* on the basis of the trace of the work, an inference that proceeds according to recurrences observed in the text or by comparing the work under discussion with other works. In both these cases, we adopt a process of 'seriation' suited to extracting a poietic significance: the first is internal to the work, while the second has recourse to external traces.

4 The trace forms the subject of an esthesic activity (involving perception). It, too, reveals itself in an indirect and more or less complex way:

(a) on the level of the interpreter, through an interpretation of the score and/or libretto;
(b) on the level of the audience, through words, critical judgements (written or spoken), applause or booing.

It will be noted that all these results of esthesic activity are themselves symbolic forms. The discourse of the musicologist is necessarily located in the realm of esthesics, but the production of the musicological discourse, by taking place after the event and starting from cold, is an activity of the second degree.[11]

5 Every production of a trace is a constructive activity to the extent that it produces a new symbolic form which potentially has the ability to change the state of a given symbolic field, which it may do by provoking a reinterpretation of previous symbolic forms or by opening up new creative dimensions. The musicologist's discourse is also a construction: we do not have direct access to the poietic and esthesic processes or to the immanent organization of a work; we retain in our discourse what we consider pertinent by reference to these three points of view.

6 Traces are symbolic forms because they put into play networks of associations and relations generally termed meaning(s). Borrowing from Peirce's terminology, we use the term interpretant for those elements which constitute the symbolic processes. This word has the advantage of indicating that our comprehension of a symbolic form is an interpretation and, as such, requires a critical hermeneutical act.

7 In music there are two types of meaning:

(a) immanent meanings; in other words, those which establish links between musical forms pure and simple;
(b) extrinsic meanings; in other words, those which establish a link between what is generally termed the 'musical' element (effects, feelings, images) and socio-cultural, ideological, political, artistic, and philosophical contexts.

In the immediate experience of a work of music, these two types of meaning are generally confused. Only an aesthetic, analytical, and musicological apriority helps us to distinguish them or, rather, helps us to deny one or other of the two types according to an a priori ontological conception of music which places the emphasis either on its 'formal' character or on the various manifestations of its expressive dimension.

In music, immanent or extrinsic meaning results from the link between the musical forms (the trace) and the situation (or context), be it musical (intrinsic or extrinsic to the work) or non-musical.

8 On the level of immanent meaning, there are three types of interpretant:

(a) for each of the musical parameters (pitch, length, intensity, timbre), certain *features* (intervals, rhythmic figures, motifs, phrases, large-scale forms, harmonic patterns, and so on) are called into play; at the same time these features are combined in specific ways;

(b) these features are subject to a *hierarchical organization*, extend-
ing from single note to large-scale form;

(c) these features acquire a *stylistic relevance* that is pyramidal in
form; they are relevant to a particular work, to a particular
period in the composer's oeuvre, to his works as a whole, to
the style of an epoch, to the system of reference as a whole
(tonal, for example), or to the totality of those phenomena
that are considered musical (universals).

The interpretants and the various combinations of immanent
interpretants are infinite in number.

9 The networks of interpretants that make up the different types
and levels of meaning exist only for the interpreters of the trace; in
other words: the composer; the performers (past and present); the
audience (past and present); the writers of specialized forms of
metadiscourse (musicological, historical, analytical, aesthetic, and
critical). Only by taking account of all the criteria which play a part
in the semiological process is it possible to define the 'judgement
of fidelity' and say in what it consists.

The Nature of the Judgement of Fidelity

What I intend to call the 'judgement of fidelity' constitutes a complex semiological phenomenon which avails itself of several symbolic
forms, together with the networks of interpretants attached to them.

Wagner creates a work with a turbulent genesis that is set against a
philosophical, literary, and musical background. This poiesis produces a complex trace in the form of the libretto and score. Taken in
hand by the performers, who interpret it on the basis of their knowledge of Wagner and their personal poiesis, the trace becomes a
spectacle. In its turn this spectacle constitutes a symbolic form.
Audience and critics (including the writer of the present article) are
placed in an esthesic situation not only by reference to the production but by reference to what they know about Boulez and Chéreau,
to say nothing of Wagner's oeuvre as a whole, the composer's poietic
work, and the creative artists who influenced him — and for whom
one could of course undertake a similar tripartite semiotic analysis,
and so on *ad infinitum*. The general public expresses judgements that
are more or less complex, applauding or booing, voicing their pleasure or indignation, talking during the interval, offering critical evalu-
ations and writing journalistic accounts, analytical pieces, and even
whole books. These traces left by the audience can be explained in
their turn, not only on the basis of what the audience retained of the
performance, of what they know about Boulez and Chéreau, about

Wagner's oeuvre and his poietic work, and of the interpretation they place upon it, but also on that of their own personal poiesis. It goes without saying that the way I approach the work of Chéreau and Boulez is itself conditioned by the theoretical model and perspective I have been summarizing here.

Why is it necessary to draw on my tripartite conception of semiology in order to deal with the problem of fidelity and the way we judge fidelity? First, because every element which may have played a crucial role in the creative process is not necessarily inscribed in the trace at our disposal. It follows from this that what one can read in the score or libretto according to our present-day frames of reference does not necessarily correspond with the composer's poietic universe. On the other hand, perceptive approaches, although partly orientated to the organization of the trace, are certainly not totally guaranteed or determined by that trace: the producer's act of perception when confronted by the libretto, the conductor's vis-à-vis the score, and the spectator's vis-à-vis the scenic and musical realization of the work all involve a veritable act of re-creation. In consequence, creative strategies and perceptive approaches do not necessarily correspond. To say 'what Wagner meant' is never to read his intentions directly but to construct hypotheses about his intentions and his poietic universe based on traces which we can read and contextual types of information — historical, sociological, philosophical, ideological, aesthetic, musical, and so on — which we have at our disposal.

The judgement of fidelity is therefore the juxtaposition of one listener/spectator's interpretation of the production and musical performance with another interpretation — the conception which this same listener/spectator has of the 'real' Wagner and of the 'essence' of the *Ring* and which he or she arrives at by selecting interpretants bound to diverse symbolic forms to which he or she has access. It must not be forgotten that, over and above the libretto and the score of the *Ring* (although these are, of course, at the heart of the problem), the philosophical writings of Feuerbach and Schopenhauer, Chéreau's production, Boulez's interpretation, and even the present article are all relatively autonomous symbolic forms and can be subjected, in turn, to a process of semiological tripartition: they have been produced, they have left a trace, and they are the object of the processes of perception, comprehension, and interpretation.

The Production from the Semiological Point of View

Since I have examined Chéreau's production in detail elsewhere, I do not need to restate the grand stylistic features which characterize it. Chéreau has been accused of treachery. This is not surprising, particularly when one lists the poietic sources of some of the gestures and images which gave this *Ring* its forcefulness and quality.

First, there were the cinematic images, some of which are explicitly cited by Chéreau,[13] while others may have been recognized by the audience — Freia and King Kong, the large wheel from *Modern Times*, Hagen/Brando on the waterfront, Hunding's henchmen and Samuel Fuller's *Forty Guns*, Wotan and Prince Salina from Visconti's *Leopard*, Fellini's *Casanova*, and Peter Brook's *Lord of the Flies*.

Second, architectural images — and it is certainly an impressive list which the designer, Richard Peduzzi, drew up, including, as it does, Desiderio, Khnopff, Degouve de Nuncques, Vitruvius, Serlio, Palladio, and Vignola.[14]

Third, images of Renaissance engineers — Ramelli, Besson, Valturio, Strada[15] — and Foucault's pendulum from the Musée des Arts Décoratifs.

Fourth, images of painters such as Dürer, Böcklin, Francesco de Nome, and Ingres; but also *Tintin in Peru* and *The Temple of the Sun*,[16] together with photographs of a dam. For the costumes, a nineteenth-century German master craftsman's clothes, including a three-cornered hat, provided the model for Alberich, while Erda was dressed as a Berber tribeswoman with a Kabyle necklace. Other images came from *L'Illustration*, *Femina*, and similar magazines.

Nor can one forget other stage productions: Mime, for example, was taken over from Joachim Herz's Leipzig production, designed by Rudolf Heinrich.[17] Boulez remembered the Japanese No theatre and thus provided the idea of having hooded stagehands manoeuvring the dragon.[18] We also rediscover the white lace from Vitez's *Phèdre*, perhaps also the gestures of a lion tamer driving back the lions with his lance (Wotan driving away the valkyries), to say nothing of images from Chéreau's own productions: 'In 1975, the children in *La Dispute*, whose father could have been Bond's Lear, reminded me in a naive sort of way of *Die Walküre* — which wasn't as wide of the mark as all that.'[19] In this way Chéreau discovered the 'possibility of summarizing [his] own previous productions in the *Ring*'.[20]

These are all the personal elements in this *Ring*. And this applies as much to Peduzzi as to Chéreau himself. It is a question of animating the myth, of retelling it for a modern audience. In order to do so, both producer and designer drew on their album of private images. It must be emphasized at once that there is of necessity an arbitrary element in this process: in falling back on a world which is not and which cannot be the world of each and every spectator, since it is the result of visits to various towns which Chéreau and Peduzzi have explored, of visits to the cinema and of books which they have read, they have inevitably translated this *Ring* into images in a way which cannot avoid being profoundly original. It is certainly an unusual way of working: 'We didn't proceed logically, we didn't start out with the opening sets, with Wagner's opening stage direction, we didn't work through the *Ring* in proper sequence, asking ourselves how to interpret one stage direction before passing on to the next. The images which we amassed had to be classified, and this classification came later'.[21]

The impression that emerges from all this is of an exuberant anarchy, as though what we are allowed to see today, presented with such sensitivity, care, and talent, were the result of some happy chance.

In proceeding in this manner, Chéreau operates in exactly the same way as Wagner. By reading the Eddas in parallel with the libretto, Chéreau 'decodes Wagner's work, that prodigious collage which he forced himself to produce, with his vast knowledge of all these multifarious sources'.[22] Chéreau's *Ring*, like that of the composer, is a synthesis of images and obsessions to which he was subjected during the period of its gestation.

Like Roland Barthes, Chéreau insists on the reader's and critic's freedom of interpretation. And it is this highly personal reading which he shows us in the theatre.

Is he really unfaithful? To the letter, no doubt. But to the spirit?

Wagner's writings on the relationship between poetry and music show plainly that, throughout his life, he hesitated over which of them was the more dominant.[23]

But each time he approached the supreme moment of seeing his works performed on stage, the action gained the upper hand and it is the man of the theatre whom we hear speaking. To draw a comparison between what Chéreau did in 1976 and what Wagner's own performances may have been like in 1876 would be pointless. Although no one has ever seriously suggested reviving Josef Hoffmann's sets on the Bayreuth stage and of lighting them with gas, the Metropolitan Opera's recent neo-Romantic production of the *Ring* did not hesitate to draw its inspiration from nineteenth-century models: the result was an aesthetic disaster for the present-day spectator, assuming him or her to be endowed with even a modicum of taste. By contrast, there is a fundamental relevance in comparing Chéreau's production with the dramatic spirit of Wagner as producer. Indeed, by bringing together the ideas of the latter with the realization of the former, one is struck by a certain coincidence on three essential points:

1 The search for what is natural. Do not look at the conductor, but always address the other characters according to the laws of dramatic

logic. Forget the audience. Here, in a word, was a *lateral* staging. It is amusing to quote certain notes recorded by Heinrich Porges which mirror exactly what Chéreau did: Siegmund, for example, kneels for his cries of 'Wälse!'[24] while Sieglinde addresses the theme of redemption directly at Brünnhilde. One should not see a search for pseudo-authenticity in any of these coincidences: they are simply quoted here to show that two men of the theatre, working one hundred years apart, devise the same solutions when allowing themselves to be guided by the evidence of the drama.

2 The appropriateness of the staging to the text and music. Wagner certainly did not write a libretto as detailed as that of the *Ring* simply in order for his singing actors not to relate to the psychology of the characters and the subtlety of their emotions. By the same token, anyone reading Porges's account of the 1876 rehearsals is struck by the fact that Wagner asked his singers to rely on the music in making their moves. I shall no doubt be reproached for falling victim to a retrospective illusion, but when one notes so close a convergence between their points of view, it is difficult not to suggest imagining the gestures that Wagner himself must have imagined in the light of what Chéreau had to offer us.

3 A concern for detail. This was as much an obsession with Chéreau as it was with Wagner. Of course, the gestures Wagner wanted could not be those which Chéreau obtained from the best of his interpreters, since a new style of production is always being defined by reference to the style which immediately precedes it: Wagner was reacting against those tenors who strode to the front of the stage to bellow their arias into the audience or who confused lyric declamation with semaphoric gesture. Chéreau comes from the spoken theatre and, in presenting us with one of the most active productions ever seen on the operatic stage, sets himself apart from the static productions of Wieland and Wolfgang Wagner.

Chéreau, then, has rediscovered the spirit of a certain Wagner and has done so, moreover, not from any concern for a historical reconstruction, but because, as a man of the theatre, he looked at the libretto with the same eyes as those of the composer himself, bringing to bear the whole creative freedom and talent of a man of the twentieth century.

Let us turn now to the esthesic aspect. How was this production understood?

A certain familiarity with Chéreau's work in Bayreuth allows us to point out that audiences saw in his production things which, as producer, he himself had never thought of. This phenomenon is intrinsic to every form of human production, even if it is one which Chéreau accepts only with difficulty.

I have not escaped this rule: in my first study of this production,[25] I allowed myself to be carried away by my own interpretive zeal. In the scene between Freia and the giants, the gold is heaped up between their two staves until the goddess herself is hidden. I was not alone in seeing a resemblance between these staves and the poles that are plied by Venetian gondoliers. It was an inspired idea, I thought: Chéreau was adding a further layer of meaning to the idea of Valhalla sinking into the mud. (An unequivocal allusion to Venice is found elsewhere, in the sets for *Götterdämmerung*.) It seems, however, that Chéreau was thinking of no such thing: the staves were simply metre rules picked up, if my memory serves me right, in the wings of the theatre.

I plead not guilty. There are so many elements in this production capable of linking up in the spectator's mind that the audience can establish relations between these elements which have no connection with Chéreau's intentions. The spectator's perception is an active and constructive phenomenon. As a result, the discrepancy between poiesis and esthesis is a normal, constant semiological phenomenon. The same phenomenon found expression in one of the rare articles of any substance to be published on this production, an altogether remarkable piece of writing by Alain Satgé in which the tendency to establish links which Chéreau himself did not envisage is reinforced by the author's structuralist orientation: 'Each element draws its significance from its neighbours, but also from its fellows'. This leads Satgé to see parallels not only between Alberich and Wotan on the one hand and Brünnhilde and Gunther on the other (this on the strength of their matching costumes),[27] but also between the tripartite structure of the hydroelectric dam and that of the Gibichung hall,[28] as well as between Mime's newspaper and Erda's veil,[29] and so on.

There are also — and above all — those interpretations which Chéreau himself would deny. Satgé, for example, imagines that it was Wotan who captured the Wood Bird and put it in a cage,[30] but it is not necessary to go searching for such far-fetched ideas. Satgé himself would no doubt reply by quoting back at us one of the opening sentences of his study: 'The producer's theses are clearly less important than their methods of implementation and the coherency of their results'.[31] On a very basic level, he is right: intentions are of little importance, for what matters is the outcome. The problem is that, by adopting the very specific framework of semantic structuralism, Satgé's exegesis — since structural analysis as practised by him is necessarily a form of exegesis — creates the very sense of coherency which may not in fact exist on the level at which Satgé is working. But he is, of course, entirely free to see it in this way, just as one cannot blame

Carlo Schmid for discovering the Lido in the Rhinemaidens' scene
or the Krupps' Essen villa in Gunther's palace. These are chance
conjunctions. There are also images whose appearance is such that a
'misinterpretation' can be explained objectively. Chéreau and Peduzzi
were taken aback to hear audiences using the word *surreal* to describe
the opening act of *Die Walküre*. 'There was no surrealist aim here:
there are no intellectual *borrowings* nor is there an *intellectual system* to
reconstruct images with bits picked up here and there in different
periods; what you have here is the expression of a sensitivity — that
of the designer and mine, too — which is realized instinctively in
these particular forms rather than in others'.[32] The juxtaposition of a
dinner jacket and breastplate is not unrelated to that of Lautréamont's
'chance meeting on a dissecting table of a sewing machine and an
umbrella'. When I put the question to Chéreau himself — in other
words, by going back to the poietic source (and ignoring the hyper-
criticism that would call his evidence into question) — I discovered
in fact that the model was a late fifteenth-century painting representing the actions of the past in a present-day setting. Peduzzi deliberately wanted Hunding's house to be neither an interior nor an
exterior, but it is impossible to prevent the spectator from associating
it with a painting by Magritte.[33] Moreover, this production is so finely
judged that, unless one is in the specific position that I was in of
investigating it in detail (and even then, not all will be revealed), a
single view of the whole of the production cannot allow one to see all
that it contains.

In a word, the perception of the forms which it contains is uncon-
trollable, which is why one cannot account for the symbolic character of an opera production without appealing not only to the intentions of the artists involved and the concrete results of their work, but
also to the way in which these results are perceived. There are also
ideas by which Chéreau set great store but which, in my view, did not
come across. The hydroelectric dam, for example, was intended to
suggest not only a piece of theatrical machinery but also the idea of
energy, which was supposed to be related to the industrial wheels in
Scenes 2 and 3 of *Das Rheingold*, as well as those in the opening act of
Die Walküre and the drop-forge in *Siegfried*. It is clear that the surprise,
not to say the scandal, provoked by this dam outweighed any meaning that Chéreau wanted to give it. There are also manifest errors of
interpretation against which even the most explicit producer can do
nothing: 'I am still being congratulated for so marvellously "ignoble
and repugnant" a Mime'.[34]

The spectator's interpretation is a re-creation, therefore, a hypothesis concerning Chéreau's aims. The spectator relates this construction to the idea he or she has of the 'real' Wagner. Is the Boulez/

Chéreau *Ring* 'Wagnerian'? It is entirely typical that the judgement of fidelity presupposes a return to what seems essential.

But what is 'Wagnerian'? To begin with, it is an adjective, in other words, it describes something that *relates to* Wagner. To which Wagner? To everything that affects him both close at hand and from afar: his personality, his ideas, his aesthetic, his works — in other words, whatever features the spectator selects from the infinite corpus of all that concerns Wagner. As we can see, to define what is Wagnerian is not to pinpoint an immutable reality but to place a personal symbolic construction on what we hear and see.

In the framework of a more specialized context — that of Wagner's political ideology and, in particular, his relations with Hitler — Jean Matter makes a comment which tends very much in the same direction as my own line of thinking: 'If one can like Wagner and still refuse to say that one is a Wagnerian, it is because the two are not the same'.[35] Or, to put it another way, one can retain specific features from the Wagnerian oeuvre and 'forget' others which are quite obviously part of it but which are none the less intolerable. I would suggest that an authentically Wagnerian *Ring* would turn Alberich and Mime into repulsive Jews, but I believe that, since 1945, no producer has envisaged such fidelity. I would also claim that, by taking a diametrically opposite view of the work's profoundly anti-Semitic dimension, Chéreau is closer to this aspect of Wagner's thinking since, instead of burking the question in his production, he reveals it in a negative way.

The Semiology of Musical Interpretation

It is impossible to explain Boulez's conception of the *Ring* without also taking account of the fact that he is one of the foremost creative artists of our time. How could he approach Wagner's work and remain neutral? Can we not even go so far as to say that he interpreted the work as though, as a composer who has attempted to serialize every parameter, he himself were the one who had written the *Ring*? Boulez's reply to this is:

> Of course, concern for detail is a great obsession of mine because, for me, when a composer sits down and takes the trouble to write all those notes, all those arrangements, all those dynamic markings, it is not so that the orchestra can then respect only a tenth of them. . . . A composer would never waste his time plunging into his own labyrinth, if there were no point to it, if it were simply to mislead others. And even if my own personal aesthetic were to have some influence on what I do, where's the harm in that? After

all, what, essentially, is a work? A work is what you make of it. Of course, the work, together with its raw material, exists in its own right, but unless you transform it, it remains a dead letter, which is why, like it or not, performances undergo an evolutionary process over the years. Look at the way in which the interpretation of Baroque music was inflected, at a certain period, by neo-Classicism, which resulted in the sewing-machine approach to Bach. Now it's quite different. Almost the opposite extreme. But what's certain is that, for any interpretation, the influence of the spirit of the age is a given fact, even in relation to the works of the past.[36]

Boulez's position comprises two elements: it reaffirms that Wagner's intentions rise to the surface in Wagner's score (we recognize them inductively, therefore, to borrow from my earlier terminology), but, at the same time, it admits that Boulez's own music — or that of the twentieth century — leads him (and us) to 'read' Wagner in a new light.

What is it that predisposes Boulez to pinpoint individual details and transitions, and to insist on the malleability of the motifs?

Essentially, it is his conception of time. It would be a fundamental misconception to think that what is commonly called the formalism of Boulez's aesthetic means cutting up the musical texture into square-cut rigid forms. It is enough to listen to any one of his works to realize that this is not so. Boulez, moreover, is the first to establish analogies between Wagner and his own works: 'Long before I conducted Wagner, I was doing similar things in my own works. In *Le Marteau sans maître*, for example, certain forms or cycles develop, sink beneath the surface, reappear elsewhere, and move towards new ideas or, in *Pli selon pli*, there are quotations which, later, come from the introduction. In the fifth section of *Le Marteau*, or in "Improvisations sur Mallarmé", you also find a constantly fluctuating tempo which, as in *Parsifal*, never stops moving'.[37]

While teaching in Darmstadt, Boulez was already drawing a fundamental distinction between an amorphous (or 'smooth') time, which is static in character, and a pulsed ('striated') time, dynamic in character.[38] Boulez applies these same categories to the *Ring*:

The diatonic-chromatic contrast is part of a much more general technique making conscious use of the dialectic between fluid and fixed time. In the new time-structure with which Wagner endowed music he first conceived, and then realized, the absolute necessity for fundamental markers based on different, new criteria. Once these markers (which include the motives) are established, the evolution of the work's time-structure will be made clear by their distortion — a brilliant, revolutionary conception if ever there was one — implying that the work must be thought of as an 'open' structure never 'closed' except provisionally and unwillingly.[39]

In his very first essay on Wagner, written on the occasion of his 1970 Bayreuth *Parsifal*, Boulez underlines the ductility of the motifs and the drawing out of the tempo:

> It is not until Wagner that we find musical material that is both complete and incomplete, acceptable both as definitive and indeterminate and belonging simultaneously to the categories of past and future, with the present lying between the two, without any distortion of the internal logic of the music. ... This musical material, which is in a perpetual state of 'becoming', is probably Wagner's most exclusively personal invention. Here for the first time we find an emphasis on uncertainty, indeterminacy, a definite rejection of finality and an unwillingness to stabilize musical events before they have exhausted their potential powers of evolution and renewal.[40]

We find here all of Boulez's own basic categories: the dialectic of rigorous determination and chance, of the definitive and the incomplete, of past and future, and the exploitation of the initial musical material to the point where it reaches the very limits of its possibilities. It is the malleability of the leitmotifs, therefore, which fascinates him above all else: 'They are never limited exclusively to that [initial] tempo on their later appearances'.[41] Boulez thus overturns the traditional picture that we have of Wagner: his music is 'a music of transition, not one of return and repetition. ... It is in his restructuring, researching of time that I find Wagner's real subversive achievement'.[42] It is clear, therefore, why Boulez feels able to say of past composers with whom he feels a certain affinity: 'It is not me speaking about them but them speaking about me. It is the interest I feel in looking at myself in their mirror'.[43]

During the Bayreuth rehearsals, I was struck by how insistently Boulez rehearsed the Annunciation of Death theme in *Die Walküre*. It was as though he were looking for something: 'I wanted to check certain balances, the difference in sonority between the brass, the low register of the trumpets and the high register of the trombones. It's obvious that this will be of use to me if ever I want to write parts for low trumpets set against high trombones'.[44]

Boulez is particularly sensitive to the difference between malleable and rigid themes, since the latter allow him to establish fixed points when drawing out a flexible tempo: 'It is very close to what I'm trying to do in the works that I currently have in hand — contrasting organic things with ones that are not. In any case, what interest would there be for me to conduct a work if it were totally outside my range of activities?'[45] Boulez admits that he wrote certain passages in the third of his *Notations* under the influence of Wagner's style of writing, even though no one would have guessed the source if he himself had not mentioned it.[46]

In reply to the question whether he thought he had been faithful to Wagner, Boulez told me:

> I don't feel any concern for literal fidelity, which, in any case, is impossible. I simply believe that men and works survive thanks to people who are able to find something there which no one else had found before them. That's something I discovered recently when giving a seminar at the IRCAM [Institut de Recherches et de Coordination Acoustique-Musique]. I prefer people to analyse four bars of a work, just four bars, providing they can get something out of it for the future. In this way I can tell how imaginative they are. If they put nothing into their investigation, they can analyse music for three years and there'll still be nothing to show for it. Communication always exists in a state of ambiguity. It is of no interest if it rests only on unilateral relations. Ambiguity allows ramifications, derivatives. If explanations are too clear, it is much more difficult to diverge, and *derivation* or *deviation* is the most important thing for me.[47]

Boulez has an implicit theory of the musical text, therefore, and it is one which we feel can be related to his concept of time: Boulez refuses to regard the past from the point of view of the past. He who 'hates remembering' and 'praises amnesia'[48] has written of Wagner: 'What delight it would be for once to discover a work without knowing *anything* about it. . . . Shall we ever make up our minds to disregard context and to forget the time factors so relentlessly insisted upon by the history books? Shall we ever manage to ignore the circumstances, banish them from our memories and bury them in oblivion and take the interior essence of a work as our only guide? Shall we be able *in the first place* to lose "time" in order to rediscover it later with a new validity?'[49] 'The "freshness" of a glance — assuming, of course, that it is an original and highly talented glance — seems to me preferable to a mass of knowledge, of reminiscences which can weigh you down and handicap you'.[50]

Boulez rejects the historical explanation and instead favours the construction of a meaning that sets out from the present. It is an attitude, after all, which owes much to Roland Barthes and which he shares with Patrice Chéreau: 'In my view, it is impossible to interpret the past with any degree of profundity except by setting out from the present, filtering it through a genuinely up-to-date way of thinking.

. . . To appeal to some ideal model . . . is an illusion bound up with the scientism of the second half of the twentieth century. . . . How can the interaction between present and past be translated concretely into musical interpretation? By reconsidering the sonority, texture, formal structures, the relationship between words and music, and the temporal dimension'.[51]

It is clear from this what Boulez's conception of fidelity must be:

One does not have the right to fix the work in a definitive attitude, it continues to evolve. Anyone who claims to be safeguarding a work within its initial tradition soon finds himself standing guard over a tomb.[52]

What is fidelity, in fact? Is it respect for what is transitory? Or is it not the belief that the work is eternally capable of bearing new truths, decipherable according to period, place, and circumstance? Isn't the great work precisely the one that frustrates our expectations?[53]

The work is a constant exchange between past and future, which irrigate it as it irrigates us.[54]

True fidelity is not remembering how people were, but recalling them in order to integrate them into our own lives. It's the old parable: if the seed dies, nothing will grow. Alberich's 'sei treu', his 'be true', is exactly that: it matters little *how* you are true, only keep me alive in your thoughts.[55]

There is a twofold aspect, therefore, to Boulez's position: through his attentive regard for the score, he claims to rediscover the true Wagner but, at the same time, he defends the right to interpret the past by reference to the present. Indeed, his personal 'interest' in Wagner is taken to such lengths that we may well ask ourselves whether the second position does not contradict the first. Can one really clean up Wagner, having once subjected him to the Boulez treatment?

Behind Boulez's various statements lies a latent theory of the musical text and it is this that we must now attempt to establish.

I think the different layers should be clarified since they are clear in the writing and in the composer's mind.[56]

You have to arrive at an explanation of a score in such a way that your interpretation expresses the composer's aim and intention while not overlooking all the detail he has put into it.[57]

The composer's intentions are as clear as possible in the score.[58]

In other words, it is the score and its every detail which bear the trace of all the composer's intentions. It is clear why Boulez has laid particular emphasis on Nietzsche's remark that Wagner was a master miniaturist.[59]

One could raise an initial objection to Boulez here: since conducting is, at bottom, an art based on 'oral tradition' (in other words, it is transmitted through observation and imitation), the representatives of a certain Wagnerian 'school' could perhaps be considered a reflection — albeit somewhat faded — of what Wagner wanted during his lifetime. Boulez reacts violently to such an idea: 'No, certainly not! That kind of tradition is the worst sort of infidelity, in my view, an excuse, nothing more'.[60]

Our present knowledge of the historical background seems to prove Boulez right. If we may believe Felix Weingartner, who worked as chorus-master and répétiteur at Bayreuth in 1886, the festival's alleged Wagnerian tradition began with Felix Mottl, whose distortions of tempo in *Tristan* and *Parsifal* Weingartner mocks by reference to those of Levi, whom Mottl replaced. As for Siegfried Wagner, his status as his father's son added nothing to his mediocre abilities as a conductor.

Tradition preserves nothing, it simply allows alluvial deposits to form: 'It used to be the correct thing to go into raptures about the "wonderful chiaroscuro" of pictures that were in fact covered with a layer of bituminous dirt. When these pictures were cleaned and restored to their pristine condition, the astonishing brightness, even the violence of the colours forced people entirely to revise their original ideas of the picture. The same is true of music, where the first thing to be done with a masterpiece of the past is to clean away the accumulated dirt, which has been all too readily accepted'.[61] To remove the dirt here is to return to the details and rigorous instructions contained in the score.

It is difficult to resist the conclusion that, in order to be faithful to Wagner, one has to de-Wagnerize him. It is no doubt this, over and above the intrinsic musical beauty of the performance, which makes Boulez's *Ring* so important from a historical point of view. Indeed, if one compares the conclusions of Porges's account of the 1876 rehearsals with Boulez's conception of the work, one has the feeling that the latter's contemporaneity helps him to rediscover those aspects of the *Ring* which, although present in the score, have been hidden by decades of misconceived tradition.

As with Chéreau's production, there is clearly a meeting of minds here. When, in his essay *Über das Dirigieren* (On conducting), Wagner puts the following words into Beethoven's mouth: 'If I wrote a fermata, it was not as a joke or out of embarrassment, it wasn't because I needed time to think of what was to come next!',[62] and when, discussing the Ninth Symphony, he writes of 'the master's plainly expressed intention, as indicated in the score',[63] one might almost think it was Boulez speaking, even down to the matter of style.

Elsewhere in the same essay Wagner insists that, 'to judge from the way in which we have hitherto got to know Beethoven through public performances of his works, the real Beethoven still remains a pure chimera to us'.[64] It is clear, then, that for both Wagner and Boulez the intentions of the composer are inscribed, as it were, in the letter of the score. Throughout Wagner's prose writings the same demands recur as those made by Boulez — respect for melodic, rhythmic, and dynamic detail, the refusal to sentimentalize (which is seen as a sign of bad taste), the importance of the problem of transitions, the continuity of the musical texture, the primacy of the dramatic action, and the clear articulation of the text.

Just as there was a 'theatre of the imagination' for Wagner, which existed only in his dreams, anyone looking at the countless details with which his score teems may well be tempted to conclude that there was also a *musica utopica* for him. Throughout the history of music we find creative artists who were so demanding that they helped extend the possibilities of the instruments for which they wrote. Wagner was such a composer. We may admit, therefore, that in certain cases he may have wanted both a detailed style of writing and a fairly rapid tempo, without being entirely sure in his own mind how this might be realized. It is left to today's conductor to settle the matter one way or another. The solutions adopted by Boulez certainly do not lack logic. Equally certainly, they have the great merit of allowing us to hear another *Ring*, a *Ring* whose existence cannot be denied in Wagner's oeuvre.

Can one claim that Boulez has rediscovered the 'real' Wagner at every point? Like Chéreau's *Ring*, Boulez's is in part a *Ring* at one remove: a comparison between his own remarks and Porges's account of the 1876 festival reveals that there is not the same interest in the entries of the leitmotifs or in the solemnity of certain passages. Boulez does not deny that there is a Romantic dimension to Wagner. After all, how can Wagner be divorced from his age? 'If we look at the vast achievement of the *Ring*, we instinctively use two words not usually found in alliance — romanticism and structure'.[65] Critics have often spoken of the 'unromantic' side of Boulez's conducting, especially in connection with his recording of *Parsifal*. This was no doubt also true of his *Ring* in 1976 and even 1977. From 1978 onwards, it was much less true. 'In spite of what people think, I'm not at all opposed to expression. What I wanted to obtain initially was a framework, a respectful distance, a putting into place with reference to the text. Once that had been instilled, I gave [the performers] free rein. It's like a horse, you can't pull on the reins all the time. I tried to bring out a conception that I believed was valid. It was rather tense to begin with, because there was no convergence of forces, but now we've reached the stage where there's real collaboration'.[66] One needs to have heard the opening act of *Die Walküre* to understand the significance of this astonishing combination of firm placing (*mise en place*) and lyrical inspiration — a combination, at all events, which means that Boulez will never be taken in by the illusory nature of redemption.

We have seen in Chéreau a child of Roland Barthes and the New Criticism, and we have recognized an element of Barthes in Boulez when he suggests interpreting the past from the starting-point of the present. His attitude towards the status of the score can be described, without difficulty, as 'structuralist': even if we feel that not all of Wagner's intentions are *immediately* legible in the score (notably on the question of tempo, which only *external* evidence could really allow one to settle), Boulez does not distinguish between those immanent structures which he can detect in the musical text and Wagner's compositional intentions. For him, the latter are revealed in the former, where it is enough to know how to 'read' them. It is significant that, in all his theoretical writings, Boulez refers only once (unless I am mistaken) to Claude Lévi-Strauss, whom he quotes as follows: 'The content draws its reality from its structure, and what we call form is the *structural disposition* of local structures, in other words of the content'.[67] Yet, however unique this reference, it explains at one and the same time both Boulez the composer and Boulez the conductor. And it also explains, on a musical plane, the 1976 *Ring* in all its luminous clarity.

The Judgement of Fidelity from the Semiological Point of View

The theoretical foundations underpinning Chéreau's and Boulez's attitude to the problem of fidelity are clearly not the same as those implied by my conception. How can we approach the problem of fidelity in semiological terms?

1 There is no single meaning to a work, not least because that meaning is broken up between poiesis and esthesis, but also because, even from the poietic point of view, there is an infinite network of interpretants for the composer. The *Ring* is exemplary in this regard: throughout the twenty-six years of the work's gestation, Wagner continued to puzzle over its ultimate meaning. Starting out from the 'optimism' of Feuerbach, he settled in 1854 for the 'pessimism' of Schopenhauer, and the work's entire centre of gravity shifted from Siegfried to Wotan. His position changed again at the end of his life.

2 This does not mean that we can have no objective knowledge of the past. Moreover, in view of the relativist conception of history and

exegesis advanced in its day by the New Criticism and transmitted nowadays by theories of deconstruction and, to a certain extent, by those of dialogue (as represented by the writings of Clifford Geertz, Richard Rorty, and Gary Tomlinson), it is worth remembering that each text contains 'hard' kernels of meaning which cannot be ignored. It does not take much to see that, by refusing to stage the scene at the end of *Götterdämmerung* in which the Rhine overflows its banks, Chéreau has presented us with a different piece from the one conceived by Wagner. And yet, if the letter of the text prescribes that attendant humanity be 'shaken' by what it has seen and if it is not possible to endorse the illusory view of redemption through love, it is clear none the less that the ring is restored to the Rhinemaidens, that the initial motif of the *Ring* returns, and that, in keeping with Wagner's idea there is a return to Nature. That this is indeed Wagner's idea is clear from a comparison between this passage and the theoretical writings of 1848–52: in Hellenic times, Wagner argued, there was a perfect symbiosis between man and Nature, a symbiosis destroyed by the barbarian hordes and by a Christianity imperfectly understood; a revolution will come, however, which will allow the artwork of the future to develop and permit us to return to the primordial state. This schema evidently parallels that of the *Ring*. But what is it that convinces me that I am right?

My epistemological justification is borrowed from Erwin Panofsky, one of the most brilliant of art historians:

> Whether we deal with historical or natural phenomena, the individual observation of phenomena assumes the character of a 'fact' only when it can be related to other, analogous observations in such a way that the whole series 'makes sense'. This 'sense' is, therefore, fully capable of being applied, as a control, to the interpretation of a new individual observation within the same range of phenomena. If, however, this new individual observation definitely refuses to be interpreted according to the 'sense' of the series, and if an error proves to be impossible, the 'sense' of the series will have to be reformulated to include the new individual observation.[68]

In other words, philology and exegesis provide the means to hunt down interpretations that go across the grain: the return of the ring to the Rhine, the return of the initial musical motif, the overall structure of the *Ring*, Wagner's theories, and so on all converge in so deeply satisfying a way that it is difficult to believe that my interpretation is incorrect. How, then, can we resolve the contradiction between these stable meanings and the networks of meaning which vary according to the changes of context and meaning?

3 Let us begin by introducing the concept of *plot* propounded by the epistemologist and classical historian Paul Veyne. A number of epistemological historians, including the music historian Carl Dahlhaus,[69] agree in recognizing that there are no raw facts in history, since an event acquires its historical dimension only when taken into consideration by the historian. Dahlhaus is right to insist that concatenations of retained facts are constructions,[70] and that there are no facts beyond the reason for retelling them.[71] In advancing the notion of 'plot', Veyne proposes a term which crystallizes these observations:

> Facts do not exist in isolation, in the sense that the fabric of history is what we shall call a plot, a very human and not very 'scientific' mixture of material causes, aims and chances — a slice of life, in short, that the historian cuts as he wills and in which facts have their objective connections and relative importance. . . . The word plot has the advantage of reminding us that what the historian studies is as human as a play or a novel, *War and Peace* or *Antony and Cleopatra*. . . . Then what are the facts worthy of rousing the interest of the historian? All depends on the plot chosen; a fact is not interesting or uninteresting. . . . In history as in the theatre, to show everything is impossible — not because it would require too many pages, but because there is no elementary historical fact, no eventworthy atom. If one ceases to see events in their plots, one is sucked into the abyss of the infinitesimal.[72]

The reference to the theatre is illuminating in the context of my own line of argument: faced with Wagner's text, Chéreau cannot say simply anything. He makes a choice among the infinity of possible plots which can be constructed on the basis of Wagner's libretto. Wieland Wagner elaborated *his*. The musicologist or literary critic proceeds in exactly the same way. I have my own plot of the genesis of the *Ring*: once Schopenhauer had revealed Wotan's true nature to him, Wagner was no longer interested in what to do with Siegfried and was incapable of integrating him into the exegesis of the *Ring* which he sent to Röckel on 23 August 1856. Chéreau constructed *his* exegesis on the basis of his reflections on this same character, from which he drew his characterization of Wotan. To say that Boulez betrayed Wagner is to construct the plot of a certain Wagner who is claimed to be the only true one and to do so, moreover, on the basis of the score, the period, and a certain view of musical history. To link the return of the ring to the Rhine to Wagner's philosophy of Nature and to establish a philological truth is to construct another plot: it is a question of inventing a coherent series of facts.

But is there not a fundamental difference between the work of the

philologist and that of the producer? Between the task of the philologist and that of the producer? As Jean Molino has shown, the philologist's task consists above all in establishing localized truths: locating a
source which throws light on the meaning of an individual line of
poetry has never made it possible, *ipso facto*, to advance the global
meaning of a poem. By establishing precise facts, the philologist may
gradually contribute to a 'more correct' view of a work, but there is
no direct link between this activity and the total act of interpretation.
But what do the producer and conductor have to do? They have to
work on the libretto and score from beginning to end, without
omitting a single line, after which they have to propose a coherent
plot. But this plot cannot be that of the musicologist. In passing from
musicological exegesis to that concrete interpretation through which
artists can bring a work to life, while at the same time assigning to
that work a network of meanings, the interpretants change their
status, since they are no longer conveyed by the same type of symbolic form. We must be wary of confusing the Bayreuth stage and
orchestra pit with a university chair in musicology.[73]

Whereas the musical or literary historian reconstructs the meaning of a text with reference to its original context, the producer and
conductor, by contrast, address themselves to their contemporaries.
It is possible that, in 1876, cultivated Germans were able to grasp the
Schopenhauerian resonances of the *Ring*, since Schopenhauer was
part of the spirit of that age. It is less certain whether they would have
understood those resonances in the way that Wagner himself understood Schopenhauer. Today's producer is obliged to relate his or her
work to a different philosophical, social, and intellectual context.[74]

In conceding that a Schopenhauerian *Ring* represents the 'real'
Wagner, are we forced, therefore, to abandon hope of being able to
present a Schopenhauerian *Ring* to twentieth-century audiences?
Only one condition has to be met for such a presentation to be
possible, and that is for the zeitgeist to re-embrace Schopenhauer, a
prospect which is not in the least nonsensical, for it needs only an
influential writer or thinker to convince an entire generation to
bring about such a return, and a pessimistic, metaphysical *Ring* —
even if not the one reconstructed by Edouard Sans[75] — would once
again be possible. Basically, however, it is in the nature of human
works to become distorted in relation to the network of possible
meanings which they originally possessed.

In the second place — and this is of overriding importance —
interpreters are confronted by the totality of a text in its linear
continuity, with the very constraints of those symbolic forms (the
musical execution and staging) through which they bring the work
to life, in other words, through gestures, sung words, and notes. The

spectator and critic, too, have been confronted by a text, and they in turn have constructed the 'true' Wagner. Believing they have based their conception on the work as a whole, they contrast their own plot with that of Chéreau and Boulez. But there is no quintessentially 'true' *Ring*, only constructions which, however logical, are all partial, setting out, as they do, from the infinite possibilities inherent in the text. But no more than the spectator and critic can the producer and conductor claim to base their conception on the 'totality' of the work. Instead, they have the task — which differs from that of the critic and public — of examining the libretto and score from beginning to end, phrase by phrase, bar by bar, and, notwithstanding the unevenness and contradictions in the text, of proposing a coherent plot. Since musicological discourse differs in kind, semiologically, from a stage production or musical realization, the plots proposed by the research scholar and those advanced by the artist can never coincide. The interpretation of a work of art suffers from constraints — temporal ones above all, but nor can we overlook the impossibility of reconstructing contexts that have long since disappeared — which the musicologist and historian are spared.

During the *Ring* rehearsals, Chéreau was often heard to repeat the same significant phrases: 'That's what I wanted to stage', 'That's not what I wanted to stage'. What he meant by this is that not everything can be staged. The producer is the person who assigns meanings to a text and who, above all, makes choices. The myth recounted by Chéreau presupposes a *choice* of significant facts, a choice, moreover, which is different from that made by Wieland Wagner, for example. Those aspects of the score which Boulez believes reflect Wagner's intentions and spirit are certainly not the same as those singled out by Solti. If, at one and the same time, such divergent conceptions can all claim to be faithful to the composer's intentions, it is because the intentions used by them all to defend their own idea of 'fidelity' are not the same for all of them. Every producer, every conductor proposes a *possible* Wagner — always assuming he or she does not abandon the text completely. Time does not stand still. Chéreau and Boulez will be followed by other artists who — equally talented, equally committed, and equally serious — will take a different view of libretto and score, revealing another 'true' Wagner which, largely different from that of the centennial *Ring*, can still be justified with reference to a specific selection of aspects of the text. And critics, musicologists, and audiences will once again apply the judgement of fidelity according to the no doubt novel image which they will have formed, in the meantime, of the 'truth' concerning Wagner.

In short, works of art do not have an absolute, global, and definitively stable meaning for interpreters, critics, or audiences. At each moment in history, in each culture, a specific network of interpretants is invested with a certain weight by reference to other possibilities: if that weight reflects the spirit of the age, it will give us the feeling that we are in contact with the 'essence' of the work and close to its innermost nature. But the meanings given to human works are always constructs. This does not prevent a certain convergence on particular points from revealing itself at certain periods between interpreters and audience. Nor does it prevent these particular meanings from corresponding with given facts firmly established by the poiesis of the creator. These consensuses and parallels do not mean that those taking part in the semiological process have touched on *the* truth concerning Wagner: they merely correspond with moments of stability in the history of a work's understanding.

Chapter 6

Performing Practice

Clive Brown

Wagner's ideas about performance made almost as profound an impact on the consciousness of his contemporaries as his theories of composition. Throughout the last forty years of his life he fought continually for what he regarded as essential reforms in the performing practices of the period, and he came increasingly to see a particular style of performance as integral to his conception of his own music. He observed when submitting his detailed proposals for a new music school in Munich to King Ludwig II:

> Faced with the prevailing evils of the German theatre, I could see no other way of ensuring decent and correct performances of my more recent dramatic works than by means of model performances, to be given by a specially chosen group of artists trained expressly for the purpose of performing these works in the correct style .... What has persuaded me to make these demands is certainly not any exaggerated opinion of the individual merits of my works but simply the nature of their style and the resultant requirements with regard to a manner of execution which has nowhere yet been cultivated to the point where it has reached the certainty of a genuine style.[1]

During Wagner's long experience as a practical musician he developed firm convictions about the necessary criteria and material conditions not only for the effective performance of his own music, but also for that of his great predecessors and contemporaries. He recognized serious shortcomings in the performing standards of the period and had come to the conclusion at an early stage that the vast majority of performers and conductors misunderstood or wilfully ignored the intentions of the composer. He was insistent that in performing a composer's work the executant musician should 'add nothing to it nor take anything away; he is to be *your second self*'.[2] In his attitude towards the music of the past, though, he was guided almost entirely by instinct and, unaware of the actual performing traditions within which Gluck, Mozart, or Beethoven had worked, imposed on their music a style that arose directly from the wellsprings of his own creativity. But, however historically dubious his ideas, the power of his personality, the strength of his convictions, and, ultimately, his perceived artistic stature meant that he exercised great influence on the performing practices of the late nineteenth century; and many of his ideas continued to have far-reaching ramifications well into the twentieth century.

Among the most prominent features in nineteenth-century musical life was the growth of large-scale public music-making and the concomitant expansion of the orchestra in terms of both number of players and diversity of instruments. At the same time it was a period of extensive experimentation in the construction of instruments. Wagner was closely involved with these developments. Following the lead of Parisian grand opera, he progressively required a greater variety and quantity of wind instruments in his orchestra than had been customary in German opera and, to balance this, he fought continuously to secure the employment of larger string sections in German theatre orchestras. While the orchestra of the Paris Opéra had a regular complement of around fifty strings during the first half of the century, there were far fewer in almost all of the many German theatres. Even theatres in fairly important musical centres had comparatively small string sections: Leipzig in 1825, for instance, had only eighteen strings and Liszt premiered *Lohengrin* at Weimar in 1850 with only twenty-one strings!

The problems of balance created by the expansion of the wind section were exacerbated by the fact that rapid and radical developments in instrument building had made the individual members of the section not only more flexible, but also louder. A real increase of string sound in proportion to wind had therefore become a pressing necessity. Wagner was acutely conscious of this problem; in 1869 he commented that flautists had 'turned their once so gentle instruments into veritable tubes of violence — a delicate sustained *piano* is hardly to be attained any more'.[3] And in his directions for performing *Tannhäuser* (1852), he observed:

> As far as the *composition of the orchestra* is concerned, the wind section in this opera is not substantially larger than the complement usually found in any decent German orchestra. In consequence there is only one point to which I need to draw attention, although it is one that is very important to me. I refer to the requisite strength of the *string instruments*. German orchestras are consistently under strength as far as string instruments are con-

cerned . . . . This much is certain: that, however much we may
deride their frivolity, the French have far larger string sections in
even their smallest orchestras than we find in Germany in often
quite famous orchestras. In orchestrating 'Tannhäuser' I envisaged a particularly large string section and did so with such clear
intent that I must insist that all theatres increase their complement
of strings to exceed their usual number; and my demands in this
regard may be measured by this very simple standard — I declare
that an orchestra which cannot muster at least four good viola
players can convey only the most garbled impression of my music.[4]

The statement that Wagner required a minimum of only four viola
players may seem excessively modest in view of his later stipulations,
but at that stage he was too well aware of the stark realities of life in
German theatres to be totally unrealistic in his demands.

Nevertheless, where he was in a position to influence the situation
directly he strove energetically for improvements. His efforts are
strikingly illustrated by the remarkable report on the Dresden orchestra which he submitted while he was Kapellmeister there.[5] The
radical reforms suggested in that report were for the most part
ignored, but Wagner was successful during his time in Dresden in
securing augmentation in the numbers and quality of the string
players. When he took up his post in 1843 the opera orchestra
contained sixteen violins, four violas, four cellos, and four basses.
The following year, largely as a result of Spontini's visit to conduct *La
Vestale*, the opportunity arose to strengthen and reorganize the orchestra, since, as a journalist noted, 'eight first violins seemed too
weak for the wind in modern operas'.[6] Wagner obtained permission
to augment the strings to twenty violins, six violas, five cellos, and
four basses. He also arranged to distribute them on either side of the
conductor instead of having all the strings to the left with wind and
percussion to the right as previously. (The conductor stood next to
the stage with his back to the players: see fig. 1.) He was criticized,
however, for sometimes grouping all the cellos and basses together
in the middle instead of having them spread throughout the orchestra.[7] The traditional practice had its roots in the important unifying
function of the bass line for orchestral ensemble, but the increasing
independence of cello and bass parts, and the allotting of a melodic
function to the cellos in music such as Wagner's, made this, as well as
the practice of each cello sharing a stand with a bass, obsolete and
largely undesirable. However, Wagner retained something of the old
tradition in the Bayreuth Festspielhaus, where he divided cellos and
basses each into two equal groups and arranged them symmetrically
at either side of the orchestra (fig. 2).

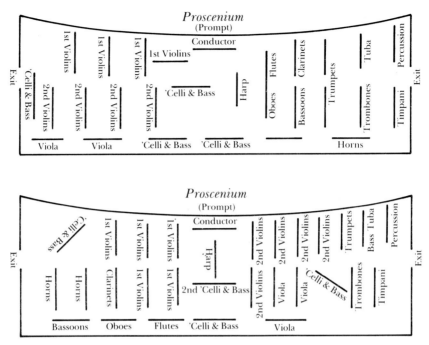

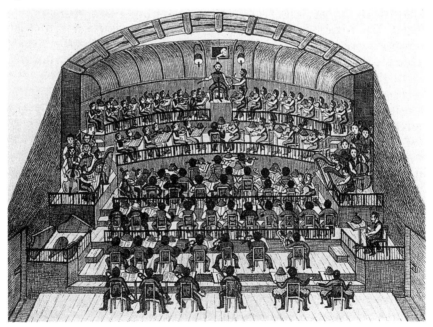

Figure 1

Figure 2

At Bayreuth Wagner finally achieved his ideal orchestral balance with sixteen first and sixteen second violins, twelve violas, twelve cellos, and eight basses; proportions of 1:1:¾:¾:½ which have remained the standard for full-size modern orchestras.

Wagner's approach to the orchestra, with respect to both constitution and playing style, was undoubtedly influenced by his experience in Paris: his appreciation of well-manned string sections was matched by his recognition of the possibilities for orchestral colour afforded by the introduction of greater numbers and variety of wind instruments. In Paris, where a demanding public expected constant novelty, opera composers were quick to expand the wind section of the orchestra. Meyerbeer employed saxophone, bass clarinet, cor anglais, valved brass, and saxhorns; he was to use the saxhorns to devastating effect in the coronation scene of *Le Prophète* (1849) in a twenty-two piece stage band. Wagner was undoubtedly attracted by the possibilities of the newer instruments. The bass clarinet, which had previously been used only for special effect (as in the Act V Trio [no. 28] in Meyerbeer's *Huguenots*), became a normal member of Wagner's woodwind section in *Lohengrin* and subsequent operas; and from *Rienzi* onwards he regularly used valve horns and valve trumpets in his scores.

At first Wagner, like Halévy and Meyerbeer, used valved brass in conjunction with natural instruments, since he regarded the valved instruments as inferior in a number of respects. But, as he explained when dispensing with natural horns in *Tristan und Isolde*: 'So much has been gained through the introduction of valves that it is impossible to ignore these improvements, although the horn has undeniably lost some of its beauty of tone and its ability to slur notes delicately'. He went on to say, however, that in the hands of fine players he believed most of this disadvantage could be obviated, and that, in any case, he was confident of an inevitable improvement of the instrument which would restore its former qualities. Even with valve horns, though, he continued to require stopped notes for special effects, and marked them with a cross in the score, instructing that, should they 'occur in keys in which they are open, it is always assumed that the player changes the key with the valve'.[8] He further stipulated that they are 'always to be accented strongly'.[9] From his other remarks it is clear that he did not necessarily expect the players to follow his instructions for the use of particular crooks (valve horns at this period were still commonly provided with a full set of removable crooks), but that the best way of producing the notes should be 'decided by the players themselves'.[10] In this, as in other respects, Wagner's conception of the sound of his orchestra looked beyond the limitations of the instruments of his own day; he was concerned not to be in the position (in which he believed Beethoven to have been) of having the full realization of his musical conceptions fettered by the imperfections of instruments. It is evident, however, that his sound-ideal for the horn was based on the tonal characteristics of the old waldhorn (hunting horn) and that the role of the horns in his orchestration was conceived in those terms.

In the case of the horn and other traditional wind instruments, Wagner was clearly not entirely happy about the tonal consequences of their 'improvement'; with the less conventional members of his wind section the correspondence between Wagner's ideas and the available instruments was even less clear-cut. By the time of the *Ring* his dissatisfaction with the tone of the cor anglais led him to commission a new instrument, and in the prefaces to the scores of *Siegfried* and *Götterdämmerung* he observed, 'For the cor anglais, which on account of its weakness does not produce the intended effect, the composer has had an "alto oboe" constructed, which he desires shall be substituted for the cor anglais in all his scores'. Wagner's stipulation has generally been ignored and the cor anglais, albeit in an evolved form, is still used.

A more radical innovation was the inclusion of the so-called Wagner tubas in the *Ring*. Wagner's original idea seems to have been to use saxhorns, which he had seen in Adolphe Sax's workshop during his visit to Paris in October 1853. He still referred to them as 'Sax'sche' instruments in a letter to King Ludwig II in September 1865, but shortly after that decided to have special tubas and also a bass trumpet constructed for performance of the *Ring*. In the *Zeitschrift für Instrumentenbau* (1884) the instruments were described as follows:

> The tubas are intended to complete the downward compass of the horns and to strengthen their tone. The shape of the tubas is that of the tenor-horn (baritone saxhorn) except that the cylinders (pistons) are moved by the left instead of the right hand, and the bell turned outwards towards the performer's right instead of pointing upwards. The tubes are of considerably wider bore than those of the horns: hence a considerable increase of power. The tone resembles that of the tenor-horn, but is softer and nobler.[11]

However, the new instruments seem not to have been entirely satisfactory. François-Auguste Gevaert observed in 1885:

> A careful examination of the score shows that, when conceiving these new qualities of tone, with a view to colouring the instrumentation of his work in a novel manner, the genial master did not always fully understand the natural laws and practical conditions

that govern the making and playing of brass instruments. Nor have German makers been able to construct the said instruments in such a manner that they can practically be played (particularly as regards the bass trumpet) without distorting Wagner's original idea.

He further remarked that the experimentation necessary to construct a workable instrument for the bass trumpet parts as Wagner wrote them resulted in a kind of valve trombone 'intermediate between the alto and tenor [trombones], whose tube is bent in the shape of a trumpet'.[12] It is likely that the first set of tubas constructed for the premiere of the *Ring* was not entirely satisfactory, for a new set replaced it for performances at Bayreuth in 1896.

Wagner's attitude to the wind instruments of his day was clearly ambivalent. On the one hand he was concerned that their technical imperfections should be rectified, just as he was concerned that the technical standard of the playing should be improved; on the other hand he undoubtedly designed his orchestration in terms of the sounds with which he was familiar; where, as in the case of the cor anglais, these did not produce the required timbre, or, in the case of the tubas, a particular sound quality was lacking, he attempted to remedy the defect.

The situation with regard to strings is somewhat different, for, while Wagner had decided views about the way he wanted his players to handle the instruments and about the numbers of strings in his orchestra, he never expressed dissatisfaction with the nature of the instruments or their basic sound qualities.

At about the time of Wagner's birth the violin, viola, and cello, and their bows, were close to achieving their modern forms in most respects. The violin chin rest was devised by Spohr around 1820 and the adjustable cello end-pin was introduced by Servais in the mid-1840s; both these aids to holding the instruments were widely adopted during the second half of the century, facilitating rapid position changing and the execution of difficult passages. The double bass was, then as now, less standardized; in the first half of the century, three-, four- and five-stringed instruments were to be found and tunings varied, but by mid-century the four-stringed bass, tuned in fourths from bottom E, was the normal orchestral instrument, and was the one for which Wagner seems to have written. Bass bows, which varied considerably in design, were normally played 'underhand', as is still the rule in Germany and Austria.

But throughout Wagner's lifetime the tone of the string instruments would have been markedly different from what we are used to today. This difference resulted from their stringing. Pure, uncovered gut was used for the E, A, and D strings; for the G string of the violin and the G and C strings of the viola and cello, the gut was usually wound with silver or silver-plated copper wire. This remained the normal method of stringing until the second decade of the twentieth century, after which a significant change in tone quality was brought about by the increasingly widespread adoption of the steel E string (which was known but scorned by professional players in the later nineteenth century); pure gut A and D strings were in turn abandoned in favour of metal-covered strings, and the subsequent use of metal and synthetic materials for the core of many modern strings has made the basic tonal characteristics of the instruments even more unlike those of the nineteenth century.

Another matter, but a very variable one, which was relevant to performance in the second half of the nineteenth century was pitch. Throughout Wagner's lifetime pitch was getting progressively higher in most places, but since there were no agreed standards it varied considerably from place to place; despite the French decree fixing $a' = 435$ in 1858, the second half of the century saw levels of over $a' = 450$ in London and Vienna. In Dresden, where pitch remained lower than in many other important German cities, Wagner's fellow Kapellmeister, Reißiger, had a tuning fork of $a' = 435$, but by 1861 the pitch at the Opera was recorded as $a' = 446$. Wagner himself was unhappy about the general rise in pitch and undoubtedly insisted whenever possible on keeping it down to something like the French *diapason normal* of $a' = 435$. (The official pitch of the Munich Opera in the 1870s was $a' = 435.4$.) When Wagner came to London for performances of his works in the Albert Hall in 1877, it is recorded that he 'complained bitterly of the inconvenience his singers had been put to, on account of the fact that the pitch they were obliged to sing was so much higher [$a' = 455.1$] than that which they were accustomed to'.[13]

How Wagner's music would have sounded in his own day was determined not only by such things as the timbre of the instruments, conventions of orchestra layout, and pitch, but also, and even more decisively, by the style of performance. This was partly a matter of the musicians applying their customary methods of tone production and techniques, and partly of their response to the copiously detailed marks for articulation, accent, and expression which Wagner included in his scores.

One of the most significant factors, which affected strings, singers, and some of the wind instruments, was a totally different attitude towards vibrato. Whereas, in the case of strings, flutes, oboes, and bassoons, vibrato has now come to be seen as a permanent colouring which may be intensified or removed for special effects, the opposite was the case throughout the nineteenth century: a basically non-vibrato sound was then seen as the norm and vibrato, of varied speeds and intensities, was added as a colouring for special notes within the phrase. As Joseph Joachim observed in his *Violinschule* (1902–05): 'A violinist whose taste is refined and healthy will always recognize the steady tone as the ruling one, and will use the vibrato only where the expression seems to demand it'.[14] The sparing use of vibrato by nineteenth-century string players is illustrated in a host of examples from the leading authorities of the period.[15] By the time Joachim published his *Violinschule*, the aesthetic he advocated was beginning to be called into question, but it was far from being overthrown.

The situation with respect to singing is closely analogous; the modern singer's attitude to vibrato, like the instrumentalist's, contrasts sharply with the nineteenth-century aesthetic. The violinist Charles de Bériot stressed the connection between the string player's and the singer's use of vibrato in his *Méthode de violon* of 1858; he, like Joachim,[16] equated the violinist's steady tone (with a perfectly still left hand) with the singer's normal delivery and counselled that in both cases vibrato was to be sparingly applied to intensify the expression of certain notes or passages. He observed:

> Vibrato is an accomplishment with the artist who knows how to use it with effect, and to abstain from it when necessary: but it becomes a fault when too frequently employed . . . . The voice of the singer, like the fine tone of the violinist, is impaired by this great fault . . . . Whether it be singer or violinist, with the artist who is governed by this desire to produce an effect vibrato is nothing but a convulsive movement which destroys strict intonation, and thus becomes a ridiculous exaggeration.[17]

Bériot's brother-in-law, the singer and teacher Manuel García (brother of Maria Malibran [Bériot] and Pauline Viardot-García), described the use of vibrato, for which he uses the term *tremolo*, in terms similar to Bériot's:

> When agitation is produced by grief so intensely deep as wholly to overpower the soul, the vocal organ experiences a vacillation called the *Tremolo*. This, when properly brought in and executed, never fails to produce a pathetic effect . . . . The *tremolo* is employed to depict sentiments, which, in real life, are of a poignant character — such as anguish at seeing the imminent danger of any one dear to us; or tears extorted by certain acts of anger, revenge, etc. Under those circumstances, even its use should be adopted with great taste, and in moderation; for its expression or duration,

if exaggerated, becomes fatiguing and ungraceful. Except it these especial cases just mentioned, care must be taken not in any degree to diminish the firmness of the voice; as a frequent use of the *tremolo* tends to make it prematurely tremulous. An artist who has contracted this intolerable habit becomes incapable of phrasing any kind of sustained song whatever.[18]

The strictures of nineteenth-century authorities make it clear that many performers employed considerably more vibrato than they recommended, but this was universally condemned as an abuse; extensive research has failed to yield any contrary opinion. The earliest sign of a radical change of attitude seems to be Siegfried Eberhardt's *Violin Vibrato* of 1910. An increasing emphasis on vibrato had been apparent in certain violinists of the Franco-Belgian school during the latter years of the nineteenth century, but the first use of continuous vibrato in solo violin playing was credited to Kreisler.[19] At about the same time singers began to develop analogous habits. During the twentieth century continuous vibrato has become the rule, and the past half-century has seen the acceptance of ever more pervasive and obtrusive vocal and instrumental vibrato. The very different method of tone production of late nineteenth-century singers and instrumentalists can easily be heard in recordings made at the beginning of the twentieth century. In the case of singers, the sound is not 'white' except on relatively short notes; there is what Mozart referred to as the 'natural trembling' which occurs 'only to such a degree that the effect is beautiful'.[20] What is specially striking in these recordings, however, is the avoidance, except occasionally, of almost any vibrato of pitch; the normal vibrato of many modern singers varies the pitch almost as much as the neatly executed trills of late nineteenth-century singers, and is generally slower.

It may be stated with confidence that Wagner did not envisage a continuous vibrato (in the modern sense) as normal in either a solo or an orchestral context, and its consequences for the effect of his music are drastic, particularly in the vocal department. Not only does the continuous vibrato remove a level of expressiveness which was regarded as highly important in the nineteenth century, but also it often has the effect of distorting and obscuring the intervallic relationships of voices within an ensemble.

Some impression of the occasions on which nineteenth-century composers would have regarded vibrato as an effective device in the instrumentalist's or singer's performance can be gleaned from the rare occasions on which they asked for it. As a rule, orchestral string players were not expected to employ it at all (though there can be little doubt that as conservatories turned out increasing numbers of

Meyerbeer, *Il crociato in Egitto*

Example 1

non v'e più a-mor

highly trained players in the second half of the century, many individuals would have used it in the orchestra, as they did in solo playing, on expressive notes and accents). But from time to time an orchestral vibrato was demanded as a special effect: thus Carl Loewe asked for it on a swelled note for violas and cellos in his oratorio *Die Festzeiten* (p. 27 of the autograph score), and almost a century later Elgar requested it in the Larghetto of his Second Symphony (rehearsal number 86). Even for wind players in solo passages, where they might have been expected to exercise the soloist's privilege of occasionally introducing vibrato, a meticulous composer sometimes felt the need to specify it: in Meyerbeer's *Crociato in Egitto* (on p. 534 of the copyist's score in the theatre library of La Fenice, Venice), 'vibrato' is written not only for a phrase in the voice part, but also for the oboe and flute figures which imitate it in the following bar (ex. 1). Requests for vibrato in voice parts, though still infrequent, are much more common than requests for it in the orchestra. Instructions for vocal vibrato can regularly be found among the many other painstakingly detailed directions for vocal and instrumental performance which Meyerbeer included in the scores of his later operas. (However, the term *vibrato* or *vibrate*, particularly in early nineteenth-century Italian music, does not always seem merely to have meant vibrato in the modern sense; on occasion it may, as the context sometimes implies, primarily have indicated a forceful delivery of the passage in question. Peter Lichtenthal's *Dizionario e bibliografia della musica* [Milan 1826] defines vibrato as 'marcato fortemente', or 'strongly marked'.)

Wagner's scores seldom ask specifically for vocal vibrato and even more rarely for instrumental vibrato. An instance of the latter occurs, however, in *Siegfried* (Act III, Scene 3, p. 1086 of Eulenburg score), where the word *vibrirend* appears in the first and second violin parts.

In vocal lines, the instruction 'vibrato' and 'ad lib vibrato' occurs in *Das Liebesverbot* (nos. 2 and 10), while in *Die Meistersinger* (Act I, bars 772 and 774) it is indicated with a wavy line; and in *Siegfried* (Act I, Scene 3, p. 277 of Eulenburg score), the word *bebend* (trembling) also has a wavy line and is directed to be sung 'mit schütternder Stimme' (with shaking voice). The wavy line was used to denote vibrato by a number of nineteenth-century composers. In *Siegfried* (Act III, Scene 3, p. 997 of Eulenburg score) Wagner used another symbol, a horizontal line, to indicate a less pronounced vibrato; Heinrich Porges, in his account of the rehearsals for the *Ring* in 1876, remarked, 'The strokes [lines] above the E and B of "zitternd" indicate that here Wagner wanted that gentle vibrato — not to be confused with the bad habit of a tremolando — whose importance in expressive singing he often spoke of'.[21] The absence of such indications elsewhere in Wagner's scores cannot be taken to mean that he absolutely excluded vibrato in other contexts; Porges, again, refers to a passage in Act I, Scene 2 of *Die Walküre*, where the words 'wo Unheil im Hause wohnt' should be 'sung broadly, the initial violence giving way to an anguished vibrato'.[22] All this confirms the view that Wagner adhered to the prevailing aesthetic of a basically non-vibrato sound. He would certainly have expected his singers and players to use vibrato only where the dramatic expression called for it.

Intimately related to the use of vibrato was that of portamento, which was likewise regarded as an indispensable constituent of expressive singing and playing, but highly damaging if abused. García observed that it 'should be employed rarely, and with extreme judgement; for, by its too frequent use, singing would be rendered drawling. Some singers, either from negligence or want of taste, slur the voice endlessly either before or after notes; thus the rhythm and spirit of the song are destroyed, and the melody becomes nauseously languid'.[23] Violinists agreed closely with singers on the artistic and technical aspects of portamento; Joachim expressed the consensus view when he commented: 'The use and manner of executing the portamento must naturally come under the same rules as those which hold good in vocal art'.[24] He went on succinctly to characterize the two principal methods of employing it:

> The *portamento* used on the violin between two notes played with one bow-stroke corresponds, therefore, to what takes place in singing when the slur is placed over two notes which are meant to be sung on one syllable; the *portamento* occurring when a change of bow and position is simultaneously made corresponds to what happens when a singer for the sake of musical expression connects two notes, on the second of which a new syllable is sung.

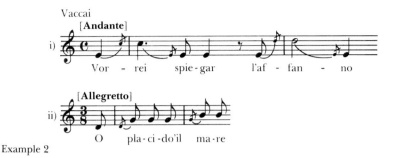

Example 2

It should be stressed, however, that the term portamento covered every degree from a finely controlled *sostenuto*, in which the connection between notes was more implied than audible, to a pronounced *glissando*; the mode of execution was expected to be appropriate to the dramatic context. Most authorities were agreed that if a portamento were used between two syllables or words, the voice should make the portamento on the first syllable, briefly anticipating the second note. García disapproved of the opposite procedure, that is, beginning to sing the second syllable at the pitch of the first and then sliding to the second note; however, this option was described by Nicola Vaccai in his *Metodo pratico* of 1832,[25] though he remarked that the other method was more usual. Vaccai's examples (ex. 2) clearly illustrate these two practices. (A rare instance where Vaccai's second method is specifically indicated by a composer is to be found in Meyerbeer's *Huguenots* [p. 765 of the 1836 full score]). Another situation in which an audible *glissando* was regarded as particularly effective was when the voice moved in descending semitones; this was described by August Ferdinand Haeser in 1828.[26]

While Wagner seems generally to have been content to leave the introduction of vibrato to the discretion of singers and instrumentalists (presumably trusting to their good taste), he was careful in his later operas to indicate the places where he required portamento. In *Der fliegende Holländer*, the first of his operas to contain unequivocal indications for portamento, he several times used the words *con portamento* or *portamento* in the vocal line to indicate that whole phrases should be sung in this manner. One instance is a characteristic descending chromatic line, when the Dutchman sings 'Dies der Verdammnis Schreckgebot' (no. 2); another, where two words separated by the interval of a diminished fourth are also joined with a slur, occurs a few pages later at the words 'Wann brichst du an in

meine Nacht?' Elsewhere in this score portamento between individual notes set to different syllables is indicated by slurs, but there
seem to be no instances of more than two syllables being slurred in
this way. In *Tannhäuser* the slurring is somewhat more extensive and
instances of three separate syllables under a slur are not uncommon.
In this and later scores Wagner discontinued the practice of writing
the word *portamento*, but continued to indicate its use with slurs;
occasionally, when he required a very pronounced portamento, he
not only used a slur but also the German 'sehr getragen' (very
sustained), as in *Die Walküre*, Act III, Scene 2 (p. 847 of Eulenburg
score). *Lohengrin* contains many long slurs in the vocal lines, often
over several bars. The same is true of *Tristan und Isolde*, where these
slurs are of particularly frequent occurrence; slurs over only two or
three syllables are relatively uncommon. Numerous instances of slurs
in the vocal line can be found in all the later operas, where their
presence relates to specific techniques of legato and portamento
which were seen by Wagner as essential to the delivery.

The question of portamento in the string section of the orchestra
in Wagner's operas is more problematic. Several authorities in the
period prior to the middle of the nineteenth century had specifically
prohibited orchestral players from using portamento, but there is
considerable evidence to suggest that their prohibitions were frequently transgressed. As early as 1799 a writer in the *Allgemeine
Musikalische Zeitung* had objected to players in the Magdeburg theatre
orchestra making audible slides, and he concluded, 'I have now
noticed this disfiguring embellishment in the orchestras of many
places'.[27] A few years later Salieri complained forcefully about the
same practice in Vienna.[28] By the 1830s there is evidence of the
deliberate use of expressive portamento in an orchestral context in,
for instance, Spohr's fingerings for the string parts in his Fifth
Symphony (1836); clearly, Spohr's rejection of orchestral portamento
in his *Violinschule*, published four years earlier, applied only to the
arbitrary introduction of the device by individual players.[29] Meyerbeer,
too, indicated portamento in the first violin part of *L'Etoile du nord*
with the instruction 'glissez ... avec le même doigt' (slide ... with
the same finger; 1854 full score, p. 184). There are many fingered
orchestral parts from the second half of the nineteenth century in
which portamento seems to be implied, and there is no reason to
believe that the deliberate and prominent use of portamento in the
earliest orchestral recordings was a feature of very recent origin
(though it may be that these recordings capture the practice at its
most extreme point).

There can be little doubt that orchestral portamento was part of
Wagner's sound-world. Whether he positively wanted it is another

matter, but there are undoubtedly many places in which the notation seems to envisage it: for instance, the passage on the G string for first and second violins beginning at bar 22 of the prelude to *Tristan und Isolde*, or the falling major sixth in violins and cellos in *Siegfried* (Act III, Scene 3, p. 1083 of Eulenburg score), where the portamento of the voice on the same notes, a bar later, is anticipated.

The progressively more intensive and sophisticated use of performance directions of all kinds in Wagner's scores mirrors the general tendency of nineteenth-century composers to attempt to control the details of performance ever more closely. As a result of the absence of adequate, universally accepted conventions for conveying finer nuances, new markings were brought into use and the meanings of many older ones modified or extended. Since Wagner's death the process of modification has continued in conjunction with changing approaches to style and technique, and it is by no means certain that Wagner's marks convey the same things to modern performers as they did to his musicians. The signification of an articulation or accent mark can only be determined by a knowledge of the traditions by which a composer had been influenced and of the way in which he developed its use in his own music.

In Wagner's earlier works his repertory of articulation and accent markings is relatively restricted and straightforward, but it becomes richer and more subtle in the later ones. In the period between *Rienzi* and *Tristan und Isolde* he began to utilize new markings and to refine the meaning of old ones. From the first Wagner used *fp* and > as accent markings; ^, as an indication to accentuate strongly and firmly, is introduced in *Rienzi* (often associated with the word *marcato*); and *sf*, extremely rare in early works, begins to be used regularly in *Tristan und Isolde*.

One of the most intriguing features in Wagner's notation of accentuation and articulation is his changing attitude towards the use of staccato dots and strokes. Many theorists have maintained that the stroke shortens the note more than the dot, usually removing three-fourths and one-half of the value of the note, respectively.[30] Heinrich Christoph Koch, however, stated that there was no universal agreement about which was the shorter staccato, while Abbé Vogler and Justin Heinrich Knecht seem to have maintained that strokes were both stronger and longer than dots.[31] (This may thus have been the sense in which Vogler's pupils Weber and Meyerbeer used them.) Spohr, who used only one staccato mark, regarded the degree of separation as a matter of taste, applying the same mark to everything from *martelé* to *grand détaché*.[32] When both marks were used, though, the stroke certainly seems to have had a stronger implication of accent than the dot. In early nineteenth-century printed music, strokes were normally associated with *forte* passages and vigorous delivery while dots usually occurred in quieter, gentler contexts. There was, however, often little correspondence between the use of these two signs by publishers and the composers' autographs.

In the period preceding *Rienzi* Wagner made no clear distinction between the two marks. In some early autographs the dot seems to be exclusively employed, in others the stroke (the orthography is not always easy to interpret), but there appears to be no intentional difference. In *Rienzi* and *Der fliegende Holländer*, the predominant form of staccato becomes the dot; strokes are occasionally used, but almost entirely on isolated notes. This use of the two marks tallies with their employment by Weber, Schubert, Berlioz, and Meyerbeer, where the stroke generally seems associated with more accented execution. Marschner certainly used the stroke in the sense of an accent; its function in *Hans Heiling* is described by that work's nineteenth-century editor, G. F. Kogel: 'The notes marked with these strokes should be executed particularly strongly (*sfz*) with powerful, short bowstrokes'.[33]

In *Tannhäuser*, however, the stroke takes over as Wagner's principal staccato mark, and dots are relatively uncommon. In later works he used dots rather more frequently, but the stroke remained the predominant staccato mark for the rest of his life. The distinction between these marks is rarely ambiguous in Wagner's mature autographs; for while the strokes are elongated in a vertical direction, the dots (like his dots of prolongation) are usually somewhat elongated in a horizontal direction (fig. 3).

Wagner's change of notation in *Tannhäuser* may be connected partly with his adoption of a wider range of accent signs which obviated the necessity of that function for the stroke, but it seems likely that it came about more as a response to the refinement of bowing style that was spreading with the influence of the French school at that time. He may have been influenced in this by his close contact with Lipiński, leader of the Dresden orchestra. There was a growing tendency among string players for the stroke to be associated with more powerful, somewhat accented bowstrokes such as *martelé* (normally near the point, but sometimes near the heel) or a short and weighty *détaché*, while the dot often, though not exclusively, implied lighter bowstrokes such as *sautillé* (hüpfender Bogen) or *spiccato* (springender Bogen). This distinction is found in the *Violinschule* (1864) by Ferdinand David, leader of the Gewandhaus Orchestra from 1836 to 1873, and an influential figure in German violin playing; it is also the distinction specified sixty years later by Schoenberg in the preface to his Serenade Op. 24. This may broadly

Figure 3

have been the signification of the two marks intended by Wagner (though sometimes he used dots in *forte* passages where they seem to imply an unaccented *détaché*). Where he deliberately left separate notes in faster-moving *forte* passages without a dot or stroke, it is possible that he envisaged the *grand détaché*, a style of bowing for which the Dresden orchestra had been renowned in the 1840s and which Wagner found to be of such good effect in Gluck's Overture to *Iphigénie en Aulide*.[34] Naturally, he would have expected wind instruments to match the articulation and attack of the strings.

Other categories of note-length and accent are indicated by various marks used in conjunction with slurs. Dots under slurs were undoubtedly intended by Wagner to mean the same thing as the pianist's *portato*, not, as in the case of many string-playing composers, a sharply separated staccato in one bowstroke; this was a point of some confusion at the time, as is illustrated by Brahms's correspondence about his Violin Concerto with Joachim.[35] Wagner also used the horizontal line under a slur. When it occurred over repeated notes it indicated a more sustained *portato*; over isolated notes or in melodic passages, it had a rather more specialized meaning. Clarification of this usage survives in a transcript of Wagner's instructions at rehearsals of *Parsifal* in 1882. In one passage (rehearsal number 45) he asked that the quavers should be 'very sustained and held [sehr

getragen und gehalten], not merely slurred, a true portamento'; and
at the repetition of a similar passage (no. 48), 'very dragged [sehr
gezogen], the quaver very clear, very distinct, the short note is the
main thing'.[36] In these passages lines over the quavers were not
present in Wagner's autograph, but, presumably as a result of his
intervention in the rehearsal, they were included in the 1883 printed
score. (Wagner also used the horizontal line, as mentioned above, to
indicate a gentle vibrato, but in that instance it is written outside, not
inside, the slur.)

   Wagner's accent and articulation marks clearly have much to tell
about the manner in which he envisaged his music being performed.
They are intimately related to his conception of the rhythmic structure of his mature works, in which he urged his singers to abandon
the traditional modes of operatic delivery and 'to give precedence to
the "little" notes, before the "big"'.[37] He was insistent that, as his
'alter ego'[38] Liszt put it, there should be 'an end to mechanical,
fragmented up-and-down playing, tied to the bar line, which is still
the rule in many cases'.[39]

Another area in which Wagner sought greater precision of notation
was ornamentation. In his operas up to *Lohengrin* he used a variety of
conventional ornament signs: in the later operas, with very few
exceptions other than trills (which according to Edward Dannreuther
[*Ornamentation* (London 1893–95) part 2, p. 172] were normally
meant to start on the main note), he dispensed with signs and either
indicated his ornaments with small notes, or incorporated them into
the musical text in normal-sized notes. In the earlier operas he
regularly used the sign ϕ for turns; he does not seem to have employed a different sign to indicate an inverted turn, but in his later
works, where the turns are written out, some begin from above and
others from below. The Vorspiel to *Götterdämmerung*, for instance,
has inverted turns and direct turns closely juxtaposed. A written-out
inverted turn also occurs in the 1855 version of his *Faust* Overture;
this example is particularly interesting, since in the 1839–40 version
of the overture the turns are indicated by Wagner's usual turn sign.
Whether Wagner originally envisaged an inverted turn in the overture is open to question; in view of his generally careful attitude
towards notation, it seems unlikely. There was, however, some laxity
in these matters at the period Wagner wrote the overture. Bernhard
Romberg, in his 1840 *Méthode de violoncelle*, having illustrated the
signs for different types of turn, admitted: 'There are however some
composers (among whom I include myself) who write in such haste
that they do not take the trouble to mark this ornament in such a way
as to show whether they intend it to be made from above or below'

(p. 86). Romberg then explained that in his music the context determined how the turn should be executed. If the following note were higher, it should begin from above; if lower, from below. But this convention certainly did not apply to Wagner.

How Wagner wished the turn signs in earlier operas to be interpreted was by no means clear even during his lifetime. In his piano versions of the Prayer from *Rienzi* and the March from *Tannhäuser* (Act II, Scene 4), Liszt realized the turn signs as direct turns. Hans von Bülow, however, apparently without any authority from the composer, insisted for a while on performing the turns in *Rienzi* and others of Wagner's earlier operas as inverted turns. This was the subject of considerable controversy at the time and though Bülow later changed his mind, other conductors adopted the habit. Dannreuther reported (*Ornamentation*, part 2, p. 174) that at Munich in the 1890s for instance, the inverted turn was routinely used in *Rienzi*; this practice was perpetuated by Karl Klindworth's vocal score, in which the signs are realized as inverted turns. Wagner himself seems to have added to the confusion over the meaning of his turn signs, for when present at rehearsals of *Tannhäuser* in Vienna in 1875, he asked the conductor, Hans Richter, to take the turns (marked by the sign for a normal turn) which follow the words 'So stehet auf!' in Act II, Scene 2 as inverted turns. In the revised vocal score of *Tannhäuser* (1876), prepared by Joseph Rubinstein under Wagner's direct supervision, however, these turns were written out as normal turns, and they also appear thus in Klindworth's vocal score.

In his attitude towards tempo and tempo modification Wagner made, perhaps, his most obvious impact on the future. During the late eighteenth and early nineteenth centuries, the generally accepted view was that a tempo held good until another tempo, or an instruction such as *ritardando* or *accelerando*, was indicated. Most theorists recognized that relaxation and tension in the music ought to exercise a limited degree of influence on the pulse; Hummel observed: 'Many persons still erroneously imagine that, in applying the metronome, they are bound to follow its equal and undeviating motion throughout the whole piece, without allowing themselves any latitude in the performance for the display of taste or feeling'.[40] But the true *tempo rubato* as understood by Mozart, Hummel, Spohr, Baillot, and even, apparently Chopin consisted of keeping the accompaniment essentially steady, while some beats in the melody were lengthened and others shortened. This practice was still being advocated in the second half of the nineteenth century.[41] Any real flexibility of tempo was only envisaged as taking place at the subtlest level. In orchestral performance the ideal was steady maintenance of the tempo throughout a movement. A writer, probably Schumann, in the *Neue Zeitschrift für Musik* in 1836 recommended that a conductor should only beat at the beginning of a movement or at tempo changes, but conceded that it might be helpful to beat regularly in very slow tempi.[42] This seems to have been close to the practice adopted by Mendelssohn, and under the general conditions of rehearsal and performance at that time it certainly ruled out any substantial modification of tempo.

Wagner did not share this view. He observed, in 1869, that 'modification of tempo' was 'not merely entirely unknown to our conductors, but precisely because of their ignorance, treated with foolishly dismissive contempt';[43] and he later remarked that it was not surprising that such a work as Beethoven's *Eroica* Symphony was misunderstood when played in strict time, but that in the past 'it was nowhere played otherwise'.[44] Wagner regarded each section of a movement as having its own appropriate tempo, and believed that the fundamental *adagio* element in lyrical melody should be emphasized. He claimed that he only expected this to take place in a discreet manner, but accounts of performances which he conducted suggest that, in fact, his modifications of tempo were quite extreme. During his conductorship of the Philharmonic Society in London in 1855, one of the most frequent complaints concerned his distortion of tempo; Henry Chorley described Wagner's conducting of a Beethoven symphony as 'full of . . . ill measured rallentandi',[45] while Henry Smart objected to his tempi in every respect: 'Firstly he takes all quick movements faster than anybody else; secondly he takes all slow movements slower than anybody else; thirdly he prefaces the entry of an important point, or the return of a theme — especially in a slow movement — by an exaggerated ritardando; and fourthly, he reduces the speed of an allegro — say in an overture or the first movement — fully one-third, immediately on the entrance of its cantabile phrases'.[46] This aspect of Wagner's attitude to orchestral performance, which has much in common with Liszt's approach to solo performance, was the direct forerunner of the highly flexible and subjective performances of Mengelberg, Furtwängler, and many other conductors in the twentieth century.

In Wagner's later works, frequent changes and modifications of tempo are specified in the score, though there is no reason to think that these are the only places where flexibility is permissible or desirable. Porges records, for instance, that in *Siegfried* Act I, Scene 1 (p. 62 of the Eulenburg score) Wagner asked for a rallentando, not marked in the score, to round off the scene.[47] With regard to tempo Wagner trusted the instincts of the conductor who was in tune with his general principles and with the dramatic meaning of his music.

After *Tannhäuser* he abandoned the practice of including metronome marks, remarking that things would be in a sorry state 'if conductor and singers are to be dependent on metronome marks alone' and that 'they will hit upon the right tempo only when they begin to feel a lively sympathy with the dramatic and musical situations and when that understanding allows them to find the tempo as though it were something self-evident, something that did not require any further searching on their part'.[48] He himself was capable of taking the same music at considerably different tempi in response to the dramatic mood of the moment.

In 1840 Wagner expressed the view that the composer's greatest concern is 'to ensure that your piece of music is heard exactly as you yourself heard it when you wrote it down: that is to say, the composer's intentions must be reproduced with conscientious fidelity, so that the ideas which it contains may be conveyed to the senses undistorted and unimpaired'.[49] Much later he insisted on the importance of the 'model performances' which would fix the 'mode of rendering' for his works. Modern performances of Wagner's operas are undeniably very different from the ones which he would have directed and experienced, in terms of both staging and musical style. Much can be learned about the way Wagner would have expected his operas to be performed, and much can be gained from a creative response to that knowledge. It is well worth considering what he wrote in 1878 about the masterpieces of another composer whom he greatly admired:

> It is clear from Mozart's operas that the very quality by which they transcended their age brought with it the curious disadvantage that they were condemned to outlive that age when the vital conditions that governed their conception and execution no longer existed. . . . To what torments of existence is the departed soul of such a masterpiece exposed when harried back to life by a modern theatrical medium for the delectation of a later generation! . . . There is scarcely an opera producer alive who has not taken it into his head at some time or other to stage *Don Giovanni* in a contemporary setting, whereas every intelligent person should be telling himself that it is not this work which must be tailored to suit our times but we ourselves who must adapt to the time of *Don Giovanni* if we are to find ourselves in harmony with Mozart's creation.[50]

Chapter 7

The Reception of Wagner in Vienna, 1860–1900

Amanda Glauert

When Wagner left Vienna in the spring of 1864 it seemed unlikely, or even impossible, that he would return. Financial embarrassments forced the composer unceremoniously to flee his apartment in the suburb of Penzing and he was subsequently warned to cut his ties there completely.[1] Though Wagner had chosen Vienna as a base for his artistic operations in 1861, his feelings about the city were always equivocal. From visits as a young man he gained an idea of the capital's artistic richness: 'Vienna remained for a long time my idea of creativity rooted in the originality of the people'.[2] With these words he suggested a vision of Vienna as a birthplace for the *Volk*, Wagner's 'artists of the future'.[3] Yet he could not help observing that for the present the Viennese public demanded little from their theatres beyond a diet of Hérold's *Zampa* and Strauss waltzes.[4]

In the heroic time of 1848, Wagner still relished the challenge of conquering such a public. As political disturbances threatened his plans for theatrical reforms in Dresden, he visited Vienna to propose linking its five imperial theatres into one institution, to make a 'suitable terrain' for his 'art-work of the future'.[5] However, in 1861 when Eduard Devrient urged the composer to try again to arrange performances of his works in Vienna, Wagner was more reticent. His growing desire, during the period of exile from 1849, for perfect artistic fellowship with his audience, or for entire control in performance, lessened the attraction of battling in Vienna's open market-place. Wagner's reply to Devrient was that he preferred special treatment by a smaller theatre such as Karlsruhe to inclusion in the routine repertory of the Vienna Opera.[6] Wagner had indeed resolved, through the composing of *Die Walküre*, to bring an end to all compromises with theatrical tradition.[7]

Such resolve broke when the management of the Vienna Opera refused to release any of their singers to Karlsruhe and insisted that if Wagner wished to use their resources, he must transfer his performance plans for *Tristan und Isolde* to Vienna itself. Wagner agreed, but the following series of delays and disappointments from 1861 to 1864 showed that the composer was right to be wary of the Vienna Opera's ability or willingness to respond to his intentions. The ill-prepared-ness of the performers balked all Wagner's efforts and gave the hostile press an excuse for declaring *Tristan* unperformable, a charge which they maintained until the Viennese premiere of 1883.[8] By the end of 1861 Wagner had returned to a performance ideal of 1850, of wanting a theatre of his own; as he wrote to Hans von Bülow, this was perhaps the only way of being entirely free from 'the operatic non-sense of our time'.[9]

At this stage Wagner still envisaged his theatre being situated in a big city such as Vienna, Berlin, or Paris, because such a location was necessary to draw out large enough audiences for the specialized nature of his work. Wagner told Bülow he favoured Berlin over Vienna, as one might expect from his recent experiences. It is more significant that the composer admitted to his work being a speciality. He seemed to be acquiescing in the general view of Vienna, that his support would only ever come from a select, rather than a broad-based, audience. To many observers, evidence of partisanship cast doubts on Wagner's apparent successes. As Friedrich Hebbel re-ported on one of Wagner's Viennese concerts of 1862–63: 'He does not by any means command unanimous or even great applause, however vociferous they are in the Theater an der Wien, where the experiment is taking place, or however often they call him back to take another bow'.[10]

Wagner's answer to the partial nature of his success was that his work must be regarded as a speciality only for the time being.[11] However, the time when the speciality would become general fare seemed to be postponed further and further into the future, until Wagner's vision of his work being written for the Volk seemed little more than a worthy ideal. In his preface to the published text of his *Der Ring des Nibelungen* of 1863, the composer now envisaged his own theatre occupying one of Germany's smaller cities, so as to avoid 'collision with any of our larger standing theatres, and . . . with the regular theatre-public of our great cities and all its habitudes'. Wagner wished to extend an invitation to the German nation as a whole, making the performances available 'not to the local public of a city, but to all the friends of Art, both near and far'. However, he saw him-self as freed from the immediate need of winning such an audience by 'an association of well-to-do, art-loving men and women, with the immediate object of collecting the needful funds for a first perform-ance of my work', or by the support of a wealthy German prince.[12]

In 1863 Wagner excused himself from resolving any contradic-tions in his plans for a Stage Festival by announcing that he had no

hope of the plans being realised in his lifetime; indeed, he did not
even think he would finish the musical composition of the *Ring*.
However, when King Ludwig II of Bavaria offered the composer his
support in May 1864, the prospect opened of ideal becoming reality
and of Wagner being able to follow through his intentions. Even the
severance from Vienna was reversed, since the king settled all Wagner's
debts. In fact, the subsequent plans for performances in Munich
revealed the same equivocation about the audience Wagner had in
mind as the plans of 1863. Wagner decided not to offer his performances to 'common curiosity' and invited only those with 'a more
serious interest in my art'. This was once more presented as a temporary measure, responding to Ludwig's wishes and the need to con-
centrate on the purely artistic challenge of performing *Tristan*: 'How
we are to allow the general population to have a share in the heights
and the profundities of art, to what extent we are prepared to help
them to that share, will also emerge in their turn'.[13] To emphasize
the provisional nature of these performance conditions, Wagner
wished the Munich Festival Theatre to be built in wood rather than
stone,[14] even though the king had plans for a much grander building. If Ludwig had followed the composer's simpler conception, he
might have lessened the political resentment which drove Wagner
from Munich in December 1865. As Wagner began his plans for a
Stage Festival in Bayreuth in the 1870s, he resumed his notion of a
temporary theatre, for the wooden theatre was to be 'merely the
outline of our idea and [we are] handing it over to the *nation for
completion* as a monumental edifice'.[15]

Whatever Wagner's views of the eventual Bayreuth theatre's physical permanence, Bayreuth's artistic permanence was never much in
doubt. As the composer wrote to Heinrich Porges in 1872, he wished
the details of the Bayreuth *Ring* rehearsals to be recorded in order to
help to establish a 'fixed tradition' of performance.[16] This idea was
strongly taken up by Hans von Wolzogen, the editor of the *Bayreuther
Blätter*, who saw the preservation of 'Wagner's tradition of pure
performance style' as one of the main aims of the journal.[17] Porges
believed that such permanence was not possible in the usual theatres, because 'in the public life of our time art does not occupy the
position which is its due'. It was the aim of the Society of Bayreuth
Patrons to offer an alternative context for developing 'a classic tradition of performance in authentic style of original German musical
and music-dramatic works'.[18]

If the Society of Bayreuth Patrons had carried out their suggestion
of cultivating other examples of 'original German' works alongside
Wagner's, the idea of Bayreuth representing a complete alternative
musical culture, rather than the reflection of one composer's will,

might have gained more credibility. The performance of Beethoven's Ninth Symphony at the laying of the Festival Theatre's foundation stone imparted some kind of general perspective to Bayreuth's endeavours. However, on the whole neither the composer nor his Bayreuth supporters seemed willing to let Wagner's music be compared with others'. Apart from the lack of other music being performed in Bayreuth, writers in the *Bayreuther Blätter* often made a point of comparing Wagner to non-musicians such as Luther, Dürer, or Goethe. Any contemporary composers who were discussed in the journal's pages often presented a flattering inferiority, since they showed the Master's influence upon the lesser genres of the lied or fairy-tale opera.[19]

At moments Wagner showed signs of concern at the narrow attitudes of his Bayreuth supporters, as when he urged Wolzogen and the *Bayreuther Blätter* to gain the perspective of the 'mountain top'.[20] He also wished to broaden the nature of the audiences, at least to let in 'indigent nationals'.[21] It was difficult for him to claim a wide popular success when the Bayreuth audience was made up entirely of members of the Society of Patrons.[22] Wagner admitted that his greatest experience of popular adulation came not from Bayreuth, but from the Viennese public.[23] However, in Bayreuth both performers and audience were described by Porges as submitting wholly to the composer's will,[24] conditions which could not obtain in Vienna, even when Wagner returned in the most favourable circumstances.

When the composer revisited the capital in March 1875, he was able to relish a new artistic independence from the Viennese establishment, since he was conducting concerts on behalf of Bayreuth, to raise money for the 1876 *Ring* performances. The concerts were a great success, though partly because Wagner was fortunate enough to pander to Viennese pride. The critic Theodor Helm described how the audiences responded enthusiastically to their own singer Amalie Materna as Brünnhilde, while Wagner's *Kaisermarsch* prompted much nationalistic fervour.[25] When Wagner reappeared later in the year to supervise performances of *Tannhäuser* and *Lohengrin*, he was surrounded by admiring crowds wherever he went.[26] *Lohengrin* was already established as a great favourite with the Viennese.[27] However, certain aspects of the performances showed particular respect for Wagner's wishes. They were given without cuts, despite the usual practice in Vienna, and showed an attention to detail which confirmed that Wagner had had a hand in all elements of the production.[28] He also had the benefit of the conductorship of Hans Richter; the latter had begun his reign at the Vienna Opera with a performance of *Die Meistersinger* earlier that year and was later to conduct the first Bayreuth Festival.

Nevertheless, when Wagner was finally called upon to respond to
the public ovations after the last performance, he dismayed his
hearers by saying the whole had been a success 'as far as the present
resources would allow'. This remark aroused much resentment and
indeed became notorious.[29] His scornful dismissal of the city's artistic
capacity undoubtedly spurred on the Viennese critics in their hostility to the Bayreuth Festival in the following year. They answered the
composer's slight by implying that he had now created an artificial
public which he ruled like an aristocratic despot.[30]

Such judgements could not necessarily be easily dismissed in
Vienna, where the critics wielded an unusual amount of power.
Wagner himself attributed some of the outcome of his dealings in
Vienna in the early 1860s to the influence of Eduard Hanslick,[31]
while later both Hugo Wolf and Anton Bruckner knew what it was to
suffer from critics' boycotts in Vienna.[32] Wolf attributed some of the
critics' influence to the natural indolence of Viennese audiences.[33]
Their conservatism was undoubtedly encouraged by the pride with
which they might identify Mozart or Beethoven as *their* composers.
This was exploited by certain critics at Wagner's death. The *Neue Freie
Presse* pointed out that while money was being collected for a Wagner
memorial, Mozart had not been given such an honour. When Wilhelm
Jahn came to conduct the *Faust* Overture in Wagner's memory at a
Philharmonic concert on 25 February 1883, the public responded
with a demonstration in Mozart's favour. Afterwards the critics declared that the 'natural' composer Mozart had triumphed over the
'unnatural' Wagner.[34]

It was incidents such as this which justified the forming of the
Vienna Wagner Society into a 'battle unit' against Viennese
philistinism.[35] The Wiener Akademischer Wagnerverein was founded
in 1873 to help raise funds for the Bayreuth Festival; it was one of
many Wagner societies that were linked to the work of the Society of
Bayreuth Patrons. Written into its statutes was also the general aim
'to promote the knowledge and appreciation of Wagner's reforms in
music and drama through discussion and performances'.[36] Wolzogen
emphasized, through the pages of the *Bayreuther Blätter*, the importance of people coming to know and accept the whole of Wagner,
writer as well as musician.[37] Thus, although there seemed no particular lack of Wagner performances in Vienna, with Richter ensconced
as conductor of the Vienna Opera and Philharmonic concerts, the
battle for greater understanding had to continue.

While the Vienna Wagner Society's aims initially coincided with
those of Bayreuth, their methods of promoting a sense of Wagner's
significance were rather different. Their internal concerts were run
essentially as members' evenings without critics being invited,[38] but

the programmes of such concerts were by no means narrow or inward-looking. The memorial festival on Wagner's death began with a performance of Beethoven's Third Symphony,[39] confronting any trend to isolate Wagner from Vienna's musical tradition. In the society's reports of 1885 there are references to a memorial concert for Bach and Handel, performances of works by Arcadelt, Palestrina, Schütz, Schubert, Goetz, and Berlioz, as well as references to works by Liszt and Peter Cornelius, accepted satellites of the Master.[40] It is noticeable from the pages of the *Bayreuther Blätter* that other Wagner societies concentrated far more exclusively upon performing excerpts from Wagner's music dramas. Theodor Helm even refers to the Vienna Wagner Society performing a series of Brahms songs in their 1877–78 concert season, despite his music being identified as opposed to Wagner's.[41] In one sense the society thus held itself apart from partisan struggles; it sought to help Wagner by standing generally for an intelligent and informed response to music.[42] It seemed to aim for a truly broad alternative culture of the kind that failed to materialize in Bayreuth.

In one area, however, the Vienna Wagner Society did allow itself to become embroiled in partisan battles. Under the artistic leadership of Josef Schalk, it engaged in energetic championship of Anton Bruckner, to counter his neglect by the Philharmonic Society and the Viennese critics. Schalk was involved in arranging and performing two-piano versions of Bruckner's works; he also wrote an article on the composer for the *Bayreuther Blätter*,[43] which caused a sensation in Vienna.[44] It might seem that the society had no option in supporting Bruckner, since he was criticised as an example of the Wagner school.[45] However, the contrasting response of Bayreuth to such issues showed that Schalk and others had in fact made a significant choice.

For Bayreuth often dismissed the whole idea that there was a Wagnerian school of composers. Wagner's biographer Carl Friedrich Glasenapp wrote in 1888: 'As to where we are to look for the true "school" of Richard Wagner, there can no longer be a shadow of a doubt. Not in the scores of "New-German" composers, but in the theatre on the Bayreuth hill, within whose walls the creative spirit of the Meister is still working with undiminished power in each performer and each singer'.[46] Such an attitude reflected some of Wagner's own feelings in his final years. As Nietzsche wrote: 'Obviously, it makes very little difference to Wagner whether musicians compose henceforth in a Wagnerian manner, or whether they compose at all; indeed, he does all he can to destroy the miserable belief that a new school of composers should form around him. Insofar as he directly influences musicians, he tries to train them in the art of great execution'.[47]

However, Bayreuth could not maintain such a line indefinitely. Though, as a genius, Wagner might appropriately be seen to defy direct imitation,[48] his work had to be seen to leave some kind of effect upon others, just as a comet leaves a tail as it passes through the heavens.[49] The problem was to provide examples of composers who reflected the whole of Wagner, style and spirit, without caricaturing him or threatening his innate superiority. In his essay *Hat Richard Wagner eine Schule hinterlassen?*, Arthur Seidl undertook to produce just such a list and was congratulated by Wolzogen for being the first Bayreuth Wagnerian to show the rest the correct path.[50] Bruckner's symphonies were deliberately not included in such a list of Wagnerian offshoots, since they adopted the Master's forms, harmonies, instrumentation, and rhythms without Wagner's poetic content.[51]

Schalk's article on Bruckner showed that he was prepared to be more flexible in his view of a Wagnerian 'school'. He saw the absolute nature of Bruckner's symphonies as part of Wagner's general spiritual view of music as the 'eternal feminine'.[52] There was certainly no question of Schalk not being dedicated to all aspects of Wagner's art, literary and musical.[53] In some ways his championing of Wolf alongside Bruckner in the Vienna Wagner Society completed the picture of Wagner's significance, since Wolf's songs followed Wagner in poetic content, though often not in style. The reports of the society continued to group Bruckner and Wolf together, as examples of Wagner's influence in the complementary spheres of the symphony and song.[54] Schalk confirmed that he did not intend to place either composer alongside Wagner himself.[55] Nevertheless, the way each was singled out for comment and the number of times their works were performed in the society[56] showed they were deemed worthy of consideration in their own right and not just as part of a group of Wagnerian after-effects.

The frequency with which Wolf's songs were performed in the Vienna Wagner Society aroused particular opposition. A year after regular informal gatherings to hear Wolf perform began in 1887, the critic Hans Paumgartner, an influential member of the society, wrote to the Viennese *Abendpost* complaining that the society was developing a Wolfian cult and bringing disgrace on Wagner's art.[57] Bayreuth also seemed aware that Wolf's songs might pose some kind of threat. In December 1889 Wolzogen enthused at great length over Wolf's ability to bring out the variety and nuances of poetry in his Mörike songs.[58] His enthusiasm continued in the editorial advertisement for the Goethe songs in January 1890, but he now rebuked those who were calling Wolf the 'new Schubert'. The accompanying recommendation to Wagner societies to use the songs to fill out their programmes was both an endorsement of Wolf and a reminder of his rightful position, as foil to the Master rather than genius in his own right.[59] From this time Wolf's name appeared less and less in the *Bayreuther Blätter*, to be overtaken by those of Martin Plüddemann and Hans Sommer, song composers who showed less bewildering variety in their music and more obvious allegiances to Wagner.[60] In his essay of 1892, Seidl had placed Wolf within his list of the Wagnerian 'school', but in the years 1898 to 1900 he revised his opinion and tried to show that enthusiasm for Wolf's songs as a Wagnerian product was misplaced.[61]

Schalk was clearly not afraid if his support for Wolf separated him from Bayreuth or other Wagnerians. When it was discovered that the Vienna Wagner Society's statutes did not allow any money to be given to Wolf, since all its resources were to be employed for Bayreuth's purposes, Wolf's supporters formed their own smaller group within the society.[62] It is not surprising that those who wished to keep the society's focus upon Wagner began to register their unrest in partisan demonstrations and eventually, in 1890, formed their own New Vienna Wagner Society.[63] Yet more was at stake for Schalk and other Wagnerians than merely the welfare of Hugo Wolf. Schalk saw his policy of promoting Wolf and Bruckner as a way of ensuring that Wagner's significance did not fall into the past and thus become part of a new conservatism. He quoted Wagner's own words that the concept of the monumental was antithetical to art. Schalk believed Bruckner and Wolf helped one to see Wagner with the eyes of the present, just as Wagner had given a new perspective to the Classical masters. They were the confirmation of Wagner's place within history, the sign that he had encouraged a development larger than himself and so gained a true universality.[64]

By placing Wagner within the flow of history, Schalk was opposing not only Vienna's reactionary critics, but also the Bayreuth establishment. For both believed that Wagner's art was a world in itself, even if the former group implied that this world was artificial and must soon die, and the latter that Wagner's world was the only real one and would outlast any other. Most important, Schalk implied that one must reach out beyond Wagner himself in order to perceive his significance, rather than relying upon the composer's own view of his art. Wagner himself spoke of the aim of the artist needing to be completely absorbed into his work,[65] and of true art being part of the irresistible flow of life.[66] This might conflict with the evidence in Bayreuth of his wishing to impose his personal will on all aspects of his creation. However, arguments over which represented the Master's true intentions — the Bayreuth Wagnerians with their emphasis on fixing an internal tradition, or Schalk's more open view — would become less crucial if Wagner's words and wishes ceased to be binding.

Schalk himself was not quite ready to follow through the implications of the freedom he suggested. Although he took a stand against conservative Wagnerians in promoting Wolf and Bruckner, he still wanted to control the audiences' responses to their music to serve his idea of Wagner. Bruckner used to call Schalk 'Herr Generalissimus', in ironic deference to his role in persuading the composer to revise his work and in providing poetic programmes for his symphonies.[67] In one sense Wolf presented fewer problems than Bruckner, since he shared Schalk's interest in Wagner's literary and philosophical significance.[68] However, Wolf's independent personality made him more sensitive to the equivocality of being supported partly for his usefulness to the Wagnerian cause. When his song *Heimweh* was used for a nationalistic demonstration in the Vienna Wagner Society in February 1889, Wolf resolved not to perform there any more.[69] Schalk persuaded him back, but Wolf retained a certain hostility to all Wagner societies: 'Whatever is not tied with an umbilical chord to Wagnerism does not exist for them. Whoever feels the urge to free himself from such bonds is decried as an apostate'.[70]

Such vehemence might seem surprising from one who, in his music criticisms for the Viennese *Salonblatt* a decade earlier, had enthusiastically joined battle for Wagner in a most obviously partisan way. Some attributed his later outbursts against Wagnerians to artistic pique or egotism.[71] However, it is also possible to see them as the inevitable outcome of the tensions within Viennese Wagnerian circles. Both Schalk and Wolf retained vestiges of the Bayreuth notion that Wagner's supremacy should be beyond question. Schalk referred to Wagner as 'him before whom we all bow in deepest reverence',[72] while Wolf said it was Wagner who had first turned us lumps of clay into human beings.[73] Yet when such a line was imposed on Wolf, in ways which affected how his music was performed or how it was critically received, he began to assert his right to question the Wagnerians and even Wagner himself. For he clearly recognized that some of the responsibility for encouraging a suppression of critical faculties had to be laid on Wagner and the music dramas themselves. In Wolf's words, they acted as 'an intoxicating drug' and Wagner himself was 'a supergod, provoking fear, not love, from his followers'.[74]

Wolf was thus driven along a path away from unquestioning devotion to criticism of Wagner, a path already taken by Friedrich Nietzsche, though with certain crucial differences. Nietzsche found himself completely isolated from the Bayreuth Wagnerians; there seemed no midway between absolute loyalty and complete rejection of Wagner, despite the philosopher's continuing sense of indebtedness for much the Master had done.[75] Wolf, by contrast, remained accepted by his supporters in the Vienna Wagner Society, however intractable he became.[76] Friedrich Eckstein speaks of Schalk and Wolf continuing to spend much time discussing Nietzsche's views of Wagner together, particularly *The Case of Wagner*, which first appeared in 1888.[77] Wolf differed from Schalk in approving Nietzsche's love of Chopin and Bizet's *Carmen*,[78] though he would also argue on Wagner's behalf in these debates.[79] The issues for and against the Master never seemed entirely resolved in Wolf's mind, and in his letters Wagnerian and Nietzschean ideas intermingled freely.[80]

A similar mixture of influences was seen in the artistic and philosophical discussions of the famous Café Griensteidl, which Wolf frequented from the late 1870s. Here Wagner was discussed alongside not only Nietzsche, but also topics such as Shelley, Ibsen, neurology, psychiatry, and socialism. Wagner by no means ruled in these debates; some of his *Religion und Kunst* (Religion and art) aroused much disagreement when it appeared in 1880. However, this circle did not exist in opposition to the Vienna Wagner Society. There was a large overlap between the two circles and members of the society were described as joining in the discussion of 'all possible kinds of problems concerning Wagner'.[81]

When the Viennese critic Max Graf completed his own survey of 'Wagner-Probleme' at the beginning of the twentieth century, he saw himself as part of a new generation of Wagnerians emerging in Vienna. They were sceptical of the heroic, all-conquering picture of the artist painted by the Wagnerian 'old guard'. Though they gave Wagner an apparently more limited role, they were a generation who had actually lived and breathed his music. While first-generation Wagnerians, such as Schalk, had to fight to establish Wagner's importance, the new generation was able to take it for granted.[82] They approached his music through their own situation, seeing reflected within it the modernist concerns with sickness and renewal. Graf made a point of stressing the suffering of the heroes in Wagner's music dramas, as they looked to new worlds but were unable to bring them into being. Wagner became seen as one who had realized the need for a new culture, even if he had not been able to realize it himself.[83] The modernists were primarily concerned with the search for a future after Wagner. However, they created new pictures of his significance in the process, which brought the composer with them into the present. After the incipient struggles of the Vienna Wagner Society, such a generation confirmed that freedom from any narrow loyalty to Wagner helped open the way for his music to become part of a greater history.

Chapter 8

Taking the Waters at Bayreuth

Matthias Theodor Vogt

Wagner's detractors have always found it easy to write off the Bay-reuth Festival as a musical steam bath designed for earnest Teutons. Wagner scholars, by contrast, seem not to have noticed that in this apparent contempt lies rather more than a grain of truth: for even the often subtropical temperatures inside the Bayreuth Festival Theatre are intimately related to the composer's festival ideal. And this ideal, in turn, is bound up with the ideology of hydropathic cures.

In *Mein Leben* Wagner explains that the crucial breakthrough in writing the *Ring* brought with it the idea of a festival: 'This exhilarat-ing turn of events gave a great fillip to my spirits, and at once the decision matured in me to realise my original sketch for the *Nibelungen* in its entirety, irrespective of whether any part of it would be actually performable in any of our theatres'.[1]

The 'turn of events' in question was bound up with the annual income of eight hundred thalers which Julie Ritter made over to Wagner in November 1851. (Wagner himself had asked Ferdinand Heine, his friend in Dresden, to approach Frau Ritter on the subject, so her offer of support was something less than a total surprise.)

But the place and background of Wagner's decision make it un-likely that, by reducing his resolve to purely economic factors, as *Mein Leben* sets out to do, he was doing justice to the complexity of his thinking. At the time when he took his decision — a decision so central not only to the *Ring* but to the history of the Bayreuth Festival — Wagner was taking the waters (a 'water diet', he called it) at the hydropathic centre of Albisbrunn, near Zurich, a nine-week ordeal from which he resolved to return only when 'fully restored to health'.[2]

The following is an attempt to relate Wagner's attitude towards water and hydropathy to a detailed account of his concept of a festival — in other words, to the genesis of the *Ring*. This will be followed by what might be called a sanatorial view of the festival. But first let us take a look at the cultic role which water has played in society generally.

Water: Swimming, Bathing, and Balneology

Wagner's Age and Its Attitude towards Water

Water now flows freely from taps in every household and at least one shower is part of the fittings of almost every home in these temperate regions of ours, so that personal hygiene at home is taken for granted, while even quite small places pride themselves on their luxury in-door swimming pools. Only the surfeit of different types of mineral water on supermarket shelves can offer a dim reminder of water's mythic qualities.

We tend to forget how recent our relationship with water as a therapeutic agent really is. As early as 1697 the empirical philosopher John Locke had recommended that boys be taught to swim, but in Germany it was not until 1817 that General von Pfuel officially opened a military swimming pool in the River Spree; not until the late 1850s were the first public swimming baths opened in Berlin. After that there was no holding back. By 1873 swimming was part of the syllabus of Prussia's teacher-training colleges, and by 1899 there were no fewer than seventy-seven municipal baths at the public's disposal in Berlin alone, an *embarras de richesses* which was due, not least, to pressure from doctors anxious to halt the spread of disease.

Wagner lived to see this gradual state recognition of the prophylactic powers of water. The aim, of course, was public health, but behind it lay far older beliefs, including a magic awe of water which could still be observed as late as the early nineteenth century. During Wagner's youth, we know of cases where young people were banned from swimming in rivers on the pretext that to do so offended against common decency.[3] By the end of his life a different view of water had gained acceptance, an attitude which, in the main, still typifies today's society.

Cultic Ritual

'Of all the different heathen cults', Max Höfler wrote in 1888, pointing out links with his own age, 'the one which is best preserved today is the cult of water'.[4] Central to this cult was the concept of purification through bathing in rivers, in other words, in water which was not stagnant. (Siegmund, after all, calls for 'Ein Quell!

Ein Quell!', rather than simply 'Wasser!', — the water he wants
should be from a spring.) Thus Charlemagne set aside special days
for bathing in rivers; and even as late as the seventeenth century,
suicides in rural areas were not buried on land but committed to
swift-flowing rivers.

The cult of springs and fountains as a prototype of flowing water
was widespread throughout the Alpine region, where it took the
form of veneration for the primeval Norns, a veneration echoed in
Wagner's *Ring*, where the First Norn sings:

Im kühlen Schatten	In the cooling shade
rauscht' ein Quell:	a spring welled forth:
Weisheit raunend	whispering wisdom
rann sein Gewell':	it rippled along:
da sang ich heil'gen Sinn.	there I sang my sacred song.

(*GS* VI, 178)

Ideas such as these can be traced back at least to ancient Egypt. As
part of the cult of Isis, the waters of the Nile were channelled
through the goddess's temple: the aim of the cult was to wash away
sins, mystery cults in general being a subdivision of purification cults.
Traces of many such cults can be found in the *Ring*: most striking of
all is the correlation between the cult of Isis and the end of
Götterdämmerung, where the Rhine overflows its banks. We are often
unaware how tenacious cults may be (not only churches and opera
houses are repositories of such beliefs). Suffice it to mention those
fearless swimmers who take the plunge on New Year's Day not only in
London's Serpentine but in other countries, too: in Rome in the
years around the birth of Christ, it was votaries of the cult of Isis who
hacked away the ice on the River Tiber to cleanse themselves in its
waters.[5]

Mystery cults demanded a very high price of those who sought
initiation, a price involving surrogate symbolism, as in the self-castra-
tion of would-be priests of Cybele. A close reading of the text suggests
a similar symbol in the opening scene of the final part of the *Ring*:

Ein kühner Gott	A dauntless god
trat zum Trunk an den Quell;	came to drink at the spring;
seiner Augen eines	one of his eyes
zahlt' er als ewigen Zoll.	he paid as toll for all time.

(*GS* VI, 178)

It is difficult to imagine a more unequivocal formulation of the
supreme significance of water in terms of the symbols, characters,
and dramaturgical framework of the narrative than in this act of
partial self-immolation on the part of the chief of the gods.

How close Wagner came, again and again, to ancient cultic beliefs is clear from Hagen's use of the optative 'fließe' (flow) when exhorting the vassals to make preparations for Gunther's wedding with Brünnhilde:

Starke Stiere	Sturdy steers
sollt ihr schlachten:	you should slaughter:
am Weihstein fließe	let Wotan's stone
Wotan ihr Blut.	flow with their blood.

(*GS* VI, 217–18)

Under Emperor Claudius (AD41–54) the cult of the Great Mother, Cybele, publicly sanctioned, quickly spread to the whole of the empire. Unlike the earlier state religion, the cult of Cybele was a redemption cult; in other words, it sought to answer a question hitherto inconceivable: What followed after death? In the sacrificial steer, or taurobolium, the cult discovered a ritual which combined redemption with purification in a highly impressive way. According to the early Christian poet Prudentius, the priest descended into a trench covered by a platform of planks pierced with fine holes, on which a bull, magnificent with gold and flowers, was slain, its blood raining down on the hierophant's head and clothes. Soaked by the gore, he would then emerge from the pit, presenting himself to the faithful as an object of veneration.[6]

Descent into the pit betokens dying. The blood which bespatters the priest was believed to possess the power to cleanse the adept of his sins. Baptised by the blood, he rises out of the pit and enters on a new life. The parallel with the episode in the *Nibelungenlied* in which Siegfried kills the dragon does not need underlining: the hero of the lay achieves a subtle kind of immortality in the form of his inviolability through bathing in the dragon's blood. In the *Nibelungenlied*, of course, the Rhinegold does not play the role which Wagner gives it in the *Ring*, where its function is to purify, the act of purification involving water rather than the blood which a genuinely Germanic heroic opera might otherwise have suggested. In order not to duplicate the mystery of purification and thus deprive it of its persuasive power, Wagner suppressed the scene where Siegfried bathes in the dragon's blood and replaced it with Brünnhilde's blessing.

Societal Factors

A name no doubt well known to Wagnerites is that of Hans Foltz. The Nuremberg barber, surgeon, and Mastersinger is the author of the oldest surviving essay on bathing in German, a work that dates from 1480. Among the remedies he prescribes are soaking in mineral water for a hundred hours during a three-week course of treatment intended to combat skin diseases. Humoral pathologists believed the resultant 'bathing rashes' a desirable reaction,[7] so that Wagner's rashes in Albisbrunn and his positive reaction to them have, as it were, a healthy tradition.

Bathing for reasons of hygiene has an equally long tradition among the Germanic peoples. We know that bathrooms existed from at least the seventh century on every farmstead in rural areas. Not until the seventeenth century did the cultivation of flax produce a change in clothing habits which affected the lower orders, too. As soon as clothes could be washed or replaced at reasonable cost, there was far less need to bathe, with the result that bathing, and the culture bound up with it, fell slowly into decline in rural areas.

The ancient view was that water was 'the best of all the elements'[8] — a viewpoint which took on a whole new meaning when social bathing came into vogue. To what extent such baths were also brothels, as Hans Peter Duerr has claimed, is a question we must leave open. More important in the present context is the widespread feudal practice of visiting thermal spas, a practice which, independent of the age's love of water, was already well attested by Michel de Montaigne in his *Journal de voyage* of 1580–81. In 1793 Duke Friedrich Franz I of Mecklenburg-Schwerin donated the princely sum of seventeen thousand thalers to establish the first coastal resort on German soil, at Heiligendamm, although opportunities for swimming were not among the duke's provisions. By 1800 spas had become the meeting-places of Europe, the possibilities for contact which they offered on more or less neutral ground being used, above all, for political ends. In 1818, for example, the Holy Alliance of Austria, Russia, and Prussia was renewed in Aix-la-Chapelle, but even more famous are the Carlsbad Decrees of 1819, which gave rise to that reactionary climate in which the young Wagner grew up and against which he later rebelled.

By 1850 Baden-Baden, with its thirty thousand annual visitors, was the leading resort in Europe, following by Bad Homburg with ten thousand, Carlsbad with nine thousand, Teplitz (to which we shall soon be returning) with eight thousand, Bad Ems with seven thousand, Bad Kissingen with five thousand five hundred, Bad Schwalbach with four thousand, Bad Nauheim with two thousand and Schlangenbad with fifteen hundred.[9] Their guest lists read like previews of the ones for Bayreuth before the First World War.

In 1857 the *Balneologische Zeitung* pointed out a highly important aspect of this 'balneological epidemic' — the effects of the Industrial Revolution on what had once been feudal institutions. 'If we take a closer look at the state of health of the less affluent members of society, we shall see that it was incomparably better before the railways opened up in Germany and that it has grown perceptibly worse as each new section of track has been laid'.[10] It was precisely because Bayreuth lacked a railway link that it had virtually no local industry in 1871, thus making the sleepy Bavarian town a perfect place for Wagner, whose festival ideal had little time for industry.

Spa casinos attracted not only those in search of health and companionship but also gamblers such as Dostoyevsky. There was, however, a further concern on the part of many of those who took the waters which should not be underestimated. Since the early Renaissance, the medieval fear of Nature's darker forces had gradually been transformed into a longing to return to Nature which was later seen as typically Romantic. It was this feeling, no doubt, which prompted Goethe to spend no fewer than 1114 days — in other words, some three and a quarter years — at watering-places during his life.

The nineteenth-century artist's nostalgic desire to return to Nature and wallow in thermal baths is well summed up by Justinus Kerner (1786–1862), a writer much in vogue around 1850 and one whom Wagner often read. In his pseudo-medical treatise *Das Wildbad im Königreich Württemberg* (The thermal springs in the kingdom of Württemberg),[11] Kerner offers what almost amounts to a code of conduct for festival visitors:

> The waters of the thermal spring have this advantage over many spas in that it is not easy for people to go there if they are not really ill or if they want only to indulge the world and its pleasures. . . . Healing springs are all that bubble here; here there are no faro tables, no theatres, no tables groaning with sumptuous food. For Heaven's sake! . . . Let those who are genuinely ill visit these salubrious springs. Let them come in love and trust: for if they place their trust in simple, bracing Nature and if they organize their way of life accordingly, they will find a cure for their ailments. Those who really want to get better and who do not intend merely playing with water must bear in mind, above all, that only a simple lifestyle, healthy and natural, accords with the silent simple greatness of Nature in this place of healing.[12]

Medicinal Springs and Anti-scientific Hydropathic Centres

The use of mineral springs for medicinal purposes characterizes many cultures — Celtic, Greek, and Germanic, if not the traditional state religion of the Romans — although it is not always clear where the dividing line should be drawn between medical and cultic aims.[13]

The oldest known case of a spring being used for medicinal ends is St Maurice's Spring at St Moritz in the Engadine, which, dating back to the Bronze Age, is known to have been in existence for over three and a half thousand years. Wagner himself took the waters there in 1853.

In 1815 Christoph Wilhelm Hufeland (1762–1836), Goethe's doctor and the private physician to Queen Luise of Prussia, published his *Praktische Uebersicht der verschiedenen Heilquellen Teutschlands* (Practical survey of the various medicinal springs in Germany), an introduction to Germany's mineral springs which attests to an almost superstitious belief in the healing powers of spring waters, traditional faith in the efficacy of such cures making up for a lack of understanding of how such procedures actually worked. A few years earlier, in 1803, Johann Wilhelm Tolberg (1762–1831) had opened the first salt-water bath at a salt-works outside Magdeburg. Only slowly did scientific methods gain acceptance in balneology, which under the pressure of an increasingly materialist and mechanistic trend in medicine, was generally regarded with some suspicion during the hundred years or so that followed Hufeland's publication. If attitudes slowly changed, it was due above all to men like Friedrich Wilhelm Beneke (1824–82), who, in 1859, devised a form of treatment for circulatory disorders. But even in cases where medicine was powerless to help, doctors would pack off their patients to watering-places and balneatic resorts. Hundreds of consumptives, including cases of galloping tuberculosis where the risk of infection was not sufficiently clear to their fellow patients, together with syphilitics, who were treated with mercury, making them sweat out the poison in communal salt-baths, flocked to such spas in the desperate hope of a cure. In 1894, for example, Hans von Bülow, by now incurably ill, allowed himself to be talked into making the journey to Cairo, only to die there shortly after arriving. In much the same way Wagner himself, having spent lengthy periods during the 1840s and 1850s taking the waters, hoped that, at the end of his life, he might find relief from his countless afflictions by wintering in Italy, beneath whose southern skies he died.

The years around 1850 witnessed the culmination of a wholly different tradition in balneology involving trends which, half progressive, half anti-progressive, reproached scientifically orientated medicine for having lost sight of the wholeness of the human body and soul. In advancing such a view of man, these theories could call on a long tradition: as early as 1784 Heinrich Matthias Marcard (1747–1817), a hydropathic doctor from the old principality of Pyrmont, had published a 'Dietetics of the Soul'. In the neo-naive trust which adherents of hydrotherapy (essentially a kind of critique of progress) placed in the power of water to heal all ills, we find traces of those heathen traditions which, given the lack of medical knowledge at the time, appear in writings on hydrotherapy as an early branch of hygienics: in 1738 the Silesian physician Johann Sigmund Hahn (1696–1773), whose writings Wagner himself was to study in 1851, had published his *Unterricht von Krafft und Würckung des frischen Wassers* (Information on the power and effect of fresh water), in which he declared that 'water has the power to cleanse and to wash away'.[14]

It was around 1830 that Vincenz Prießnitz, a farmhand hailing, like Hahn, from Upper Silesia, though lacking Hahn's medical training, caused something of a stir. Prießnitz discovered a means of fortifying both body and central nervous system by pouring cold water over the patient's naked body while standing him by an open window. He found supporters all over Europe, to the great misfortune of countless souls such as tuberculosis cases, who, adopting his methods, died in their thousands during the 1830s and 1840s. The hydropathic centres which he established sprang up like mushrooms after a shower and included the one at Albisbrunn, not far from Zurich, on the River Albis, which was run by a certain Dr Christoph Zacharias Brunner,[15] thanks to whose radical management the place enjoyed an excellent reputation.[16]

Sebastian Kneipp (1821–97) had already been given up by his doctors in 1847. With the help of Hahn's little treatise, he cured himself by hydrotherapeutic means and later went on to evolve the science of physiotherapy. Kneipp's autobiography *Meine Wasserkur* (1886), translated into English as *My Water-Cure*, became a bestseller, as did his later *So sollt ihr leben!* (*Thus Shalt Thou Live: Hints and Advice for the Healthy and the Sick*), one of the earliest books to expound a healthy lifestyle (a genre which now accounts for 10 per cent of all books sold). At least as far as laymen are concerned, current thinking on the complex issue of 'health' derives in essence from Kneipp's ideas on the one hand and from Eastern spiritual beliefs on the other, beliefs, in short, which Wagner imbued from the mid-1850s onwards, not least in the wake of his reading of Arthur Schopenhauer.

Aiming at a holistic way of life, Kneipp preached a return to Nature in terms of both body and mind. Wagner, by contrast, was looking for ways of fleshing out his aesthetico-political total work of art; he subjected himself to the rigours of a hydropathic regime in order to turn its key ideas to his own artistic advantage. What attracted Wagner was spelt out by Ludwig Diemer (1814–76) in 1855: 'The idea of sweating out all that was sinful and impure by means of the Prießnitz method led thousands upon thousands to visit hydropathic centres'.

Wagner and Watering-Places: The Cold-Water Cure

Wagner Takes the Waters

'I mistrust everything connected with the theatre of today', Wagner wrote to his niece Franziska on 4 June 1850, 'and I feel the same about actors as the police do about those people whom they consider rogues until such time as they find compelling proof to convince them of the opposite. How many of you ever get round to noticing that you're really dealing with the most unspeakable rabble; even fewer of you escape from this morass to find solace in artistry pure and simple'.[17]

In spite of Wagner's declared contempt for all that was bound up with the theatre, scarcely five months were to pass before he conducted not only *Don Giovanni* (in his own revision) but five other operas, too, in Zurich's Aktientheater. Their success was to guarantee him a place in the musical life of the town, leading not only to the first ever Wagner Festival — a concert programme devoted entirely to his own works and performed three times in May 1853 to mark his fortieth birthday — but also to his decision, the following June, to embark on plans for the first performance of the *Ring*: the festival was to have taken place in 1856 on the banks of the River Limmat, but the deficit incurred by the May concerts soon put paid to his plans.

Don Giovanni had marked Wagner's début as a conductor, in the tiny spa of Bad Lauchstädt, on 2 August 1834. He had come to Bad Lauchstädt straight from another watering-place, Teplitz (modern Teplice), where, in the June of that year, he had found a cure for his first recorded attack of erysipelas (a skin disorder caused, in Wagner's case, by nervous tension) and, at the same time, had written the prose draft of *Das Liebesverbot*. The same basic pattern of taking the waters during the summer months, when he felt at his most creatively inspired, accompanied Wagner during his years in Dresden. By far the majority of his works were conceived and sketched in spas. In June 1842 he drafted *Tannhäuser* in Teplitz; in July of the following year (again in Teplitz) he read Jacob Grimm's *Teutonic Mythology*, discovering many ideas there for several later works; in the summer of 1845, this time in Marienbad (modern Mariánské Lázně), he sketched both *Lohengrin* and *Die Meistersinger*, while the initial idea for *Parsifal* was already germinating within him. In a word, we are reminded (not least by Wagner's own account of the matter) of Archimedes, who is said to have leapt from his bath in Syracuse, shouting the word 'Eureka' and running home without stopping to dress. If there is truth in the saying that many ideas are snatched from the air, it is equally true that Wagner found *his* ideas in water.

The New Religion of Hydropathy

From the middle of 1850 onwards, two of Wagner's closest friends, Theodor Uhlig and the painter Ernst Benedikt Kietz, bombarded him with hydropathic literature. Uhlig recommended the writings of J. H. Rausse (the pseudonym of H. Friedrich Franke). Rausse had founded a hydropathic centre in Mecklenburg, which he ran according to Prießnitz's principles, and, prior to his death in 1848, had been director of a similar institution at Alexandersbad, north-east of Bayreuth.[18] What attracted Wagner to Rausse's writings, he later told Uhlig (qualifying his earlier enthusiasm), was 'above all their fresh approach to Nature',[19] which did not prevent him from finding out as much as he could about water, dietetics, and other ways of getting better, joining in a discussion that raged in countless pamphlets, articles, and books. After all, he himself had already addressed one aspect of the discussion a short time earlier in his own article *Kunst und Klima* (Art and climate), a piece which, apparently unconnected with art, had appeared in a periodical launched only recently under the catch-all title of *Deutsche Monatsschrift für Politik, Wissenschaft, Kunst und Leben* (German monthly for politics, science, art, and life).

Wagner's first reply on the subject is dated 9 October 1850, and in it he scoffs at hydrotherapy, adopting a tone which he himself was shortly to frown on. Yet even here, in two or three apparently unconnected phrases, we already find him sketching out a framework of socio-political ideas which, still indebted to revolutionary thinking, was to characterize his attitude to water in all its later manifestations: 'Next time I'll write at greater length, especially on the subject of your views on water! I only drink water when I feel thirsty, and yet I am far less sanguine than you!' And he goes on without a break: 'What do you want to experience? — be true, implacably true, rejoice in the truth, for its own sake alone, and you'll have enough to be going on with! We shall not put the world to rights, but what does that matter? Should we therefore start to tell lies?' There seems little doubt that what Wagner had in mind here was the cause of revolution. Even more important, however, is the sudden switch from 'water' to a way of life which sets store by the 'truth', followed by the precipitate outburst: 'How happy I am, now that it has become increasingly clear to me how empty and worthless everything is that relates to the state and to public life and art! After all, everyone knows now that they are thoroughly miserable'.[20]

Two weeks later Wagner noted down a chain of ideas which was, I believe, to remain of central importance throughout the coming twelve months: 'Look, just as we need a water cure to heal our bodies, so we need a fire cure in order to remedy (i.e. destroy) the cause of our illness — a cause that is all around us'.[21] But within the year, I would argue, Wagner must have realised that a 'fire cure' — in other words, revolution — could no longer be achieved, either by himself or by anyone else: 'We shall not put the world to rights, but what does that matter?' During the twelve months in question Wagner developed an altogether different kind of hydrotherapy, a musical panacea designed to improve society — in other words, his festival.

In judging Wagner, we need to bear in mind his tendency to make conceptual links between disparate ideas. His early Paris essays are remarkable for a linguistic brilliance indebted to Heine and Börne, but all the more astonishing is their unquestionable ability to draw the most startling conclusions. Unlike his revolutionary essays, which are concerned with affairs of the moment and written in a style of eruptive inconsequentiality rather than one of logical coherence, the aesthetic writings that date from his early years in Zurich tend to disprove the artistic reproach that they are no more than an exercise in self-help. 'The argumentative, hectoring tone, carried to extremes in the aesthetic essays of the Zurich period, undoubtedly ruined his style', according to Martin Gregor-Dellin.[22] It is not only Wagner's essays, however, which betray such constitutional confusion in their increasingly vegetative line of reasoning; even in his dramatic sketches and drafts he clearly lacks the gift of concision or careful self-correction. The fate of *Götterdämmerung* is eloquent proof of this failing: events that had once been merely recounted in *Siegfrieds Tod* were now portrayed on stage in the prefatory parts of the cycle, without corresponding cuts being made.

> That we can all be redeemed from the current state of so thoroughly unnatural a condition only by means of this radical element is certain. . . . Superfluity and deprivation, these are the two destructive enemies of present-day humanity. . . . Everything is superfluous that encloses the walls of a town . . . . Until now we have encountered expressions of enslaved human nature only in *crimes* that disgust and appal us! — Whenever murderers and thieves now set fire to a house, the deed rightly strikes us as base and repugnant: — but how shall it seem to us if the monster that is Paris is burned to the ground, if the conflagration spreads from town to town, and if we ourselves, in our wild enthusiasm, finally set fire to these uncleansable Augean stables for the sake of a breath of fresh air? . . . Just wait and see how we recover from this fire cure: if necessary I could finish painting this picture, I could even imagine how a man of enthusiasm might here and there summon together the living remnants of our former art and how he might say to them — who among you desires to help me perform a drama? Only those people will answer who genuinely

share that desire, for there will no longer be money available, but those who respond will at once reveal to the world, in a rapidly erected wooden structure, what art is. — At all events, it will all happen quickly, for you can see there is no question here of gradual progress: our redeemer will destroy with furious speed all that stands in our way! . . . Look, just as we need a water cure to heal our bodies, so we need a fire cure to remedy (i.e. destroy) the cause of our illness — a cause that is all around us. Shall we return then to a state of Nature, shall we reacquire the human animal's ability to live to be 200 years old? God forbid! Man is a social, all-powerful being only through *culture*. Let us not forget that culture alone grants us the power to enjoy life to the full as only mankind can enjoy it. . . . Water will restore us to our former health, but we shall not be truly healthy until we can also drink wine without harm to ourselves![23]

Thus Wagner's train of ideas comes full circle: (1) hydropathy as a means of curing the ills of the body; (2) a fire cure as a means of curing the ills of society; and (3) reform of the theatre: the above quotation is prefaced by a two-page report on the way in which Wagner had stood in for Karl Ritter at the Aktientheater in Zurich, an incident which Wagner recalls not without a certain pride: 'To cut a long story short, let me say only that, completely unnoticed, what was once a *flea-pit* has now been transformed into an institution in which my public seeks only *true artistic enjoyment*'.[24]

The theoretical foundations for the musical language of the *Ring* were laid in the winter of 1850–51. In a preliminary announcement to Theodor Uhlig of 12 December 1850, Wagner uses a distinctively watery simile in setting forth the tripartite structure of *Opera and Drama*: opera (part I) or, rather, the music in opera is 'a life-bearing organism', drama (part II) a procreative force, while 'the poetic intent' is 'the fructifying seed'. Finally, in part III, Wagner planned to describe 'the birth of the poetic intent through the consummate language of music'.[25] In the same letter he returns to the subject of hydropathy, commenting on Uhlig's poor state of health, before continuing: 'I, too, am undertaking a kind of Water Cure; in addition to morning baths, I'm drinking cold water in bed'.[26]

The water cure soon began to show results. 'I, too, have become a semi-aquarian', Wagner wrote to Uhlig on 20 January 1851: 'I've been following your advice with the Neptune Belt [a cold-water poultice wrapped round the torso]! I hope it will do me some good. On the whole I feel noticeably better than last year: I'm working very hard, i.e. uninterruptedly, and appear not to be suffering as a result; it also helps, no doubt, that my domestic affairs are now a little calmer — that is, clearer, wiser, more sensible — or however you like to put it — !'[27]

A slightly different emphasis emerges from another letter to Uhlig from the end of August 1851. Uhlig had just returned to Dresden, following his visit to Zurich, and had given Wagner a number of Rausse's books on hydrotherapy: 'For the last six days I have been on a strict water diet. . . . My head feels much lighter, sometimes even somewhat dull; I suppose this is one of the short-term effects'.[28]

Albisbrunn

And finally comes the decision:

> My dearest friend! I am going to the hydropathic centre. — I have just returned from Albisbrunn, where I spoke with the doctor and agreed that I should move in on Monday, the 15th. — I cannot stand doing things by halves: the diet on its own was a waste of time. But such is my present state of health that, had I set about composing 'Young Siegfried' [the libretto of which Wagner had written during the spring of 1851 while taking a series of sulphur baths], I should perhaps have been incurable by next spring. I now feel a great desire to sort out the matter once and for all: the thought of being completely well again is altogether novel, but it is bound up for me with Things and Plans of the greatest Importance [as the use of capitals, normally scorned by Wagner, makes abundantly plain].[29]

The visit to Albisbrunn was planned to last from 15 September to 23 November 1851; for part of that time Wagner was joined by Karl Ritter and Hermann Müller, a soldier whom Wagner had got to know in Dresden at the time of Müller's affair with Wilhelmine Schröder-Devrient. Minna was less than wholly delighted, not least when, as a result of over-exertion, Wagner developed a fever, and over-excitement caused a recurrence of erysipelas. He leapt to his own defence: 'I'll not hear a word against my cold-water cure, that is something quite different, and I now have every confidence that it will be a complete success'.[30] It is, however, scarcely surprising that Minna should have protested at the drastic treatment to which Wagner subjected himself at a time when his health was not of the best:

> My daily routine is now as follows, lst, half-past-five in the morning wet pack until 7 o'clock; then a cold bath and a walk. 8 o'clock breakfast: dry bread and milk or water. 2nd, immediately afterwards a first and then a second clyster; another short walk; then a cold compress on my abdomen. 3rd, around 12 o'clock: wet rub-down; short walk; fresh compress. Then lunch in my room with Karl

[Ritter], to prevent insubordination. Then an hour spent in idleness: brisk two-hour walk — alone. 4th, around 4 o'clock: another wet rub-down and a short walk. 5th, hip-bath for a quarter of an hour around 6 o'clock, followed by a walk to warm me up. Fresh compress. Around 7 o'clock dinner: dry bread and water. 6th, immediately followed by a first and then a second clyster; then a game of whist until after nine o'clock, after which another compress, and then around 10 o'clock we all retire to bed. — I am now bearing up quite well under this regimen: I may even intensify it.[31]

From a purely medical point of view, such treatment could scarcely promise success, and, in his *Annals*, Wagner was forced to admit: 'Drag out pitiful existence with unsuccessful cure'.[32] Such an approach was distinctly antediluvian: much the same sort of treatment would have been meted out by Hans Foltz, involving, as it did, drenching and soaking patients until they came out in a bathing rash, followed by water and yet more water administered from above and behind. Without implicit faith in the healing powers of water *per se*, such treatment must have been intolerable. But just such faith sustained Wagner, a faith which was founded in nothing but blind conviction and which can be seen as a protest against the march of progress. 'For me', he concluded in *Mein Leben*, 'this was something of a new religion', but his energetic advocacy of it long after his return from Albisbrunn began to bore his friends, who finally demanded that he study chemistry and medicine instead of regaling them with half-digested theories.[33] His devotional attitude to this 'new religion' ended abruptly, however, when the doctor in charge of a hydropathic clinic at Mornex, near Geneva, where he stayed in 1856, advised him to abandon such treatment, while offering him accommodation in a cottage in the clinic grounds, since 'vous n'êtes que nerveux' (you're only suffering from nerves). For the rest of his life Wagner preferred a change of climate to hydropathic cures. At the same time, however, his nine weeks in Albisbrunn, where 'the avoidance of any other kind of intellectual labour soon resulted in growing strain and nervous irritation',[34] were not without important repercussions: his 'new religion' brought with it a crucial breakthrough for the *Ring* and hence for Wagner's festival ideal.

Wagner's Festival Ideal

Heroic Operas

According to Wagner's own account, it was Jacob Grimm's *Teutonic Mythology* which, in 1843, introduced him to the subject-matter of the

Ring. In the conscious reappraisal of the past which constitutes *Mein Leben,* he considered his bathtime reading in Teplitz to have been a total 'rebirth'.[35] Only a few years later his enthusiasm for the past was rekindled by Droysen's translation of Aeschylus and by the former's *Didaskalien,*[36] which 'helped to bring the intoxicating vision of Attic tragedy so clearly before me that I could see the *Oresteia* with my mind's eye as if actually being performed'.[37] At least as important as the *Oresteia,* however, was the concept of catharsis which Droysen, appealing to Aristotle's *Poetics,* described as the central pillar of the theatre of ancient Greece and glossed as the purging or purification of the protagonist, who represents the community of spectators moved by the hero's fate.[38]

Myth as a subject for opera, the action as a form of purification, and the performance as a quasi-religious festival are constitutive elements of the later *Ring.* They had still not crystallized out when, taking time off from his articles for Röckel's revolutionary *Volksblätter,* Wagner completed the earliest draft of *Siegfrieds Tod, Die Nibelungensage (Mythus),* on 4 October 1848. But his thoughts kept turning away from myth and back to historical subjects. He toyed with the subject of Friedrich Barbarossa and, early in 1849, penned that curious essay *Die Wibelungen. Weltgeschichte aus der Sage* (The Wibelungs: World history from legend), with its etymological musings.

What Wagner was looking for was a character who could embody his revolutionary hopes for fundamental change. His thoughts turned initially to great figures from history: between 1848 and 1850 there were plans for works on the lives of Friedrich I, Jesus of Nazareth, Alexander the Great, and Achilles. But his reading of Hegel had made it clear that historical facts were not universally valid: history could never predicate the future.

Nevertheless, 'world history from legend' showed the way. By going back a stage further, into the prehistoric past, Wagner was able to bypass the historicity of the past and hold up a mirror to his own age. His Siegfried was the hero who — unlike some exotic Egyptian prince who, for that very reason, could elicit only astonishment — would be the potential progenitor of both rulers and the ruled among the composer's audience, shaming those who did not stand by their oaths and deeds in a similar spirit of self-sacrificial duty and opening the eyes of others to the failings of their perjurious colleagues.

And yet it was heroes rather than gods that peopled Wagner's prose draft for *Siegfrieds Tod,* noted down in October 1848, the month in which he had finished his outline of the Nibelung legend. Only in the scene where Siegfried assumes the shape of Gunther does a supernatural element enter the work. The draft was versified in November. The following month Wagner read it aloud to a circle of friends, who failed to grasp the work's linguistic form, but even more important was the objection raised by Eduard Devrient, who pointed out that the plot's prehistory was constantly taken for granted rather than shown on stage. Wagner's response was to preface the poem with Siegfried's farewell to Brünnhilde, after which he added the Prelude for the Norns — the first mythic scene that he wrote.

Meanwhile, a mythic scene of a somewhat different order was unfolding in Dresden. In the elections held on 10 January 1849 the Radical Democrats had polled sixteen thousand votes, the Liberals six thousand six hundred, while the Conservatives had failed to take a single seat. If the legally elected members of Parliament (including several who, until then, had been living in exile or serving terms of imprisonment) had sat it out and sought, in that way, to affect the general mood, the king of Saxony would, sooner or later, have had to accept the new constitution, and a substantial improvement in political and economic conditions would inevitably have followed. But the Romantically inflated belief that the revolution would, of itself, bring about a new situation played into the hands of the king and his prime minister, who fanned the flames of unrest till insurrection broke out in the streets of Dresden in May 1849 and toppled the Saxon government. Revolution as myth triumphed over revolution as an almost tangible possibility, driving one of its keenest supporters, the court conductor, Richard Wagner, into self-exile for more than a decade.

He fled to Weimar, where Liszt attempted to obtain a commission for him to write an opera for Paris. But Paris, to Wagner, was like the Augean stables which revolution alone could cleanse, so the failure of his efforts was a source of self-congratulation. He drafted *Wieland der Schmied*, begun in Zurich in January 1850 and completed in Paris three months later. Chained to an anvil, his tendons severed, this Nordic Daedalus represents the alienated *Volk*. Finally Wieland forges a pair of wings for himself and flies away to a life of freedom, having first taken care to set his oppressors' court on fire. The motifs of magic, redemption, and fire are variants on the Nibelung theme, which Wagner had not lost sight of.

'I've already acquired some manuscript paper and a rastrum from Dresden: whether I can still compose, God alone can say', he wrote to Uhlig on 27 July 1850.[39] Liszt, he went on, had told him that he could reckon on a commission to write *Siegfrieds Tod* for the Court Theatre in Weimar, involving an advance which would, he thought, allow him to go on eking out his existence. But in making it clear to Liszt that he would 'never write *Siegfried* in a vacuum',[40] he had put his finger on one of three points which still stood between him and the completed *Ring*. It required the visit to Albisbrunn, in November 1851, to precipitate the decision 'to realize my original sketch for the *Nibelungen* in its entirety, irrespective of whether any part of it would be actually performable in our theatres'.[41] By return of post he sent back the two-hundred-thaler advance which Weimar had paid him, defining 'freedom', at least for the present, as disregard for the need to have his works performed. But by August 1850 he had not yet reached this point, and so he broke off composition of *Siegfrieds Tod* while working on Scene 2.

Myth

The work was still an heroic opera. No doubt it was up-to-date, and no doubt, too, it took account of the progressive tendencies of his latest operas, even breaking new ground in respect of its use of words (none of his friends who heard him declaim it could have known of the close correlation between phonological sound and musical pitch,[42] so their dismay is not altogether surprising), while Wagner's definitive break with the old division into arias and recitatives could be seen, at a glance, from the text. From a dramaturgical and structural point of view, however, the work is little more than a latterday *Lohengrin*, an attempt, in Wagner's words, 'to present a crucial turning-point in the whole vast action, and to present it as a drama suited to our present-day stage'.[43]

The 1848 scenario, *The Nibelung Legend (Myth)*, had already traced the *Ring* in outline, from the theft of the Rhinegold to the end of the gods, anticipating the form in which we know the work today. It was in Albisbrunn that Wagner made up his mind to 'realize' this 'original sketch . . . in its entirety'.[44]

He wrote to Liszt on 20 November 1851: 'According to my newly acquired [!] and innermost conviction, a work of art — and hence the basic drama — can make its rightful impression only if the poetic intent is fully presented to the senses in every one of its important moments; and *I* least of all can now afford to sin against this insight which I now recognize as true. In order to be perfectly understood, I must therefore communicate my entire myth, in its deepest and widest significance, with total artistic clarity; no part of it should have to be supplied by the audience's having to think about it or reflect on it.'[45] Thus the seed of disaster was sown in the form of Wagner's fear of leaving anything out, to say nothing of his love of repetition, which reflection and a surfeit of dramatic underlinings did nothing to discourage. The letter goes on:

> I cannot contemplate a division of the constituent parts of this great whole without ruining my intention in advance. The whole complex of dramas must be staged at the same time in rapid succession . . . : the performance of my Nibelung dramas must take

place at a great festival which may perhaps be organized for the
unique purpose of this performance. It must then be given on
three successive days, with the introductory prelude being performed on the preceding evening. Once I have achieved such a
performance under these conditions, the whole work may then be
repeated on another occasion, and only after that may the individual dramas, which in themselves are intended as entirely independent pieces, be performed as people wish: but, whatever happens, these performances must be preceded by an impression of
the complete production which I myself shall have prepared.[46]

Wagner was still in Albisbrunn when he wrote the earliest sketches
for *Die Walküre* and *Der Raub des Rheingolds* (as he initially thought of
calling it). Thus the Gordian knot was cut, allowing him to write the
libretto of *Die Walküre* the following June and that of *Das Rheingold*
between 15 September and 3 November 1852. The existing parts
were then revised and a new ending added to *Siegfrieds Tod*, prior to
the private printing of the poem in February 1853. Not until the
autumn of that year did he begin composition of *Das Rheingold* under
the impression, as he later claimed, of the sea at La Spezia.[47] A
further twenty years were to pass before the full score of *Götterdämmerung* was completed in Bayreuth, on 21 November 1874.

Festival

The third of the points which Wagner resolved when he took the
decision in Albisbrunn to write the entire *Ring* without regard to
financial support was that of a festival performance.

He had just received Karl Ritter's report on the first performance
of *Lohengrin* in Weimar, a production which, under Liszt's direction,
had been adequate musically but a failure in terms of its staging. It
was under this impression that Wagner wrote to Kietz on 14 September 1850: 'But you know me well enough by now to realize that I no
longer expect any results either from this or from similar efforts
made on behalf of our cause in general or of me in particular. But
since I am still alive, and since, with the best will in the world, I can
live only in the *here and now*, I must needs do something that accords
with my temperament.' There follows a speculative plan based on
what he would do when his assistant's uncle died:

I am genuinely thinking of setting Siegfried [*Siegfrieds Tod*] to
music, only I cannot reconcile myself with the idea of trusting to
luck and of having the work performed by the very first theatre
that comes along: on the contrary, I am toying with the boldest of

plans, which it will require no less a sum than 10,000 thalers to bring about. According to this plan of mine, I would have a theatre, made of planks, erected here on the spot [in Zurich], have the most suitable singers join me here, and arrange everything necessary for this one special occasion, so that I would be certain of an outstanding performance of the opera. I would then send out invitations far and wide to all who were interested in my works, ensure that the auditorium was decently filled, and give three performances — free, of course — one after the other in the space of a week, after which the theatre would then be demolished and the whole affair would be over and done with. Only something of this nature can still appeal to me. I shall receive the sum when Karl Ritter's uncle dies.[48]

This happened in November 1851. In the event, however, it was not Karl himself who inherited the estate but his mother who, as mentioned above, increased Wagner's annual allowance.

But by November 1851, as noted earlier, Wagner had made up his mind to expand the work to the four-part *Ring*. And so he wrote to Theodor Uhlig on the twelfth of the month to tell him of his plans to produce the cycle at a special festival:

With this new conception of mine I am moving *completely* out of touch with our present-day theatre and its audiences: I am breaking decisively and for ever with the formal present. . . . A *performance* is something I can conceive of only *after the Revolution*; only the Revolution can offer me the artists and listeners I need. The coming Revolution must necessarily put an end to this whole *theatrical business* of ours: they must all perish, and will certainly do so, it is inevitable. Out of the ruins I shall summon together what I need: I shall *then* find what I require. I shall then run up a theatre on the Rhine and send out invitations to a great dramatic festival: after a year's preparations I shall then perform my entire work within the space of *four days*: *with it* I shall then make clear to the men of the Revolution the *meaning* of that Revolution, in its noblest sense. *This audience* will understand me: present-day audiences cannot.[49]

In referring to the revolution, Wagner was thinking quite concretely of the elections due to take place in the spring of 1852. During the early part of 1850 he had gone to Paris to follow up plans for *Wieland der Schmied* (plans, it must be said, for which he had little enthusiasm) and had attended a vast electoral meeting, which had inspired him with revolutionary hopes for the 1852 elections. It appears that what he was planning was nothing less than a message of greeting addressed to the French *avant garde* by those still loyal to the revolution — and planning to do so, moreover, with a work that was based on Germanic mythology. The coup d'état organized by Louis-Napoléon (later Napoléon III) on 2 December 1851 put an end to all these prospects, and Wagner and Uhlig decided to go on dating their letters 'December 1851' until such time as new elections were called in France. He had, however, already resolved to write the four-part *Ring*, and with it had come his decision to mount his own production, a decision taken during his cold-water cure in Albisbrunn near Zurich.

The Festival Hill as a Magic Mountain

The festival was to take place 'on the Rhine', and so indeed it did, at least in a figurative sense. In German-speaking countries, the Rhine is the archetypal river, far more so than the Danube, for instance, from where Wagner had transferred certain episodes from his literary sources, relocating them in Germany. And in flowing water, guilt not only could but *had* to be washed away, in keeping with the heathen tradition cited at the outset of this chapter. Hagen himself, at the end of *Götterdämmerung*, commits a kind of ritual suicide, which traditionally had to take place in flowing water. The whole of the story of the *Ring* aims at this washing away of guilt.

The idea that is central not only to Prießnitz's cold-water cure but also to Wagner's revolutionary theories[50] is that of purification. Indeed, I would even go so far as to claim that it was in Albisbrunn that he realized that a festival performance of the four-part *Ring des Nibelungen* could have the same socio-cathartic effect as his cold-water cure had had, and that it could do so, moreover, by means of an art embedded in Nature.

The decisive step that was taken in Albisbrunn was from an heroic opera (in one or two parts but promised, at all events, to Weimar) to the representation of myth with its totally different requirements. This step, moreover, brought with it a sense of liberation for the whole of Wagner's later oeuvre. If the early parts of the *Ring* had been tentative in their compositional approach, he was now free to write both *Tristan* and *Die Meistersinger* in his new-found style; and after the *Ring* came *Parsifal*. That this latter work, with its Sacred Bath and Spa March (to quote Wagner's own description of the March to the Holy Grail in conversation with Cosima on 27 December 1877), is very much a dramatisation of Vincenz Prießnitz's principles is manifestly plain, albeit irrelevant to the present discussion.[51]

Of course, we need to make a minor adjustment to the image of Archimedes which, as mentioned above, Wagner used to describe his visits to the watering-places of Teplitz and Marienbad during the 1840s: Archimedes-Wagner did not climb into his bathtub in

Albisbrunn only to discover his principle by chance; rather, he clambered into it because he hoped to find the principle of the *Ring* already there. In support of my hypothesis that water was of fundamental import for the work, I may cite the fact that, according to the original conception of *Siegfrieds Tod*, Siegfried's Rhine Journey would have been the overture; the link between the beginning and the end which was later forged by the Rhinemaidens' vocalization in the opening scene of *Das Rheingold* was not, therefore, something new, since it merely restored what was there from the outset.

Hagen's ritual suicide is emblematic of this inner connection: at all events, it is for him alone, and for that other suicide, Brünnhilde, that the Rhine overflows its banks. According to the stage directions for this final scene:

> Hagen who, since the incident with the ring [when the dead Siegfried's arm had been raised in a threatening gesture and Brünnhilde had entered to slip the ring from his hand], has been watching Brünnhilde with increasing concern, is seized with extreme alarm at the sight of the Rhinemaidens. He hastily throws aside his spear, shield, and helmet and plunges into the floodwaters like a man possessed . . . . Woglinde and Wellgunde twine their arms around his neck and, swimming away, draw him with them into the depths. Floßhilde leads the way as they swim towards the back of the stage, holding the regained ring aloft in a gesture of jubilation.[52]

The ring which Alberich had earlier cursed is purified at last and restored to the children of Nature. The world of the gods goes up in flames, taking with it the symbol of empty power, while the human survivors, children of Nature once more, refuse to be cowed by the sight, but stand, undismayed by the rising flood-tide and watching, 'deeply stirred'[53] (in other words, in a mood of religious awe), as the glow from the fire grows in the sky. Thus a fire cure is reserved for the gods, a water cure for their mortal counterparts. But such a cure offers no prescription for the new beginning which has now become so necessary if the human race is to rise again from the ashes.

This inner connection, already contained, in part, in the basic idea behind *The Nibelung Legend (Myth)* and partly (we may suppose) thought out in advance in a series of vivid images, may well have attracted Wagner to Prießnitz's theories, so that, at least as far as the *Ring* is concerned, he hit on the notion of taking the waters only as an afterthought. If cold-water cures proved crucial, it was partly in terms of the type of decision he took and partly because they persuaded him of the need to hold a festival, a festival born of the spirit of hydrotherapy.

But the first decision has to be taken by members of the public. As with a cold-water cure, they must leave the big city behind them, so that they feel not only a sense of inner distance from the city but, by extension, an inner closeness to the impending performance. If Wagner's initial plan was to stage the *Ring* on the banks of the Rhine, it was certainly not Cologne that he had in mind. When Ludwig ordered Gottfried Semper to design a stone-built theatre along the lines of a temple, Wagner did what he could to undermine the project and finally won the day.

Wagner's decision to turn his back on the city is bound up, of course, with the loathing he felt for the conditions which have always existed in theatres in every major town and city. Above all, however, the model performances he planned were a protest against the custom of hurrying off to the theatre after a tiring day at the office, in search of mere entertainment, while mind and body were still elsewhere. Wagner demanded exclusivity for his work as an artist, taking up arms against the tradition of underrating the type of art which he himself was promulgating and of using it for social, non-artistic ends. Even the emperor would have to come to him in order to see the *Ring* — as, indeed, he did in 1876. This readiness to travel to Bayreuth represents an important breakthrough in art's struggle to gain acceptance not only for its beauty of form but, more especially, for the message it implies.

A central point in Wagner's festival concept was that Nature herself should be pressed into serving the cause of art. As far as I am aware, the Festspielhaus in Bayreuth is the only theatre of any size that was consciously planned without a foyer. The public is therefore obliged, not least by the length of the intervals, to promenade around the grounds, an idea modelled, in part, on the frequent walks which Wagner would undertake in the course of his daily routine while taking the waters in Albisbrunn. Their spiritual basis, however, stems from the passage by Justinus Kerner, cited above, where he speaks of the 'silent simple greatness of Nature in this place of healing'.[54] The Festspielhaus is thus drawn as far as possible into its natural setting.

'Get rid of the ornaments', Wagner wrote on an early plan of the theatre, demanding instead the simplest possible type of building which would give the impression of being provisional. It was to be a building in which the lighting and stage technology would be as perfect as possible, so that, quite apart from the unplanned excellence of the acoustics and the intended high standards on stage and in the pit, the audience would be held in thrall as though by some magic spell. Wagner productions make their mark through the very intensity of the experience.

This experience is now conditioned in various ways, an essential part of the process — which Wagner himself both preached and practised — being the way that the visitor's day is strictly divided up. It was never necessary to lay down rules of conduct, since these emerged of their own accord: shopping expeditions or visits to casinos were out of the question in Bayreuth — anyone who did not stay at home and study the vocal score or at least read some of the secondary literature on the subject (which even then was already voluminous) would go for a walk. After lunch (the search for something to eat, which, in 1876, seems, for Tchaikovsky at least, to have been more memorable than the music itself, appears to have borne unpredictable fruit), the early start and effort of sitting still and concentrating for long periods on seats which, at that time, were rather more comfortable — not least because of their sudorific properties, even if their occupants were forced to wear unduly formal dress — suggested a siesta. The walk up the hill to the Festspielhaus was a chance to stretch one's legs, and, after sitting for at least an hour — two in the case of the regrettably protracted opening act of *Götterdämmerung* — the visitor was happy to flee the airless and overheated auditorium in search of a little fresh air and exercise; and the same was true of the second interval, when it was also possible to have a bite to eat. And after the evening's performance was over, Bayreuth's brewers (at the beginning of the nineteenth century, there were no fewer than two hundred brewers in a town of ten thousand inhabitants) offered the ideal nightcap. This strict division of the day's activities had two important consequences: concentration on the performance and a palpably healthy way of life.

During my years on Bayreuth's Green Hill, what impressed me most of all was a charming couple from France who had been coming to the festival for almost half a century. It was they who first made me think of writing this essay when they told me they needed to come to Bayreuth for reasons of health. Although the time they spent there was certainly tiring, filled as it was with intense experiences, each of which they savoured to the full, they always returned to France refreshed and fortified for the rest of the year. Those who mock the festival are, therefore, probably wrong: for, although a visit to Bayreuth is unlikely to lead to redemption, any more than Wagner's cold-water cure in Albisbrunn could restore his ruined health, it helps the visitor to stand aside from everyday life through the help of a conscious awareness of art and the feeling that he or she is close to Nature. From the point of view of medical history, Wagner's 'mystic abyss'[55] turns out to be a fountain of youth, but, unlike its models, it works, keeping its visitors healthy and itself eternally young.

Chapter 9

Wagner on Record: Re-evaluating Singing in the Early Years

David Breckbill

The performance history of every musical repertory is subject to high and low points if the works it encompasses remain continuously before the public for an extended period, and Wagner's operas are no exception. For more than a century they have been performed conscientiously and haphazardly, in note-complete renditions and cut by as much as a third, in concert and in excerpts. Most of all, they have been performed very frequently. Periodizing the history of Wagner performance is thus less a statistical exercise than an evaluation of the appropriateness of the numerous styles through which Wagner's works have been encountered by audiences over the decades. Historians have used evidence in a variety of ways to buttress arguments that one era or another was notable. Ernest Newman (writing in the 1940s) concluded that 'the 1876 performances [of the *Ring* at Bayreuth] were equal at their least good to the average good of today, and, at their best, better than the present-day best',[1] and that the Bayreuth *Parsifal* 'was better sung and acted in 1882 than it is as a whole today'.[2] One can recognize in Newman's gratuitous and methodologically naive comparisons a desire to believe that performances supervised by a genius of Wagner's magnitude must have been better than those to which he (Newman) was accustomed — a strain of wistful hero worship which many would endorse. On the other hand, I recently heard a person involved in a long-established *Ring* festival assert that the 1980s and 1990s constitute a 'Golden Age' of *Ring* performance. Underlying this sentiment is not only a parochial and self-aggrandizing belief that what one knows is best, but also the tendency to believe that as technical standards rise, so do general performance standards. Since in at least cosmetic respects technique in general has never been more impressive than it is today, it might seem logical to conclude that ours is indeed a Golden Age.

On the other hand, a growing minority opinion holds that Wagner

153

performance of our time is in a state of crisis. So thoughtful a commentator as Samuel Lipman, for example, does not scruple to use a word such as 'travesty' to describe 'present-day Wagner performances, in and out of the opera house'.[3] Whether one accepts or rejects this assessment, Lipman's critique at least differs in kind from those of Newman and the apologist for today, who developed their opinions comfortably ensconced in unexamined assumptions. By contrast, Lipman reaches his conclusion after having listened to Wagner recordings from the 1920s and 1930s, which have begun to recirculate in increasing profusion over the last two decades. Recordings introduce into discussions of performance style a note of confirmability, since they do not change[4] and therefore can serve as an ongoing point of reference for increasingly elaborate historical accounts of performance styles. This does not prevent silly things from being said about and claimed for certain recordings; further, no one can prevent someone else from hearing what she or he wants to hear, or believes she or he is hearing, in any particular recorded performance. Nevertheless, recordings do fix performance style in a way that prose accounts of performances will never manage to equal, and therefore may serve as a cornerstone in any historical account of performance style.

The evidence provided by historical recordings causes Lipman to assert that Wagner singing — and especially conducting, although singing is the focus of the present essay — between the two world wars was far superior to what we normally encounter today. Those who glance back fondly at earlier eras of Wagner performance through the medium of recordings have not always chosen such lofty models,[5] but the practice of looking to the past rather than to the future for models of Wagner singing has become firmly engrained. Even in the 1960s historically-minded reviewers of new recordings occasionally compared Wagner performers of that era unfavourably with those of the inter-war years, but the difference in quality between the two periods did not seem profound;[6] perhaps the satisfaction of filling out the Wagner discography in complete recordings employing the latest technological breakthrough, stereophonic sound, diluted any nagging pessimism about the performances. By and large, however, Wagner singers who began their careers in the 1960s fared less well in critical assessments than did those who had dominated or emerged in the 1950s (Hans Hotter, Wolfgang Windgassen, Birgit Nilsson, and so on). By the time a new generation of Wagner singers came to the fore in the late 1960s and 1970s — the generation of Helga Dernesch, René Kollo, and Gwyneth Jones — the general feeling was that these singers were markedly inferior even to their immediate predecessors. Conrad L. Osborne, reviewing simultaneously (in

1971) a new recording of *Lohengrin*[7] and one from three decades earlier,[8] put it this way:

> Whatever their individual weaknesses, these singers of two operatic generations back display command of certain niceties of Wagnerian singing that are unexplored by their successors [in the new recording under discussion]: (1) Some command of mezzavoce — at least the ability to sing a reduced dynamic without losing all sense of firmness and resonance in the tone; (2) a feeling for the turn as an expressive device — an embellishment, yet integral to the line, and done with a flourish rather than picked at; (3) a natural use of some portamento and old-fashioned legato, and an unashamed use of the *portando la voce* effects specifically phrased in by Wagner and quite essential as a means of guiding the vocal line onward. Styles may quite legitimately change, but these are elements of the Wagnerian grammar.[9]

Osborne thus recognized a style in Wagner singing which cannot be abandoned without detriment to the music but which by 1971 had begun to fall into disuse. In general, the trend he sensed then has continued, albeit with even more objectionable accretions and fundamental flaws which make the decline seem to have been increasingly precipitous.

The inter-war period of Wagner singing, glorified by the increasingly long memory with which recordings provide us, is the last era in which a considerable number of singers were capable of dealing successfully with the demands of Wagner's operas. At their best, these singers possessed firm tone, flexible phrasing, and vivid declamation, all combining to achieve urgent, heroic, sharply drawn characterizations. Frida Leider, Lotte Lehmann, Lauritz Melchior, and Friedrich Schorr, as leading members of that contingent, will remain household names among Wagnerians as long as their records can be heard. Their first appearances on the international scene roughly coincided with the introduction of electrical recordings (1925–26), and although each of the four made acoustical Wagner recordings, it is the records they made using the new process that are most celebrated.

It seems strange that the era prior to the inter-war years is so poorly remembered; except in the minds of specialists and record collectors, no Wagner singers until the time of the quartet just named have had a lasting place in the history of Wagner performance. Indeed, the only group of singers before the inter-war contingent who are still automatically associated with Wagner's music are those with whom the composer himself worked in Dresden, Paris, Munich, and Bayreuth: Wilhelmine Schröder-Devrient, Joseph Tichatschek, Albert Niemann, Ludwig Schnorr, Franz Betz, Amalie Materna, Karl Hill,

Emil Scaria, and others. Because we can no longer hear performances by the most important singers of this group, we have long since
adopted a Newmanesque stance towards them. In light of Wagner's
much repeated concern that his music be well sung, and of the fact
that these were the singers he chose and/or admired in his music, we
assume that they must have represented the kind of singing he had
in mind. Yet Wagner's death after only two Bayreuth Festivals prevented the singers he assembled there from realizing or establishing
a fully formed style under his supervision. As competing factions and
ideologies emerged in the composer's absence, Wagner singing after
Wagner's death is generally thought nowadays to have been in decline except in a few isolated pockets of enlightenment. Further, the
general consensus is that this dark age was unexpectedly brought to
an end by the emergence of the inter-war singers.

Can a four-part periodization, derived from standard views of the
most important eras in Wagner singing, be accepted as a working
hypothesis for further study? Yes and no. The time-spans of the four
segments — (1) Wagner singing in the composer's own day, especially at Bayreuth, (2) Wagner singing in the years following the
composer's death until (3) the outstanding inter-war period, followed by (4) a prolonged, gradual, but decisive decline since 1940 —
need no significant revision. One dislikes being as harsh towards the
contemporary scene as the periodization suggests one must be, especially since the Wotan of James Morris, for example, would most
likely have been viewed as a fine interpretation at any point in the last
seventy years. The fact that this characterization has been greeted so
rapturously, however, demonstrates the dearth of worthwhile counterparts in current Wagner performances, and so the provisional
characterization of the fourth period may be allowed to stand as a
stimulus to ongoing discussion.

What must be challenged in this periodization is the assessment of
the quality of the first period and the function of the second. Specifically, the few recordings of the singers with whom Wagner worked
have been seriously misinterpreted to suggest that, in general, they
could boast customary virtues of good singing which their successors
lacked. Moreover, far from being characterized by inadequate singing, the period from Wagner's death to the inter-war years was a
dynamic era in which conflicting styles and ideologies competed for
supremacy. The interaction between singers who represented these
differing ideologies, further influenced by audiences with equally
diverse expectations, helped to forge a stylistic synthesis which made
the inter-war period a natural summit in the history of Wagner
singing. Evidence for this assertion can be discovered in the many
early (that is, acoustical) Wagner recordings.[10] These have generally

been the province of record collectors, not of those primarily interested in charting the history of performance style. Unfortunately, scholars of performance history who have thought to consult recordings have often lacked the experience with records which would make their conclusions either novel or adequately contextualized. The present essay, therefore, seeks to revise ways evidence provided by recordings might profitably be used to elucidate the first two segments of this tentative periodization.

For those interested in learning at first hand how the singers with whom Wagner worked sounded, their recordings possess an inevitable charm. Wagnerians are not as fortunate as Verdians, who can sample the work of the first Otello, Iago, and Falstaff in those roles but we do have recordings by five singers who participated in the 1876 and 1882 Bayreuth Festivals. The following list gives the roles they sang and the extent of their recorded Wagner repertory:

Lilli Lehmann (1848–1929): Woglinde, Helmwige[11] and Wood Bird in 1876. Thirty-eight published recordings for Odeon (1906–07), including Sieglinde's 'Du bist der Lenz'; an unpublished recording of Isolde's Liebestod is also extant.[12]

Marianne Brandt (1842–1921): replacement Waltraute at *Götterdämmerung* in 1876, one of three Kundrys in 1882. Three recordings for Artistikal, released on Pathé (Vienna, September 1905); no Wagner titles.[13]

Hermann Winkelmann (1849–1912): first of three Parsifals in 1882. Four recordings for Berliner (Vienna, May 1900), including two excerpts as Walther von Stolzing and one as Lohengrin; six recordings for G&T (Vienna, early 1905), including one excerpt each as Tannhäuser, Walther, and Lohengrin; at least five recordings for Favorite (Vienna, 1905), including one excerpt each as Tannhäuser and Walther.[14]

Luise Belce (later Reuss-Belce) (1862-1945): a solo Flowermaiden in 1882. A brief outburst as Ortrud from a live performance at the Metropolitan Opera on 7 February 1903, captured on a Mapleson cylinder.[15]

Adolf von Hübbenet (1858–1903): Second Squire in 1882. Two one-line interjections as Mime in *Siegfried* from a Metropolitan Opera performance of 19 March 1901, captured on a very dim and noisy Mapleson cylinder.[16]

Apart from the von Hübbenet recording, which may as well not exist for all that can be deciphered of his singing, two of these singers can under no circumstances be regarded as duplicating on record the kind of singing they did under Wagner's supervision. Lilli Lehmann had become a leading dramatic soprano, even though her native vocal endowment seemed most suited for a lighter repertory — the kind in which she appeared at Bayreuth in 1876, and in which she would have appeared in 1882 had not amorous turmoil caused her to decline Wagner's invitation to be leader of the Flowermaidens. Whatever her virtues and leading characteristics as a singer, they cannot safely be attributed to Wagner's influence. After Wagner's death, Luise Reuss-Belce was increasingly associated with Bayreuth and became one of the foremost practitioners of the much denounced Bayreuth style — a style which had been developed only *since* Wagner's time. Her belief that her singing was what Wagner had really wanted was at least partially formed and perpetuated in her by Wagner's widow, Cosima.

This leaves Brandt (sixty-three at the time of her recordings) and Winkelmann (who was fifty-one and fifty-six when he made his records) as the most direct representatives of the kind of singing Wagner sponsored in his operas. Infirmities of age afflict them both, although Brandt's singing seems better preserved than Winkelmann's. One comes away from hearing their recordings fairly confident in being able to identify the style — Wagnerian or not — with which they were comfortable. Winkelmann's delivery is oppressively soulful ('lachrymose' was Lilli Lehmann's non-pejorative description of his singing as Parsifal at Bayreuth in 1883), but, despite brittle short-breathedness, he does seem to aim at a lingering quality which suggests slowish tempos and sustained line. His attacks and especially releases are far from clean, often incorporating a brief falsetto squeak or sob as the sound begins or ends.[17] By far the best part of the voice is the top, and many of his phrases and interpretive decisions seem calculated to show this range to best advantage: it is not coincidence that in his two recordings of Tannhäuser's Song of Praise to Venus he selects the third stanza, since it has the highest notes and the highest tessitura. Few of his recordings are as choppy, desperate, and — frankly — ghastly as his Favorite version of this aria, but in general he seems to have been a sloppy singer (his 1900 Prize Song substitutes the words from a later stanza for a couple of lines), and a vain one. Brandt makes a decidedly better impression, with a fruity voice, wide range, some agility, a grand manner, intentionality of phrasing, and a genuine trill. Her registers are beginning to come apart by 1905, but the variety and sweep of her singing — with intonation at least no more unreliable than Winkelmann's — provide a suitably scaled context for some hard attacks. It is perhaps difficult to imagine this voice endowing the opening portion of the Garden Scene in

Act II of *Parsifal* with ideal seductiveness,[18] but the rest of her Bayreuth assignments would seem to have been well within her grasp.

Most commentators have bent over backwards to be generous to these recordings, glossing over the unpleasing aspects of Winkelmann's singing in particular, in order to perpetuate the myth that Wagner's singers were paragons. This orthodoxy has been passed down from generation to generation of record collectors. P. G. Hurst, noting Winkelmann's appearance in the leading tenor roles during the 1882 Drury Lane season of Wagner opera (*Tristan, Die Meistersinger, Lohengrin,* and *Tannhäuser*) under Hans Richter's direction, goes on to praise the casting of those productions: 'These singers, among whom were [Rosa] Sucher, [Therese] Malten, [Marianne] Brandt, and [Eugen] Gura, comprised probably the best exponents of the Wagnerian idiom, for they sang under Wagner's personal direction, and before it became the vogue to abandon lyrical methods in favor of the ugly declamatory style which has supplanted them'.[19] Michael Scott is briefer — '[Winkelmann's] style antedates the Bayreuth barkers'[20] — and David Hamilton more cautiously circumspect: 'What [Winkelmann's] recordings, and Brandt's, do suggest is that the singers Wagner chose for his own performances possessed such traditional virtues as firm, rounded tone and a strong legato, which they did not sacrifice to an excessively vigorous declamatory style. Over the next thirty years, this would not always be the case'.[21] However, both leave undisturbed the notion that, all in all, Wagner's singers displayed so-called traditional virtues and that it was the Bayreuth style of the subsequent decades that is to blame for the bad singing that became a byword in German performances of Wagner into the next century.

The fallacy of this assumption is that it stems directly from negative propaganda generated by one faction and directed at an opposing camp in the ideological strife which surrounded Wagner singing after Wagner's death. When to this attitude is added a charitable interpretation of the few recordings of singers who participated in a certain limited group of performances from two decades and more earlier, the error is compounded. It must be granted that singers who worked under Wagner's supervision and survived long enough to make recordings would have possessed a healthy vocal method, one which was based at least in part on 'traditional virtues'. It is hardly surprising that Winkelmann and Brandt fall into this category. Nor is it surprising that singers who did not possess such a technique failed to make careers which lasted to 1900 and beyond — that is, to the time when it would have been possible for them to make records. What is surprising is the apparent unwillingness of many commentators to believe that the casts Wagner assembled at

Bayreuth were far from the homogeneously fine-singing troupe which legend makes them out to have been.

A closer examination reveals that the Siegfried in 1876, Georg Unger, was practically a vocal novice, lacking such traditional virtues as a usable head voice and reliable intonation, and possessing baritonal sound which not only was not a thing of beauty but which limited his flexibility. Unger was the first in a long line of Bayreuth casting experiments based on a singer's promise rather than on his or her achievements, and so might be regarded as an aberration; but the same cannot be said of Albert Niemann, whose Siegmund was regarded as one of the glories of the 1876 festival by Wagner, Lilli Lehmann, Angelo Neumann, Julius Stockhausen and most German observers. Yet Camille Saint-Saëns, who had heard Niemann as the Paris Tannhäuser of 1861, remarked that by 1876 the voice itself was but a shadow of its former self. A few years earlier Eduard Hanslick gave extended and admiring attention to Niemann's artistry, but this did not prevent him from concluding that he was a natural — that is, untrained — vocalist, that his voice was more compelling in volume than in delicacy and charm, and that his real strength was his declamation, his 'complete fusion of word and tone, of poem and composition'.[22] Near the end of his career, between 1886 and 1888, Niemann participated in two seasons at the Metropolitan Opera in New York. Much later, the American critic W. J. Henderson recalled the first American performance of *Tristan und Isolde* (1 December 1886): 'It was a great performance and in dramatic intensity has not yet been surpassed. The music [read: singing — Henderson admired the conducting of Anton Seidl immensely] of the drama has been better done. Mme. [Lilli] Lehmann [Isolde] and Emil Fischer [Marke] did most of the singing in the first New York *Tristan*. . . . Albert Niemann . . . came to us an old man with remnants of a voice, who sang in shattered and brittle phrases, but . . . poured into the last act of *Tristan*, as he did in the death of Siegfried, the vials of all agonies. He was heart-rending'.[23] In short, connoisseurs of 'fine' singing (as defined by international standards), even those who found Niemann's performances deeply moving and impressive, did not consider his voice or singing *per se* (without taking his utterance of words into account) to be the foundation upon which his greatness was constructed; and yet all German observers praised him highly — Lehmann even for his 'singing'.

Other of Wagner's singers likewise committed sins that made them questionable exponents of 'traditional virtues'. Heinrich Vogl, Wagner's Loge, was received with praise by Hugo Wolf when Vogl first appeared in Vienna in June of 1884, but by later in the same year, Wolf had begun to perceive some characteristics worthy of ridicule:

Herr Vogl, from Munich, was the Tristan, or, to speak in his manner, the Trrristan. Compared with this continuous rattle, as, for example, in the upward surging expiation oath: 'Tr(rr)ug des Her(rr)zens! Tr(rr)aum der(rr) Ahnung ew'ger(rr) Tr(rr)auer(rr)! Einzger(rr) Tr(rr)ost,' etc., the most hellish racket of the most decrepit, unlubricated coach on our potholed pavement must fall upon the ear as a siren song. The listener is assailed by a sensation of chewing mill wheels, which is quite an imposition. His sensitivity to such disaster may well be somewhat dulled by now, to be sure, Herr [Franz] von Reichenberg [Wagner's Bayreuth Fafner] having taken every conceivable pain to accustom the public to clamorous consonants.[24]

Wolf found Vogl's Loge to be an epoch-making achievement, but could not refrain from framing his praise in terms of his earlier criticism: 'Was it really Herr Vogl? I doubt it, for I would have recognized him by his *rr*. It was Loge himself'.[25] It is too easy to assume that Vogl went without his enthusiastic emphasis of consonants on this occasion, however. Lilli Lehmann's appraisal of his 1876 Loge, which includes remarks on Vogl's 'exaggerated accent, that was specially suited for just this role, and that sounded not merely sharp but both sharp and biting',[26] suggests that even when Wolf heard him as Loge this characteristic of his singing was present, although in this role it did not clash with the character he portrayed. Vogl seems always to have treated consonants in this way, which leads one to doubt whether he ever attained the traditional virtue of strong legato.

Edvard Grieg, in his report on the 1876 Bayreuth *Ring*, wrote that Schlosser as Mime 'declaims more than he sings, which brings out the words of the text more distinctly. This may be the answer to music-drama'.[27] Further examples would be redundant in making the point that the vast majority of Wagner's Bayreuth singers can be shown to have lacked or ignored 'traditional virtues' as we understand them. Suffice it to say that Wagner's singers of the 1870s and 1880s were typical German singers of their time, not only in their various levels of technical accomplishment but also in the diversity of styles they represented. Those who declaimed well did not always sing to the satisfaction of those accustomed to the best in French and Italian singing, while those who sang well often gave the impression of not being completely familiar with the Wagnerian style.[28] In general, a broad spectrum of styles was represented among German singers. To the extent that the 'German style' of singing in the nineteenth century could be characterized as a unified style, however, it undoubtedly relied less on 'traditional virtues of firm, rounded tone and a strong legato' than did Italian, French, and English singing of the same time. At the very least, the assertion that Wagner's singers were invariably top-rank, or that their compelling qualities were based on or encompassed traditional virtues, is open to scepticism.

Recordings are of some help in allowing us to hear other singers who were linked with Wagner in one way or another. Gustav Walter (1834–1910) gave the first concert performances of Siegfried's Forging Songs, under Wagner's direction in Vienna in 1862, and not only made three impressive commercial recordings (at the age of seventy!) in 1904 but also recorded at least two brief selections, including Lohengrin's Arrival, for the Phonogrammarchiv of the Österreichische Akademie der Wissenschaften in 1906.[29] Walter's recording of Schubert's *Am Meer* is of legendary and timeless expressivity, with tapered phrases, purposefully sustained line, and affectingly appropriate timbre. The *Lohengrin* is less remarkable, but the plangent tone and unhurried elegance persist. This style, typical of Viennese tenors, is quite unlike the image we would associate with Siegfried today, however, and must likewise have differed from Wagner's conception of the role, since this is one feature that even the wildest dreamer could not have perceived lurking in Unger's musical nature.

The young Julius Lieban sang Mime in Angelo Neumann's 1881 Berlin production of the *Ring*, and Wagner appears to have been deeply impressed by his performance;[30] Lieban lived to make many records, among them six sides from the *Siegfried* Mime in 1912–15.[31] Lieban's Mime seems underinflected after the vivid 'characterizations' which have become customary in this role, but especially in the Act I Siegfried/Mime scene he displays an extensive yet subtle tonal palette and apt expressive variety. A rumour that Wagner heard and admired the great Italian baritone Mattia Battistini, who made many records, including excerpts from the role of Wolfram (sung in Italian) has yet to be decisively substantiated.[32] In any case, these additional recordings again suggest that singers who both worked with Wagner and lived to make records did possess enough 'traditional virtues' to enjoy long careers. Many others were associated with styles and training which precluded that possibility.

While Wagner was alive, the diversity of the singers he chose went largely unnoticed because all bore the composer's imprimatur (at least *faute de mieux*), and because the German observers whose descriptions are primary in this matter expected such diversity. Upon Wagner's death, however, battles over his artistic heritage flared up and in many cases brought previously unperceived differences into the open. In Germany it was widely held that the musical content of Wagner's music dramas resided in the symphonic orchestral writing. From a vocal standpoint, this meant that Wagner singers were expected first and foremost to make the words comprehensible as a kind of verbal counterpoint to the orchestra. Stated in the most provocative terms, beautiful singing was mistrusted as an 'operatic' trait, irrelevant and inappropriate to the drama which Wagner's works were intended to project. This point of view was associated with the Bayreuth style under the leadership of Cosima, Wagner's widow. Its antithesis was achieved particularly in the second half of the 1890s on the great international stages — the Metropolitan Opera and Covent Garden — and persisted as an unachieved ideal there and elsewhere for some time afterwards. This second approach stemmed from a view that Wagner marked the summit of grand opera, and its advocates held that singers trained in an 'operatic' milieu were ideally equipped to perform Wagner's works by observing universally applicable principles of good singing. The gradual infiltration of the Wagnerian canon into the French and Italian repertories from the 1870s on buttressed this notion, since in those countries indigenous and sharply defined styles determined the way Wagner would be sung. A middle ground between these two poles was inhabited by the majority of German singers who, like their foreign counterparts, applied to Wagner the style with which they were comfortable. In the 1880s and 1890s Wagner became the most prestigious component of the German repertory, so that the demands of Wagner's works shaped German singers much more than they did those for whom Wagner represented a judicious supplement to the repertory.

Recordings suitable to serve as trustworthy stylistic documents began to be made only some two decades after Wagner's death. During those years, stylistic diversity in Wagner singing had become more clearly defined as individual theatres developed distinctive Wagnerian ideologies and sought out singers who conformed to those ideals. Recordings which document the singing of performers closely associated with important theatres tend to reveal a surprisingly extensive collection of distinct styles. A recording[33] of Elsa's Dream by Eva von der Osten, (who spent most of her career in Dresden, the bel canto capital of Germany) is vocally seamless, dramatically neutral, verbally repressed, and utterly controlled, proving that there were German counterparts to predictably 'well sung' recorded performances in French (Aino Ackté) and Italian (Nellie Melba). By way of contrast, a Pathé recording of the same passage by the Berlin singer Erna Denera[34] reveals a much sloppier and less technically sophisticated performance; Denera uses a larger range of vocal effects than von der Osten to paint and respond to the words and their meanings. Although the emotional overlay of this Denera performance is not entirely typical of contemporaneous Berlin Wagner singing, which tended to be rather prim (the contralto Marie Goetze, the bass Paul Knüpfer, and the baritone Hermann Bachmann exemplify this more restrained style), these two performances demonstrate the distinctness of approaches to Wagner in German-language theatres. (Munich and Vienna also possessed unique Wagner styles.) They also show that two performances which are valid and effective within their own stylistic parameters can be totally incompatible.

These two recordings of a passage from one of Wagner's pre–*Oper und Drama* works, which at the times of recording had been in the active repertory for over half a century, do not begin to hint at the extremes of the ideological polarities which came to bear on the vocal writing in the music dramas. One archetype can be represented by the singing of Lillian Nordica, an admired champion of the Wagner-as-grand-opera approach, recorded on Mapleson cylinders in 1903 during Metropolitan Opera performances of *Siegfried*, *Götterdämmerung*, and *Tristan*. The surging orchestra, paced urgently and flexibly by Alfred Hertz, drives Nordica to exalted rhythmic freedom and a genial, caressing treatment of the vocal line — until an opportunity for traditional virtuosity is required. Her treatment of the words 'leuchtender Sproß' in the concluding lines of 'Ewig war ich', with its high C and rapidly ascending triplet, is notable for the sudden shift to precise rhythm, snappy articulation, and impersonal brilliance that is completely out of keeping with her otherwise generous emotion. This automatic, temporary reversion to a familiar performance style suggests just how unusual Wagner's demands were for this kind of singer. Nordica's rhythmically impressionistic Wagner style was her own, but insofar as Jean de Reszke's Mapleson cylinders of Wagner — *Tristan*, *Siegfried*, *Lohengrin* — can be made out, he, like many non-German singers, matched her sweet-toned euphony.

Examples of the other stylistic extreme come from Bayreuth. Cosima Wagner believed that 'here we are duty-bound to present the action [Handlung], and to allow it to be as intelligible as possible through clear and definite pronunciation; if something must be slighted, then music must yield to the poem rather than the poem to music'. She further asserted that Wagner's music dramas contained scenes 'which are to be more spoken than sung'.[35] One limitation of early recordings is that the most tuneful excerpts tended to be the more frequently recorded; consequently, recordings of 'spoken' scenes involving Cosima's singers are comparatively few. But there are some suggestive passages none the less. Loge's one-line interjections in Mime's most extended scene in *Das Rheingold* are prime examples of conversational material. In Hans Breuer's recording of the passage, made at the Bayreuth Festival in 1904, these two lines are sung by Bayreuth's celebrated Loge, Otto Briesemeister.[36] The complete renunciation of singing tone in favour of explosive consonants at strong notes on downbeats — 'Dich, Mime, zu binden, was gab ihm die *Macht*?' and 'Dich Trägen soeben traf wohl sein *Zorn*?' — bespeaks a systematic preoccupation with vividly projecting the sound of the text.

Brittle enunciation, however, though commonly associated with the Bayreuth style, is far from a consistent trait among its representatives who made records — the stylistic diversity with which Wagner had to contend was a dependable feature of Bayreuth up to the First World War. Briesemeister's 1904 solo recording illustrates much the same treatment of consonants, but this performance is an example of the Bayreuth style at its best. Not only are the consonants emphasized, but the sounds of the words, including vowels, seem to generate the vocal line, resulting in an expressively detailed recitation of the text. This kind of performance — about a dozen recordings by Bayreuth singers of the time can be placed in the same class — seems to represent the true aim of the badly misunderstood Bayreuth style. Although they eschewed the sustained line held to be an ideal on the international circuit, Bayreuth singers achieved an historically premature synthesis of the polarized ideologies of the day. This synthesis could and did incorporate good singing, and at its best yielded one of the most densely expressive singing styles ever devised.[37]

During the second of the four eras in the tentative periodization sketched above, the style of Wagner singing represented by Denera — a style in which an emotional elucidation of the meaning of the words took precedence over beautiful singing *per se* — was the norm in Germany. Many singers with less than first-rate technical training or ability also attempted a heavily emphasized declamation intended to convey authority (recordings of the sopranos Pelagie Greeff-Andriessen and Anny Thomas-Schwartz come to mind). By the 1910s, however, German singers had begun to be exposed to the best international standards of singing. Caruso visited Germany frequently from 1904 to 1913 to exceptional acclaim, and German singers interacted among themselves and with celebrated singers of French and Italian training at the Munich Wagner festivals, Covent Garden, and the Metropolitan. The many German traditions and styles of Wagner singing began imperceptibly to merge as a result, and smoother singing became generally appreciated (recall the singing of the baritone Heinrich Schlusnus, for example). By the early 1920s, one could hear lyrical performances of Wagner by German singers, the best of whom did not sacrifice the inner meaning of words that had made earlier performances compelling despite technical crudities. Heinrich Rehkemper's recording of the Song to the Evening Star from *Tannhäuser*[38] shows just how successfully good singing and subtly expressive treatment of words could be linked in Germany by the early 1920s. The challenge of Wagner roles more heroic than Wolfram was even greater: to maintain the energy of declamation that had made earlier exponents seem forceful and decisive while simultaneously intensifying the musical line so that it would not be overshadowed or broken up by the vigorously word-based projection.[39] Those who apprehended the problem in this way, and who achieved such a synthesis, became the leading exponents of the formidable inter-war Wagner style.

In retrospect, it is evident that the excellent Wagner singing which prevailed during the inter-war period was more inevitable than fortuitous. This is not to disparage the innate endowments of the leading singers of those years, but rather to suggest that the stylistic streams which arose amid the enormous diversity of Wagner's day achieved a natural confluence in their singing. The synthesis of strong ideologies which they reflected lent their performances a vivacity and integrity that Wagner was clearly unable to instil in the majority of the singers with whom he worked. The best Wagner singing of the inter-war period, although surely not precisely what Wagner longed for, realized consistently for the first time both the fervent enunciation deemed necessary in Germany and the traditional virtues of fine singing valued elsewhere. It did so, moreover, in a way that was largely pleasing to advocates of each of the two points of view.

Since 1940 the dynamic tension which lay at the root of the inter-war Wagner style has understandably been forgotten, and we have entered a new period of diversity as the musical component of Wagner's works has gradually been subordinated to the visual. Unfortunately, this diversity lacks a foundation in the kind of aesthetic issues whose resolution could lead to a regeneration in the direction of either stylistic purpose or musical autonomy. On the other hand, Wagner's works continue to seem aesthetically imposing and to attract new audiences who would have found the visual component of Wagner performance laughable in the days lauded here as the high-water mark in vocal performance. One strength of the *Gesamtkunstwerk* is its ability to survive inappropriate or unsatisfactory performance styles in one of its parameters so long as those in other realms seem relevant to the audience encountering it. Those who claim that music is the most significant component of Wagner's works are consequently likely to rue the numerous injustices it suffers in performance today. For them, the many Wagner recordings made during and around the inter-war period enshrine a thrilling stylistic confidence and make it possible to experience Wagner's vision more comprehensively than contemporary renditions often permit. And thanks to acoustical Wagner recordings, posterity can sample something of the ideological diversity and eager experimentation which surrounded the performance of Wagner's works when they were new.

Chapter 10

Anton Seidl and America's Wagner Cult

Joseph Horowitz

Anton Seidl's funeral, on 31 March 1898, was the most impressive ever accorded a conductor. The cortège — including leading intellectuals and civic figures as well as world-famous musicians — began its solemn trek at Seidl's brownstone apartment on East Sixty-Second Street. As it proceeded down Fifth Avenue, the route was thronged by spectators, the men hatless in the rain. A hundred-piece band assembled at the Fortieth-Street corner; the dark euphony of its massed winds and muffled drums, in the Funeral March from Beethoven's Op. 26 Piano Sonata, doubled the dismal New York weather. The band, the horse-drawn hearse, the pallbearers, and bereaved friends headed east. Their destination, straddling Broadway between Thirty-Ninth and Fortieth streets, was the Metropolitan Opera House, a scene of chaos. The vestibule had been clogged for an hour. Several women had fainted in the crush. One hundred and fifty patrolmen had arrived to restore a degree of order, inside and out, before the house was opened a few minutes past midday with six policemen stationed at every door. For fully ten minutes, the inrushing women formed a surging, smothering human mass. Many who lacked tickets gained entrance by clasping hands with ticket-holders. Within fifteen minutes, every downstairs seat was occupied, with women outnumbering men twenty to one. The crowd poured upstairs. Standees were packed five and six rows deep. The house eventually contained about four thousand people. Its normal capacity was thirty-three hundred. As many as fifteen thousand had applied for tickets.

The cortège arrived at the Fortieth-Street entrance at 1.15 p.m. The pallbearers removed the coffin and conveyed it into the awesome horseshoe auditorium, whose Family Circle, five storeys aloft, inclined beyond the back wall towards some remote Valhalla. Upon the casket's appearance, the audience, overflowing two tiers of boxes and three balconies, arose with a sudden loud rustle of furniture and clothes. All heads were bowed. The procession moved down the centre aisle. The band of honour, now on stage, played a dirge. The cavernous space stirred with memories.

From the railing to the stage, the pit had been floored over, carpeted, and encircled with black cloth. Masses of harmonized flowers blanketed both this platform and the stage. Jean and Edouard de Reszke had contributed a wreath of four thousand violets. Nellie Melba had sent a wreath of violets nearly two feet in diameter. A rose wreath from Lillian Nordica quoted Isolde: 'Gebrochen der Blick! Still das Herz! Nicht eines Atems flucht'ges Weh'n! Muß sie nun jammernd vor dir steh'n'.[1] A music stand in white roses and violets bore an open score on which appeared on one page a portrait of Richard Wagner, on the other, of the departed, with the inscription 'Vereint auf ewig'.[2]

The casket was placed on a black flowered catafalque several feet high; draped in an American flag, it marked the conductor's place. The stage, lit by candles in great candelabras, was set as the cathedral from Gounod's *Faust*. There sat mourners and friends, a male chorus and the German band as well as the New York Philharmonic. The Philharmonic performed the Adagio lamentoso from Tchaikovsky's *Pathétique* Symphony and, inevitably, the Funeral March from *Götterdämmerung*.[3]

According to James Huneker, who was not a sentimental critic, Anton Seidl's funeral 'was more impressive than any music drama ever seen or heard at Bayreuth. The Metropolitan Opera House was for the moment transformed into a huge mortuary chamber. It was extremely picturesque, yet sincerely solemn. The trappings of woe were not exhibited for their mere bravery. A genuine grief absorbed every person in the building . . . ; it was overwhelmingly touching'. Another eulogist said: 'Anton Seidl held a place in the affections of the American public such as no artist had ever held before, nor, likely, will ever hold'.[4] This extraordinary encomium bears pondering.

Seidl was recognized as one of the leading conductors of the late nineteenth century. With his remote manner, Gothic features, and flowing hair, he was priestly, mysterious, charismatic. He was rumoured to be an atheist, and Liszt's illegitimate son. On the podium, according to Huneker, he 'riveted his men with a glance of steel'.[5] But it was his singular relationship to Wagner, the man and musician, that mainly accounted for the singular place Seidl held in the affections of the American public. In fact, he had materialized in the New World as Wagner's personal emissary.

He was born in Budapest in 1850. Hans Richter was one of his early mentors. Essentially, however, he was Wagner's own protégé. Between the ages of twenty-two and twenty-eight, he was a member of the Wahnfried household, a favourite of Cosima and the children.

For the first Bayreuth *Ring*, in 1876, he coached some of the principal singers, helped with the staging, and stood ready as Richter's *de facto* understudy. Subsequently, as conductor of Angelo Neumann's touring Wagner ensemble, he introduced the *Ring* to Central Europe and also to England.

Wagner himself reportedly advised Seidl to go to the New World. He arrived in 1885. At the Met, he presided over six German seasons — everything, including *Carmen* and *Aida*, was sung in German — that were among the most remarkable in the company's history. The ensemble of 1885-91 arguably surpassed that of any company in Germany or Austria. Seidl would conduct three and four times a week. During one 1889 stretch, Lilli Lehmann sang all three Brünnhildes in the space of six days, plus Rachel in *La Juive*. The entire undertaking was consumed by an infectious energy and idealism.

And yet the most profound impression was made less by the performances than by the operas themselves. Wagner dominated the repertory: 280 of the company's 490 performances were of Wagnerian music dramas. *Tristan, Die Meistersinger, Das Rheingold, Siegfried*, and *Götterdämmerung* received their American premieres between 1886 and 1889, all under Seidl's baton.[6] In the summers, Seidl would conduct *fourteen* times a week at Coney Island's Brighton Beach resort: on Wagner nights, the three-thousand-seat seashore pavilion would be filled to capacity.[7] And Seidl took Wagner on tour: to Utica and Rochester, Dayton and Cincinnati, St Louis and Peoria.

Not the least remarkable aspect of this enterprise was its reception. The Wagner acolytes read books and libretti. They attended classes and lectures. Especially for wives whose husbands were away making money and whose own professional possibilities were suppressed by Gilded Age mores, Sieglinde's ecstatic pregnancy and Isolde's orgasmic love-death became necessary opportunities for intense emotional release.[8] At the Met, the ladies were in love with Seidl; according to the *Musical Courier*, 'Middle-aged women in their enthusiasm stood up in the chairs and screamed their delight . . . for what seemed hours'.[9] The Wagner cult dominated America's musical high culture and pervaded its intellectual life. No wonder Seidl's death was experienced as an American calamity.

The implausible speed and magnitude of Seidl's American impact become plausible when seen in relation to what had gone before. America was avidly acquainted with Wagner, but mainly as a concert composer. He was esteemed as a musical dramatist, but most often encountered via disembodied orchestral extracts. America's flourishing operatic culture was predominantly Italian. German opera remained a sporadic or provincial presence.

The leading Wagner conductors were Theodore Thomas and Leopold Damrosch. Thomas mistrusted the theatre. Damrosch's allegiance to the Music of the Future was more consuming. He attended the 1876 Bayreuth *Ring*. Eight years later, at the Met, he eagerly descended from the concert platform to the opera pit. He rehearsed his first *Walküre*, a labour of love, for a period of months.

Seidl, at thirty-five, was already a seasoned opera conductor. Unlike Thomas or Damrosch, he was also a superb pianist, accustomed to coaching Wagner's own singers. He had helped prepare the Bayreuth *Ring* Damrosch attended. He had led *Die Walküre* and the other *Ring* operas dozens of times.

Much as fledgling painters visit museums to copy masterpieces, fledgling conductors and composers benefit from copying the orchestral scores of a master. The activity of inking every string figuration, every clarinet note, every accent and crescendo is a learning experience more painstaking and permanent than any afforded by the scanning ear or eye. Seidl had spent years copying full scores and parts for Wagner, sewing every strand of the complex sonic tapestry. At the keyboard, he had played and sung at Wagner's side, absorbing a second imprint, in performance, of the music he had written out.

'He gave us a new Wagner — the real Wagner', wrote Huneker. 'We all thought we knew [*Lohengrin*] perfectly well', testified another listener, 'and yet . . . many of us were greatly puzzled. Not alone were the climaxes built up in a strange manner, the *melos* brought out in a more plastic fashion, and a hundred lovely poetic details supplied that were formerly missing, but the opera . . . sounded differently'.[10] This formula of praise — the familiar made new — is so abused today that only with difficulty can we recapture its literal meaning. When we think of *Lohengrin*, we refer to conventions of interpretation culled from myriad broadcasts, recordings, and live performances — to a binding mainstream experience of the work. In 1885, when Seidl first led *Lohengrin* at the Met, those in the audience who had heard it had most likely heard only one or two others conduct it. And those conductors would themselves seldom have encountered *Lohengrin* as listeners. In 1885, different *Lohengrin* readings *were* likely to sound completely different.

And Seidl was different — not a nervous musician, like Damrosch, or stoically placid, like Thomas. He was poised and mysterious, undemonstrative and impassioned, attractive and remote. Huneker wrote: 'His eyes alone were eloquent when his other features were sphinx-like — brown, almost black . . . . It was the eye omniscient'.[11]

'Magnetic' and 'electric' are two adjectives that recur in reviews of Seidl at the Met. Three other general attributes of his conducting bear stressing. First, he was a man of the theatre. He knew all the vocal parts and all the words. He maintained eye contact with the singers. He worried over every detail of the staging. He harmonized voice and orchestra. Lilli Lehmann considered him 'a leader of singers, who felt and breathed with them'. According to Edouard and Jean de Reszke, he possessed

> an instinct which is indeed rare among orchestral conductors of the modern school; he understood singing, seemed to know by intuition exactly what the singer would do in every case and always helped him to do it well. But he did not accomplish this by following the singer slavishly. There are many conductors who can follow a singer in a ritardando such as singers love to make at the close of a musical phrase, but there are few who know exactly how to catch up the rhythm again and restore the equilibrium, as Seidl did, without apparently affecting the shape of the musical period in the least.[12]

A second predominant attribute of Seidl's conducting — and a necessary condition of the first — was fluidity. He did not beat a steady pulse. 'Herr Seidl not only attends to every mark of shading and expression with a watchful eye', wrote Henry T. Finck, 'but he indulges in various minute modifications of tempo, which are indicated by the emotional character of the music; and this it is that gives so much life and meaning to his "reading" of a score'.[13]

Third, Seidl was a master of climax, a calibrator of harmonic and structural stress who preferred paragraphs to other conductors' words and sentences. According to the *Musical Courier,* 'No conductor that we have ever heard could build up such ... overpowering, such thrilling altitudes of tone. His breadth ... was no less wonderful. With him there was the abiding sense of foundational security; his accelerandos were never feverish, a calm logic prevailed from the first bar to the last, yet he was a master of the whirlwind and rose it with a repose that was almost appalling'. Henry Krehbiel confirmed: 'The more furious the tempest of passion which he worked up, the more firmly did he hold the forces in rein until the moment arrived when they were to be loosed, so that all should be swept away in the mêlée'.[14]

The sum total was a new type of conductor of whom Seidl was America's first important exemplar (the second being Arthur Nikisch, who arrived in Boston in 1889). The apostle of the new type was Richard Wagner. In his essay *Über das Dirigieren* (On conducting, 1869), Wagner dismissed both the self-effacing time-beaters of his day and, on a higher level, the elegant Mendelssohn; in his brisk, polished Beethoven performances, with the Leipzig Gewandhaus Orchestra, Mendelssohn mistook his own discreet aesthetic for

'Beethovenian classicism'. The new podium type Wagner proph-
esied embodied Lisztian licence and charisma. With improvisatory
abandon, he would seize extremes of tempo and dynamics. For
Wagner, the 'pure Allegro' cannot be too fast; and the 'pure Adagio'
cannot be taken slowly enough: 'a rapt confidence . . . should reign
here; the languor of feeling grows to ecstasy'. 'Omnipresent tempo
modification' is ' a positive life principle in all our music'. Emotional
commitment dictates plasticity of pulse: different speeds for each
passing image or mood. 'Sustained tone', eschewing accented downbeats, is the basis for long-breathed phrasing. A deep subjectivity —
Germanic *Innigkeit* — correlates with the ebb and flow of harmonic
rhythm. In opera, the new conductor must equally be a man of the
stage.[15] In effect, the new conductor is Wagner himself. And his
prescriptions — which his essay applies to pieces by Bach, Beethoven
and Weber, as well as to *Die Meistersinger* — have the effect of
Wagnerizing all the music he touches.

This was Seidl's way. His Bach and Mozart were formidably Romantic. His Beethoven shifted speeds. In the Eighth Symphony he
followed Wagner's instructions, in *On Conducting*, to accelerate the
second movement and slow down the third. These impressions, from
written accounts, are reinforced by Seidl's own essay, 'On Conducting', published in 1895.[16]

As Wagner was an intuitive, not a trained, conductor, Seidl begins
by asserting that conducting cannot be taught; it is 'a gift of God with
which few have been endowed in full measure'. The only worthwhile
readings on the subject are by Wagner and Berlioz. 'Most of you',
Seidl instructs gifted novices, are 'too exclusively musicians'. His
detailed admonitions on 'blending the scenic action with the music
and song' are not only informative but discouragingly timely. Every
contemporary Wagnerite can cite the abuses of stage directors —
literalists and non-literalists alike — who do not hear what the music
says. Far more than is generally appreciated, Wagner's orchestra
precisely dictates gesture and movement. Wagner once provided a
performance manual for the Dutchman's monologue, 'Die Frist ist
um', including such instructions as:

> During the deep trumpet notes . . . he has come off board . . . ; his
> rolling gait, proper to seafolk on first treading dry land after a long
> voyage, is accompanied by a wavelike figure for the violas and
> cellos: with the first crotchet of the third bar he makes his second
> step. . . . With the tremolo of the violins at the fifth bar he raises his
> face to heaven, his body still bent low: with the entry of the muffled
> roll of the kettledrum at the ninth bar of the postlude he begins to
> shudder. . . . Only at the passage marked *piano* . . . does he gradu-

ally relax his attitude; his arms fall down; at the four bars of *espressivo* for the first violins he slowly sinks his head, and during the last eight bars of the postlude he totters to the rock wall at the side. . . . I have discussed this scene at such length in order to show how I wish the Dutchman to be portrayed and what weight I place on the most careful adaptation of the action to the music.[17]

Seidl, in 'On Conducting', relates how Wagner rehearsed the movements of the Rhinemaidens, in the first scene of *Das Rheingold*, for six hours:

I learned to know the meaning of every phrase, every violin figure, every sixteenth note. I learned, too, how it was possible with the help of the picture and action to transform an apparently insignificant violin passage into an incident, and to lift a simple horn call into a thing of stupendous significance by means of scenic emphasis. . . . The swimming of the Rhine-daughters is carried out very well at most of the larger theatres, but the movements of the nixies do not illustrate the accompanying music. Frequently the fair one rises while a descending violin passage is playing, and again to the music of hurried upward passages she sinks gently to the bottom of the river. Neither is it a matter of indifference whether the movements of the Rhine-daughters be fast or slow. At a majority of the theatres this is treated as a matter of no consequence, regardless of the fact that the public are utterly bewildered by such contradictions between what they see and what they hear. Wagner often said to me, 'My dear friend, give your attention to the stage, following my scenic directions, and you will hit the right thing in the music without a question'.

A second example:

In the first scene of *Die Walküre* between Siegmund, Sieglinde and afterward Hunding, there are a great number of little interludes — dainty, simple, and melodic in manner. Now, if the conductor is unable to explain the meaning of these little interludes to the singers, he cannot associate them with the requisite gestures, changes of facial expression and even steps, and the scene is bound to make a painfully monotonous impression. No effect is possible here with the music alone.

A related priority: in shaping the music, always empathize with what the singers are expressing.

Look . . . to *Tristan und Isolde* for an example. A large space of time in the first act is occupied by Isolde and Brangaene, who are alone in the tent. A few motives are continually developed, but with what a variety must they be treated — surging up now stormily, impetuously; sinking back sadly, exhausted, anon threatening, then timid, now in eager haste, now reassuring! For such a variety of expression the few indications, ritardando, accelerando, and a tempo do not suffice; it is necessary to live through the action of the drama in order to make it all plain. The composer says, 'With variety' — a meagre injunction for the conductor. Therefore I add, 'Feel with the characters, ponder with them, experience with them all the devious outbursts of passion'.[18]

Seidl's ability to identify with his singers informs many pages of his essay. The orchestra must never overmatch the voices. Wagner 'was painfully anxious that every syllable of the singer should be heard'. 'How discouraging must be the effect upon an intelligent singer to feel that, in spite of every exertion, he is being drowned by the orchestra!' An orchestral forte is not the same as a vocal forte. There is no such thing as a single 'correct' tempo; different voices ask for different speeds. For that matter, there is no such thing as a single 'correct' reading: different conductors differently experience the same overture or symphony. With the composer, as with the singer, the conductor strives for empathy. This will not always occur. Theatres demand of their music director that he 'mount the funeral pyre tomorrow with Siegfried, and be incarcerated in a madhouse with Lucia the next day. I do not believe in such versatility; conductors are only human'.

In closing, Seidl pays homage to 'not only the mightiest of all musical geniuses, but also the greatest conductor that ever lived'. Wagner conducted with his body immobile, 'but his eyes glittered, glowed, pierced . . . and electric currents seemed to pass through the air to each individual musician'. All 'hung on his glance, and he seemed to see them all at one'. Here is Huneker on Seidl: 'His contrabassist, his concertmaster will tell you that he seemed to watch each and every man throughout a performance'. Here is Victor Herbert, one of Seidl's cellists at the Met and later an assistant conductor to Seidl at Coney Island: 'We always knew by a glance from his eye just what was expected of us'. Seidl's composed gestures, like Wagner's, registered a volcano of feeling. He often wept while conducting. His usual expression, according to Henry Finck, was of 'impassioned serenity'. Krehbiel said Seidl 'was transfigured when he conducted *Parsifal* or *Tristan und Isolde*'. Finck called him 'the most emotional conductor that ever lived'.[19]

Every iota of evidence — from Wagner's essay and Seidl's, from descriptions and reviews, from the recordings of turn-of-the-century conductors like Nikisch — suggests that Seidl was more mercurial, more prone to pervasive rubato than any conductor we are likely to encounter today. 'Tempo modification' was a principle with him. At the same time, he was, as Krehbiel put it, 'an empiric'. 'He had no patience with theories, but a wondrous love for experiences. In him, impulse dominated reflection, emotion shamed logic. . . . With him in the chair, it was only the most case-hardened critic who could think of comparative tempi and discriminate between means of effect. As for the rest, professional and layman, dilettante and ignorant, their souls were his to play with.'[20]

Among the most appreciated aspects of the Met's German seasons was the espousal of opera as theatre. The stagings were admittedly flawed. But the company included, at its core, a group of bona fide singing actors. Intellectuals of the Gilded Age looked to Germany for clean streets and prompt trains, science and medicine, philosophy and *Kultur*. They revered Beethoven. They deplored 'fashionable' grand opera: Bellini and Meyerbeer, Patti and Christine Nilsson. They advocated the Wagnerian *Gesamtkunstwerk*.

During the Seidl years, singers like Marianne Brandt seemingly displaced glamorous warblers as New York's favourites. Brandt's Met début, on 19 November 1884, was as Beethoven's Leonore. Krehbiel wrote: 'On its musical side her performance was thrillingly effective, but on its histrionic it rose to grandeur. Every word of her few speeches, every note of her songs, every look of her eyes and expression of her face was an exposition of that world of tenderness which filled the heart of Leonore. . . . There was nothing of the petty theatrical in Fräulein Brandt'.[21]

Nine days later, signalling the company's ensemble spirit, Brandt took the tiny role of Hedwige in Rossini's *Guillaume Tell*. The following January Amalie Materna made her American stage début as Elisabeth in *Tannhäuser*. She performed, one reviewer marvelled, 'like a play actress'.[22] Lilli Lehmann succeeded Materna as the Met's principal soprano. Like Brandt and Materna, she had worked with Wagner in Bayreuth. Wagner insisted that his singers act. He urged the eradication of stereotypical gestures and attitudes. He made his singers gesticulate meaningfully or — even more difficult — stand absolutely still. In New York Lehmann's histrionic gift was hailed as art concealing art.

The most admired singing actor in the Met's German ensemble, however, was Albert Niemann, who sang Tannhäuser, Lohengrin, Siegmund, Siegfried, and Tristan. Niemann made his New York début in *Die Walküre* — the opera he had prepared for Wagner at Bayreuth — on 10 November 1886, at the age of fifty-five. Krehbiel (with Huneker and William J. Henderson, New York's most distinguished music critic during its most distinguished period of music criticism) left an unforgettable account which shows that Niemann's delivery — of 'Wess' Herd dies auch sei'; of 'Winterstürme' — differed from that of present-day Siegmunds:

> Those who go to see and hear Herr Niemann must go to see and hear him as the representative of the character that he enacts. . . . The first claim to admiration which [he] puts forth is based on the intensely vivid and harmonious picture of the Volsung which he brings to the stage. There is scarcely one of the theatrical conventions which the public have been accustomed to accept that he employs. He takes possession of the stage like an elemental force. . . . His attitude and gestures all seem parts of Wagner's creation. . . . When he staggers into Hunding's hut and falls upon the bearskin beside the hearth a thrill passes through the observer. Part of his story is already told, and it is repeated with electrifying eloquence in the few words that he utters when his limbs refuse their office. The voice is as weary as the exhausted body. In the picturesque side of his impersonation he is aided by the physical gifts with which nature has generously endowed him. The figure is colossal; the head, like 'the front of Jove himself'; the eyes large and full of luminous light, that seems to dart through the tangled and matted hair that conceals the greater portion of his face. The fate for which he has been marked out has set its seal in the heroic melancholy which is never absent even in his finest frenzies . . . .
>
> Herr Niemann's treatment of Wagner's musical and literary text . . . is, like the drama itself, an exposition of the German esthetic ideal: strength before beauty. It puts truthful declamation before beautiful tone production in his singing and lifts dramatic color above what is generally considered essential musical color. That from this a new beauty results all those can testify who hear Herr Niemann sing the love song in the first act of 'Die Walküre', which had previously in America been presented only as a lyrical effusion and given with more or less sweetness and sentimentality. Herr Niemann was the first representative of the character who made this passage an eager, vital, and personal expression of a mood so ecstatic that it resorts to symbolism, as if there was no other language for it. The charm with which he invests the poetry of this song . . . can only be appreciated by one who is on intimate terms with the German language, but the dramatic effect attained by his use of tone color and his marvelous distinctness of enunciation all can feel.[23]

The following February Niemann gave his apparent 'farewell performance' opposite Lehmann in *Tristan und Isolde*. The house was sold out by speculators at prices six times the norm. It included delegations from Boston, Philadelphia, and Cincinnati. Krehbiel reported:

> Herr Niemann husbanded his vocal resources in the first act, but after that both he and Fräulein Lehmann threw themselves into the work with utter abandon. . . . After two recalls had followed the second fall of the curtain a third round was swelled by a fanfare from the orchestra. To acknowledge this round Herr Niemann came forward alone, and was greeted with cheers, while a laurel wreath, bearing on one of its ribbons the line from Tannhäuser 'O, kehr zurück, du kühner Sänger', was handed up to him. The third act wrought the enthusiasm to a climax. After the curtain had been raised over and over again, Herr Niemann came forward and said, in German: 'I regret exceedingly that I am not able to tell you in your own language how sincerely I appreciate your kindness toward me. I thank you heartily, and would like to say Auf Wiedersehn'.[24]

In fact, Niemann returned to the Met the following season. A dozen years before, he had prepared the *Götterdämmerung* Siegfried in the hope of singing it at Bayreuth in 1876 — but Wagner did not want his Siegmund enacting another part. In New York Niemann prepared the role with Seidl. Krehbiel, as ever, was there: 'I chanced one evening to be a witness of his study hour — the strangest one I ever saw. It was at the conductor's lodgings in the opera house. There was a pianoforte in the room, but it was closed. The two men sat at a table with the open score before them. Seidl beat time to the inaudible orchestral music, and Niemann sang sans support of any kind. Then would come discussion of readings, markings of cues, etc., all with indescribable gravity, while Frau Seidl-Krauss . . . sat sewing in a corner'. And so Niemann was Seidl's Siegfried for the first American *Götterdämmerung*, on 25 January 1888. Lehmann was the Brünnhilde, Emil Fischer the Hagen. Brandt sang the Rhinemaiden Wellgunde.[25]

In one respect, Krehbiel's description of Niemann's Siegmund was atypical. Unlike the reviews one reads in newspapers today, most Wagner reviews in the New York press a hundred years ago were not primarily reviews of performances. Niemann and Lehmann were famous singers. Seidl was a famous conductor. But their contributions were allotted a sentence or two, versus many long paragraphs about the contributions of the composer. Krehbiel and other Gilded Age critics pondered Wagner's life story and personality, his writings, his librettos, his music — all of which was made to seem not esoteric or 'difficult', but timely and urgent.

Tannhäuser, for instance, was the first Wagner opera to be staged in America — the performance took place in the German-language Stadt-theater, on the Bowery in lower Manhattan, on 4 April 1859. The musical language — its charged chromaticism and robust orchestration — seemed daring and new. The grave speeches and weighty themes of the drama were likened to Shakespeare. 'The general idea is the struggle between the pleasure of the senses and the conviction of faith', commented the *New York Post.* 'It is but a romanticized epitome of the similar trials in every day real life'.[26] The conflict between sacred and profane seemed neither quaint nor abstract.

In the following decades, *Tannhäuser* migrated uptown from the German-American ghetto (where operagoers drank beer and ate sausages) to the fashionable Metropolitan Opera — from an immigrant milieu to the cultural mainstream. But long before *Tannhäuser* attained the Met, the *Tannhäuser* Overture attained an amazing popularity. American concert (and band) programmes of the late nineteenth century suggest that it may have been the most familiar work in the symphonic repertory. It was unquestionably Wagner's most familiar work — his Gilded Age signature. A moment's thought suggests the reason.

The overture begins with a prayer: the Pilgrims' Chorus. This becomes one polarity in a musical dialectic. Its antithesis is the Venusberg music, whose erotic maelstrom stunned its first listeners. One 1890 New York review called the *Tannhäuser* Bacchanale 'beyond comparison the most intoxicating piece . . . ever composed . . . ; if an abstainer wants to realize the voluptuous dreams of an Oriental opium-smoker, he may have the experience without bad after-effects by simply listening to this ballet music'.[27] The story of the *Tannhäuser* Overture is the story of the pilgrims and intoxicants locked in mortal combat — until the latter recede, and the former return in blazing triumph. It is a story simpler and more comforting than the story of the opera — not to mention the story of the *Tristan* Prelude, or of *Tristan und Isolde.*

And this was a microcosm of the whole. In the United States, the cult of Wagner did not, as in Europe, herald an iconoclastic modernism; there were no American decadents or Symbolists poised to discover avant-garde aspects of Wagnerism. Rather, to a remarkable degree, Wagnerism was absorbed within the dominant 'genteel tradition'. Like the *Tannhäuser* Overture, Wagner was meaningful, titillating, and, ultimately, reassuring. He stirred powerful and neglected feelings, yet left 'no bad after-effects'. He was found not to challenge but to reinforce the intellectual mainstream.

In this regard, Francis Hueffer, a German-born scholar who moved to London in 1869, was influential on both sides of the Atlantic. His article 'Richard Wagner', in the November 1874 *Century* magazine (a genteel intellectual beacon), illustrates the resourcefulness with which Wagnerites simplified and reconstituted their hero. Wagner, Hueffer stressed, 'is not negative only' — he was less a rebel than a progressive reformer, embodying 'character' (a genteel codeword for moral rectitude) as well as genius. 'He has overthrown much, but his reconstructions are vaster and more harmonious than the old fabric'. Had Wagner been born to a higher station, he might have made a 'great statesman'. Rather, copying a quintessential New World scenario, his life was struggle, his success hard-earned. Beethoven was 'the load-star of our master's early aspirations'. His political activism was an outgrowth of early discouragements, of a 'morbid despondency, in which change at any price seemed a relief. In this mood, and more from a sense of antagonism to things existing than from any distinct political persuasion', Wagner took an active part in the revolutionary risings of 1848 and 1849. Anyway, that revolt was no nihilistic deviation, but a 'dream of liberty'.

Elsewhere in the article, Hueffer dispenses with special pleadings in favour of canny omission and association. His synopsis of *Tristan und Isolde*, for instance, is confined to Act I — evading the carnal second act and the suicidal eroticism of Act III. The disturbing fatality of the love potion is cleverly soft-pedalled: it is a 'symbol of irresistible love, which, to speak with the Psalmist, is "strong as death" and knows no fetter'. The whole of *Tristan*, moreover, closely follows a respectable medieval source: Gottfried von Straßburg's 'immortal epic'.

Other Wagnerites extolled the entrepreneurial prowess of Wagner's Bayreuth project. If praise of Wagner the democratic zealot, self-made man, and Yankee businessman slanted the truth, other components of Wagner's agenda completely supported Gilded Age mores. Like Krehbiel and other earnest Germanophiles, Wagner made art a religion. Like the genteel critics of industrial capitalism, he inveighed against decadent aristocrats, greedy materialists, and depraved utilitarians. He preached uplift: new social vision, new spiritual awareness. No less than Ralph Waldo Emerson or John Sullivan Dwight, he perceived himself as a cultural missionary embattled by philistines. This is why, compared to subsequent generations of American Wagnerites, Americans of the Gilded Age were predisposed to listen to what Wagner was saying; even before they knew him as a musician, they took him seriously as a thinker.[28]

Seidl's death in 1898 left a vacuum. It terminated his flourishing eight-year tenure with the New York Philharmonic, where his predecessors, Carl Bergmann and Theodore Thomas, were also in their day the leading American Wagner conductors. At the Metropolitan

Opera, Seidl's German seasons had ended seven years before, to be replaced by star-studded Italian and French performances preferred by the boxholders. But Seidl was retained to conduct Wagner. With his passing, the Met's German wing lacked charismatic leadership until the arrival of Gustav Mahler in January 1908, and of his successor Arturo Toscanini ten months later. By the First World War, the Wagner cult — like the genteel tradition that absorbed it — had greatly dissipated; wartime Germanophobia finished it off.

The post-Seidl Wagner revival fostered by Mahler and Toscanini deserves a footnote — partly because it calibrates the impact of what had gone before. In Italian opera, Toscanini galvanized New York. In Wagner, he seemed amazingly adept — for an Italian. During his American heyday of the 1930s, 1940s, and 1950s, he would be hailed as the greatest of all Wagnerians. This, however, was not the opinion of pre-1914 critics who had heard Wagner led by Seidl, Mahler, Nikisch, Muck, Weingartner, and Mottl in New York and Boston. Huneker wrote of Toscanini's 'poetically intense' *Tristan* with Olive Fremstad: 'Toscanini is a superman. . . . He does not always achieve the ultimate heights as did Seidl, as does Arthur Nikisch. While his interpretation of *Tristan* is a wonderfully worked-out musical picture, yet the elemental ground-swell, which Anton Seidl summoned from the vasty deep, is missing.'[29]

Mahler's Wagner at the Met was received with less qualified admiration. And yet Mahler was embattled in New York. His nemesis was Krehbiel, who resented Mahler's arrogance. Money had lured Mahler to America: he needed more of it to reserve his European summers for composing. Krehbiel remembered Seidl, who became an American citizen and summered in New York's Catskill Mountains; who befriended the Amerian composer and made the Met a Wagner shrine.[30] Mahler, who did not care about New York's previous musical life, intended to reform German opera at the Metropolitan. He would make the New York Philharmonic as good as the best European orchestras. He vowed he would 'educate' its public.[31]

When Mahler died in 1911, Krehbiel wrote: 'He was paid a sum of money which ought to have seemed to him fabulous [but] the investment was a poor one. . . . He was looked upon as a great artist, and possibly he was one, but he failed to convince the people of New York'.[32] If this infamous obituary (which ran for fifty inches in the *New York Tribune*) revealed an American chauvinism, its provocation was the chauvinism of a visiting European. Its unstated frame of reference was the Wagner cult whose lingering impact it gauged.

Notes

The following abbreviations are used in the annotation:

BB   *Das Braune Buch: Tagebuchaufzeich-nungen, 1865–1882*, ed. Joachim Bergfeld (Zurich/Freiberg 1975); translated by George Bird as *The Diary of Richard Wagner: The Brown Book* (London 1980)

CT   *Cosima Wagner: Die Tagebücher, 1869–1883*, 2 vols., ed. Martin Gregor-Dellin and Dietrich Mack (Munich/Zurich 1976–7); translated by Geoffrey Skelton as *Cosima Wagner's Diaries* (London/New York 1978–80)

GS   Richard Wagner, *Gesammelte Schriften und Dichtungen*, 10 vols., 2d ed. (Leipzig 1887–8)

ML   Richard Wagner, *Mein Leben*, ed. Martin Gregor-Dellin (Munich 1976); translated by Andrew Gray as *My Life* (Cambridge 1983)

·PW   *Richard Wagner's Prose Works*, edited and translated by William Ashton Ellis, 8 vols. (London 1891–99, Repr. 1972). References to Ellis have been included for orientational purposes, although his translations have generally been edited and, in many cases, completely rewritten for the purposes of the present volume.

SB   Richard Wagner, *Sämtliche Briefe*, ed. Gertrud Strobel and Werner Wolf (vols. I–IV), Hans-Joachim Bauer and Johannes Forner (vols. VI–VIII) (Leipzig 1967–91)

SS   Richard Wagner, *Sämtliche Schriften und Dichtungen*, 16 vols. (Leipzig [1911–16])

SW   Richard Wagner, *Sämtliche Werke*, ed. Carl Dahlhaus and Egon Voss, 31 vols. (Mainz 1970–)

WWV   *Verzeichnis der musikalischen Werke Richard Wagners und ihrer Quellen*, ed. John Deathridge, Martin Geck, and Egon Voss (Mainz 1986)

Chapter 1   Conducting Wagner

1   *Musical Times*, xxiii (1882), 324. Nicholas Kenyon in the *Observer*, 14 Jan. 1990.

2   Hans Richter's diary entry for 9 May 1877 (unpublished).

3   G. B. Shaw, 6 June 1877, *How to Become a Musical Critic* (London 1960), 24.

4   Shaw in *The Dramatic Review*, 8 Feb. 1885; repr. in *How to Become A Musical Critic*, 52.

5   The orchestra's wind section had refused to play an encore of Siegfried's Funeral March because they had to save their energy for a performance later that evening of Meyerbeer's *L'Africaine*.

6   S. Bachrich, *Aus verklungenen Zeiten* (Vienna 1914), 47–48.

7   Richter wrote in his *Dirigierbuch*

(conducting book) on 15 December 1875, 'Lohengrin unter Anwesenheit und Direction des Meisters', with 'und Direction' crossed out. Wagner had declined to conduct and instructed Richter, now Kapellmeister in Vienna, to do so instead.

8   Joseph Sulzer, *Erinnerungen eines Wiener Philharmonikers* (Vienna 1910), 27.

9   *Felix Mottls Tagebuchaufzeichnungen aus den Jahren 1873–76*, ed. Willy Krienitz (Neue Wagner-Forschungen) (Bayreuth 1943), 188–96.

10 Shaw, 'Wagner in Bayreuth', *English Illustrated Magazine* (Oct. 1889), 11–12.

11 Richard Sternfeld, 'Hans Richter's letzte Rede', *Allgemeine Musik-Zeitung* (29 Dec. 1916), 744–45.

12 Victor Schnitzler, *Aus meinem Leben* (Cologne 1935), 123–24.

13 Ibid.

14 Charles Villiers Stanford, *Interludes, Records and Reflections* (London 1922), 30–31.

15 'Richter and the First English *Ring*', *Musical Times*, xcii (1951), 262–63.

16 Adrian Boult, *Thoughts on Conducting* (London 1963), x.

17 *Mottls Tagebuchaufzeichnungen* (note 9), 180.

18 Shaw, 25 April 1894, *Music in London*, III (London 1932), 195.

19 Ibid.

20 Boult, *My Own Trumpet* (London 1973), 37.

21 Boult, *Thoughts on Conducting* (note 16), xii.

22 Harold C. Schonberg, *The Great Conductors* (London 1967), 212.

23 Richard Aldrich, *Concert Life in New York, 1902–23* (New York 1941), 365.

24 Anton Seidl, 'Über das Dirigieren', *Bayreuther Blätter*, xxiii (1900), 291.

25 H. T. Finck, *My Adventures in the Golden Age of Music* (New York/London 1926), 199.

26 Ibid.

27 Ibid., 200.

28 Felix Weingartner, *Lebenserinnerungen* (Zurich 1923), 308.

29 Schonberg (note 22), 221.

30 Frida Leider, *Playing My Part*, trans. Charles Osborne (London 1966), 98.

31 Natalie Bauer-Lechner, *Recollections of Gustav Mahler* (London 1980), 109.

32 Ernst Lert, 'The Conductor Gustav Mahler', *Journal of the Conductors' Guild*, i (1980), no. 3, p. 5.

33 Schonberg (note 22), 225.

34 Bauer-Lechner (note 31), 92.

35 Ibid., 91.

36 Schonberg (note 22), 245.

37 Christopher Dyment, *Felix Weingartner: Recollections and Recordings* (Rickmansworth 1976), 64.

38 Josef Krips, 'Felix von Weingartner', *Hi-Fidelity* (December 1962), 48.

39 Wilhelm Furtwängler, *Notebooks*, trans. Shaun Whiteside (London 1989), 91.

40 Peter Heyworth, *Conversations with Klemperer* (London 1973), 92.

41 Leider (note 30), 135–36.

42 John Culshaw, *Ring Resounding* (London 1967), 45.

43 Schonberg (note 22), 257.

44 Lawrence Gilman, *Toscanini and Great Music* (New York 1938), 182–83.

45 Peter Heyworth, *Otto Klemperer: His Life and Times* (Cambridge 1983), 169 and 345.

46 Ibid., 283.

Chapter 2   Wagner and His Singers

1   Wagner's autobiographical account of hearing Schröder-Devrient in Leipzig in 1829 is probably an unconscious conflation of two different events: there is no record of her having sung the role in Leipzig in that year.

2   *GS* X, 298–99; *PW* VI, 304.

3   Lotte Lehmann, *Wings of Song* (London 1938), 77.

4   *GS* VIII, 178; *PW* IV, 228.

5   Richard Capell, 'Kirsten Flagstad', *The New Grove Dictionary of Music and Musicians* (London 1980) VI, 625.

Chapter 3   Producing Wagner

1   The word 'director' is currently used in most English-speaking countries outside the United Kingdom to mean the artist responsible for the creation of a stage production. Before 1950, however, in both Britain and the USA, a 'stage director' was a technically-orientated stage manager who had the added responsibility of co-ordinating (but rarely originating) the stage movements of a (largely unrehearsed) cast. In the 1990s several British opera companies still retain the word 'producer' for the director of an opera.

2   Typical of a composer's contemporary intervention in the working theatre is Wagner's account of rehearsing Ludwig Schnorr von Carolsfeld in *Tannhäuser* during a full run of an act with orchestra. See *BB* 162–65; English trans. 136–38.

3   '*Le Freischutz*' *GS* I, 220–40, esp. 229; English trans. from *Wagner Writes from Paris*, ed. and trans. Robert Jacobs and Geoffrey Skelton (London 1973), 138–55, esp. 146.

4   The first of eight or nine production books issued around the time of the premieres of Verdi's operas. The one for *Les Vêpres siciliennes* was 38 pages and fairly rudimentary, especially for the chorus; by 1887 the one for *Otello* had 111 pages, including 270 blocking diagrams.

5   *Franz Liszt – Richard Wagner: Briefwechsel*, ed. Hanjo Kesting (Frankfurt am Main 1988), 216 (letter of 2 May 1852).

6   *ML* 122; English trans. 113.

7   *SB* III, 390–93; English trans. from *Correspondence of Wagner and Liszt*. Translated into English, with a preface, by Francis Hueffer. Second edition revised by W. Ashton Ellis. 2 vols. (New York 1973), 94–97. In July 1850 Wagner had sent Liszt a lengthy list of detailed stage directions, including his own scenery sketches (wryly described as 'the most successful creations of my innermost

spirit'). Despite his keen championing of modern operas, Liszt was often considered to have little interest in their actual staging.

8   *SB* III, 394; English trans. (note 7), 97.

9   *GS* IV, 292; *PW* I, 337.

10   *GS* VII, 285–86 (*Das Wiener Hof-Operntheater*); *PW* III, 376–77.

11   *GS* V, 147 (*Über die Aufführung des 'Tannhäuser'*); *PW* III, 193.

12   *Richard Wagner und Albert Niemann*, ed. Wilhelm Altmann (Berlin 1924), 125–26; English trans. from *Selected Letters of Richard Wagner*, ed. and trans. Stewart Spencer and Barry Millington (London 1987), 511.

13   The cuts Wagner made in all three acts of the score for this production have (regrettably) become standard practice in many opera houses outside Bayreuth. It remains debatable whether or not he was merely being practical, having taken over the production so late. Also allowed were some transpositions in Act III and some word changes in Act I. And the opera was performed in *three* acts.

14   *BB* 165 (*Erinnerungen an Ludwig Schnorr*); English trans. 139.

15   Ibid.

16   Wagner came to like Hallwachs sufficiently to recommend him as producer for the Munich *Rheingold* premiere — while he was in agreement with its going ahead. Hallwachs also staged the Munich *Walküre*.

17   Angelo Neumann, *Erinnerungen an Richard Wagner*, 2d ed. (Leipzig 1907), 9–10; English trans. from *Personal Recollections of Wagner*, trans. Edith Livermore (London 1909), 9–10.

18   Richard Fricke, *Bayreuth vor dreißig Jahren* (Dresden 1906), 113 (entry of 1 July). Fricke's diary, reissued in Germany only in 1983, and translated by Stewart Spencer as 'Bayreuth in 1876' in *Wagner*, xi (1990), 93–109, 134–50 and xii (1991), 25–44, is the only realistic, close-quarters account of Wagner in rehearsal. He described the overblown rehearsal notes of Heinrich Porges (on

the Bayreuth music staff) and J. Zimmermann (editor of the *Bayreuther Tagblatt*) as 'inaccurate and superficial'.

19 Eduard Hanslick complained in his review of the Munich *Rheingold* premiere that everyone talked about 'swimming nixies, coloured steam, the castle of the gods and the rainbow' but 'only rarely about the music'. Quoted in Oswald Georg Bauer, *Richard Wagner: Die Bühnenwerke von der Uraufführung bis heute* (Frankfurt/Berlin/Vienna 1982), 206; translated by Stewart Spencer as *Richard Wagner: The Stage Designs and Productions from the Premieres to the Present* (New York 1983), 222.

20 Richard Fricke felt that Alberich's transformations into dragon and toad, and the rainbow bridge were the three greatest disasters of the whole *Ring* production.

21 Josef Hoffmann (from Vienna) designed the sets for the first Bayreuth *Ring*. He was a landscape painter with some experience of working in the theatre. Carl Emil Doepler (from Berlin) designed the costumes. Wagner's and Cosima's approaches to the noted Swiss painter Arnold Böcklin produced only one sketch for the dragon in *Siegfried*. (See Martina Srocke, *Richard Wagner als Regisseur* [Munich/Salzburg 1988], 28–29.) Cosima approached Böcklin again — together with the costume painter Rudolf Seitz and the architect and painter Camillo Sitte — for *Parsifal*, but only Seitz produced some sketches, which Wagner rejected. He also rejected plans by the Munich Court Theatre designers Christian Jank and Heinrich Döll before settling on the untried Russian painter Paul von Joukowsky to design both sets and costumes for *Parsifal* under his (very close) supervision.

22 Letter from Malwida von Meysenbug to Emil Heckel (a leading fund-raiser for Bayreuth in 1876), quoted in Bauer (note 19), 212; English trans. 227.

23 Quoted in Bauer (note 19), 262; English trans. 275. One French critic later hailed this scene as 'the first symbolist set'.

24 In May 1881 Wagner praised Neumann for 'following consistently my new departures in stagecraft, and keeping at its height the spirit and integrity of my style': see Neumann (note 17), 165; English trans. 160. It should be remembered, however, that Wagner was more than glad to have his newest work kept in the public eye at this time and was grateful for the royalties it provided.

25 Cosima Wagner to Count Hermann Keyserling, quoted in *Cosima Wagner: Das zweite Leben*, ed. Dietrich Mack (Munich/Zurich 1980), 630. The letter was written partly to explain why Cosima could not find a use for the theories of Adolphe Appia at Bayreuth, despite pressure from her future son-in-law, Houston Stewart Chamberlain. But this famous rejection is a little more complicated than is generally known. Having at first suggested that Appia could perhaps find a career producing Shakespeare and Goethe — where there were no model stagings to follow — Cosima looked at his submitted costume sketches for *Tannhäuser*. She did not like them but went as far as to suggest, in October 1888, that Appia could perhaps become 'costume designer and lighting consultant for Bayreuth' (ibid., 166; letter to Chamberlain of 23 October 1888). Sadly, nothing came of this.

26 Quoted in Bauer (note 19), 227; English trans. 242.

27 Adolphe Appia, *Staging Wagnerian Drama* (Basel 1982), 48–50.

28 Quoted in Bauer (note 19), 143–44; English trans. 151–53.

29 According to Peter Heyworth (*Otto Klemperer: His Life and Times* [Cambridge 1983], the performances were based, at Richard Strauss's suggestion, on the score that Wagner used for the Berlin premiere of 1844.

30 Quoted in Heyworth (note 29) 281.
31 Tietjen's extraordinary career, involving no small amount of political 'trimming', encompassed the roles of intendant of the Berlin State Theatres, intendant of the Bayreuth Festival under Winifred Wagner (both in the 1930s and 1940s, during which time he conducted and recorded a great deal), and a later return to Wieland Wagner's Bayreuth to conduct some *Lohengrin* performances.
32 His *Parsifal* sets in 1937 had drawn a bitter letter (at sight unseen!) from his aunt, Daniela Thode, Bayreuth's one-time regular costume designer.
33 Wieland Wagner to Hans Knappertsbusch, letter of May 1951, quoted in Dietrich Mack, *Der Bayreuther Inszenierungsstil* (Munich 1976), 104. Wieland's often acrimonious debates with his senior conductor (whom he much respected) are worth an essay in themselves — their correspondence included an apparently serious offer to withdraw the *Parsifal* production entirely in favour of one that more respected his grandfather's wishes. For further explanation of Wieland's production, see his famous psychological schema 'The Parsifal Cross', first published in the 1951 Bayreuth *Festspielbuch*.
34 *GS* III, 270; *PW* II, 63.
35 Wieland Wagner, interview with *Die Welt am Sonntag*, 12 August 1956, quoted in Mack (note 33), 110.
36 This production was actually the first occasion on which Bayreuth played the score as one uninterrupted act. It also saw the most scholarly attempt to date to perform the score as it stood at the work's Dresden premiere.

Chapter 4 Designing Wagner

1 Eduard Hanslick, *Aus dem Opernleben der Gegenwart: Moderne Oper*, III (Berlin 1885), 324.

2 *GS* IX, 306; *PW* V, 303.
3 Quoted by Wieland Wagner in 'What Is "Faithful Representation"?', *Die Programmhefte der Bayreuther Festspiele 1967: III — 'Tannhäuser'*, 24.
4 Illuminating eye-witness accounts of Wagner's stage practice include Richard Fricke, *Bayreuth vor dreißig Jahren* (Dresden 1906), reprinted as *1876: Richard Wagner auf der Probe* (Stuttgart 1983), translated by Stewart Spencer as 'Bayreuth in 1876' in *Wagner*, xi (1990), 93–109, 134–50 and xii (1991), 25–44; and Heinrich Porges, *Die Bühnenproben zu den Bayreuther Festspielen des Jahres 1876* (Chemnitz/Leipzig 1881–96), translated by Robert L. Jacobs as *Wagner Rehearsing the 'Ring'* (Cambridge 1983); see also Martina Srocke, *Richard Wagner als Regisseur* (Munich/Salzburg 1988).
5 Quoted by Oswald Georg Bauer, *Richard Wagner: Die Bühnenwerke von der Uraufführung bis heute* (Frankfurt/Berlin/Vienna 1982), 220; translated by Stewart Spencer as *Richard Wagner: The Stage Designs and Productions from the Premieres to the Present* (New York 1983), 237.
6 A collected edition of Appia's writings is in progress: *Oeuvres complètes*, ed. Marie-L. Bablet-Hahn (Lausanne 1983–). Valuable material in English includes *Essays, Scenarios, and Designs*, trans. Walther R. Volbach, ed. Richard C. Beacham (Ann Arbor 1989); Walter Volbach, *Adolphe Appia: Prophet of the Modern Theatre* (Middletown, Conn., 1968); and Richard C. Beacham, *Adolphe Appia: Theatre Artist* (Cambridge 1987).
7 Theatersammlung, Österreichische Nationalbibliothek, Vienna.
8 Quoted in Bauer (note 5), 52; English trans. 56.
9 Quoted in Bauer (note 5), 234; English trans. 248; for an English translation of Emil Preetorius's *Wagner: Bild und Vision* (1942), see *Wagner*, xii (1991), 75–86.
10 Although Felsenstein had directed

Wagner previously (*Die Meistersinger von Nürnberg*, Basel 1927; *Parsifal*, Basel 1928 and Cologne 1933; *Rienzi*, Cologne 1932; and *Tannhäuser*, Frankfurt 1934 and Aachen 1943), he never did so at the Komische Oper.

11 Wieland Wagner (note 3), *passim*.

12 Quoted in Geoffrey Skelton, *Wieland Wagner: The Positive Sceptic* (London 1971), 132.

13 Quoted by Joseph Horowitz, 'Of Swimming and Dancing: Staging Wagner's *Ring*', *Opus* (April 1987), 17.

14 Mike Ashman reports that Goodall preferred Götz Friedrich's staging for Covent Garden.

15 Peter Sykora, 'The Spatial Concept' in programme book for 1989 production of *Die Walküre* at the Royal Opera House, Covent Garden, London.

Chapter 5   'Fidelity' to Wagner

1 See Nicholas Kenyon (ed.), *Authenticity and Early Music* (Oxford 1988).

2 Oswald Georg Bauer (ed.), *Bayreuth 1977: Rückblick und Vorschau* (Bayreuth 1976), unnumbered pages.

3 Pierre Boulez, Patrice Chéreau, and Carlo Schmid, 'Mythologie et idéologie: Echange de vues sur la mise en scène de la Tétralogie en 1976' in *Die Programmhefte der Bayreuther Festspiele 1977: IV — 'Das Rheingold'*, 1–23 and 104–10, esp. 1.

4 E. Bouillon, *Le Ring à Bayreuth: La Tétralogie du Centenaire* (Paris 1980), 158.

5 Ibid., 218.

6 Ibid., 111–12.

7 'Mythologie'(note 3), 9.

8 Bouillon (note 4), 107.

9 Ibid., 108.

10 I have published two works on this subject: 'La Trahison de Chéreau' in *Musique en jeu*, xxxi (1978), 85–110, translated as 'Chéreau's Treachery' in *October*, xiv (1980), 71–100; and *Tétralogies (Wagner, Boulez,*

Chéreau): Essai sur l'infidélité (Paris 1983). The second part of the present article is based on pp. 19–21, 174–77, 234–46, 251–57, and 261–65 of *Tétralogies*, which still awaits an English translation. The semiological theory propounded in the first section of the present article is expounded at greater length in *Music and Discourse: Toward a Semiology of Music* (Princeton 1990). The present article is intended to complement the one published in 1980 and therefore avoids going over the same ground.

11 See my *Music and Discourse* (note 10), 153.

12 See 'Chéreau's Treachery' (note 10).

13 Pierre Boulez, Patrice Chéreau, Richard Peduzzi, and Jacques Schmidt, *Histoire d'un 'Ring': Bayreuth 1976–1980* (Paris 1980); translated into German as *Der 'Ring': Bayreuth 1976–1980* (Berlin/Hamburg 1980).

14 Ibid., 92.

15 Ibid.

16 Ibid., 61.

17 Quoted in Bouillon, (note 4), 321.

18 *Histoire d'un 'Ring'* (note 13), 54.

19 Ibid., 55.

20 Ibid., 51.

21 Ibid., 57.

22 Ibid., 55.

23 See my *Wagner androgyne* (Paris 1990), *passim*.

24 Heinrich Porges, *Die Bühnenproben zu den Bayreuther Festspielen des Jahres 1876* (Chemnitz/Leipzig 1881–96); translated by Robert L. Jacobs as *Wagner Rehearsing the 'Ring'* (Cambridge 1983), 49.

25 See 'Chéreau's Treachery' (note 10).

26 Quoted in Bouillon (note 4), 217.

27 Ibid., 203.

28 Ibid., 200.

29 Ibid., 212.

30 Ibid., 214.

31 Ibid., 198.

32 Patrice Chéreau, 'Commentaires sur "Mythologie et idéologie"' in *Die Programmhefte der Bayreuther Festspiele*

1977: VI— 'Siegfried', 17–19 and 86–102, esp. 96.

33 Quoted in Bouillon (note 4), 119.
34 Chéreau in *Histoire d'un 'Ring'* (note 13), 76.
35 Jean Matter, *Wagner et Hitler: Poète et penseur* (Paris 1977).
36 Pierre Boulez, Jeffrey Tate, and Jean–Jacques Nattiez, *Entretiens sur la Tétralogie du Centenaire* (Montreal 1982), 79–81.
37 Ibid., 190.
38 Pierre Boulez, *Penser la musique aujourd'hui* (Paris 1964), 99–100; translated by Susan Bradshaw and Richard Rodney Bennett as *Boulez on Music Today* (London 1971), 87–89.
39 Pierre Boulez, *Points de repère* (Paris 1981), 249; translated by Martin Cooper as *Orientations: Collected Writings* (London 1986), 271.
40 Ibid., 267; English trans. 253–54.
41 Ibid., 243; English trans. 266.
42 Ibid., 256; English trans. 277.
43 Said during a French television broadcast, *Apostrophes*, on Antenne 2, 18 September 1981.
44 *Entretiens sur la Tétralogie* (note 36), 191.
45 Ibid.
46 Ibid., 194.
47 Ibid., 194–96.
48 *Points de repère* (note 39), 312–23 and 388–402; English trans. 500–512 and 349–59.
49 Ibid., 237; English trans. 261.
50 *Histoire d'un 'Ring'* (note 13), 14.
51 Ibid., 16.
52 Interview in *Réalités*, No. 365 (July 1976).
53 Pierre Boulez, 'Commentaires sur "Mythologie et idéologie"' in *Die Programmhefte der Bayreuther Festspiele 1977: VI— 'Siegfried'*, 1–17, esp. 13.
54 Ibid., 14.
55 *Histoire d'un 'Ring'* (note 13), 96–97.
56 Quoted in Bouillon (note 4), 108.
57 Ibid., 333.
58 *Points de repère* (note 39), 272; English trans. 258.
59 Ibid., 16; see also Friedrich Nietzsche, *Sämtliche Werke: Kritische Studienausgabe in 15 Bänden*, ed. Giorgio Colli and Mazzino Montinari (Munich 1988), VI, 28; translated by Walter Kaufmann as 'The Case of Wagner' in *Basic Writings of Nietzsche* (New York 1968), 627.
60 *Entretiens sur la Tétralogie* (note 36), 80.
61 *Points de repère* (note 39), 514; English trans. 469–70.
62 *GS* VIII, 273; *PW* IV, 302.
63 *GS* VIII, 282, *PW* IV, 312.
64 *GS* VIII, 291; *PW* IV, 320.
65 *Points de repère* (note 39), 238; English trans. 262.
66 *Entretiens sur la Tétralogie* (note 36), 77.
67 *Penser la musique aujourd'hui* (note 38), 31; English trans. 32.
68 Erwin Panofsky, *Meaning in the Visual Arts* (Woodstock 1955), 35.
69 Carl Dahlhaus, *Grundlagen der Musikgeschichte* (Cologne 1977), esp. chap. 3; translated by J. B. Robinson as *Foundations of Music History* (Cambridge 1983).
70 Ibid., 69.
71 Ibid., 71.
72 Paul Veyne, *Comment on écrit l'histoire* (Paris 1971), 46–47; translated by Mina Moore-Rinvolucri as *Writing History* (Middletown, Conn., 1984), 32–33.
73 The idea that there is a distinction between the historical reconstruction proposed by the musicologist and the constraints of performance practice is also found in recent reflections by early-music specialists on the question of authenticity of interpretation: 'For the performer, what happens at the moment when the cautious conclusions of musicological enquiry have to be turned into action?' (Nicholas Kenyon, 'Authenticity and Early Music: Some Issues and Questions' in *Authenticity and Early Music* [note 1], 13).
74 In his contribution to *Authenticity and Early Music* (note 1), Gary Tomlinson arrives at an analogous position for early music: 'Since the meaning of a musical work does not

wholly reside in the work, it cannot be conveyed fully by means of performance. . . . The performer, in so far as he acts as performer and not as cultural historian, can only touch upon certain of these meanings' ('The Historian, the Performer, and Authentic Meaning in Music,' 122–23). Although I share this theoretical position, it remains to be explained why the feeling of fidelity or betrayal on the part of the spectator or critic cannot be circumvented, and why this problem will always have to be faced.

75 Edouard Sans, *Richard Wagner et la pensée schopenhauerienne* (Paris 1969).

Chapter 6   Performing Practice

1 *GS* VIII, 173 (*Bericht über eine in München zu errichtende deutsche Musikschule*); *PW* IV, 220–21.

2 *GS* I, 172 (*Der Virtuos und der Künstler*); *PW* VII, 114.

3 *GS* VIII, 283 (*Über das Dirigieren*); *PW* IV, 313.

4 *GS* V, 144 (*Über die Aufführung des 'Tannhäuser'*); *PW* III, 190–91.

5 SS XII, 151–204 (*Die Königliche Kapelle betreffend*).

6 *Allgemeine Musikalische Zeitung*, xlvii (1845), 97.

7 Ibid.

8 Preface to full score of *Tristan und Isolde* (Breitkopf & Härtel: Leipzig [1911], VII (this edition [Pl. No 25 000] was later taken over, unchanged, by Ernst Eulenburg, E.E. 6076).

9 Preface to full score of *Siegfried* (B. Schott's Söhne: Mainz [1901], V (this three-volume edition (Pl. No 27003, 27003a and 27003b) was later taken over, unchanged, in one volume by Ernst Eulenburg, E.E. 6120).

10 Preface to full score of *Tristan und Isolde*.

11 Quoted in François-Auguste Gevaert, *Nouveau traité d'instrumentation* (Paris/Brussels 1885), trans. by E. F. E. Suddard as *A New Treatise on*

Instrumentation (Paris/Brussels 1885), 296.

12 Ibid., 294–96.

13 Alexander J. Ellis, 'On the History of Musical Pitch', *Journal of the Society of Arts*, xviii (1880), 329.

14 Joseph Joachim and Andreas Moser, *Violinschule* (Berlin 1902–05), II, 96a.

15 See Clive Brown, 'Bowing Styles, Vibrato and Portamento in Nineteenth-Century Violin Playing', *Proceedings of the Royal Musical Association*, cxiii (1988), 97–128.

16 Joachim (note 14), II, 96.

17 Charles-Auguste de Bériot, *Méthode de violon* (Mainz [1858]), 242.

18 Manuel García, *New Treatise on the Art of Singing* (London 1855), 66.

19 Carl Flesch, *Memoirs* (London 1957), 120.

20 *The Letters of Mozart and His Family*, ed. Emily Anderson, 3d ed. (London 1985), 552, letter to Leopold Mozart of 12 June 1778.

21 Heinrich Porges, *Die Bühnenproben zu den Bayreuther Festspielen des Jahres 1876* (Chemnitz/Leipzig 1881–96); translated by Robert L. Jacobs as *Wagner Rehearsing the 'Ring'* (Cambridge 1983), 109.

22 Ibid., 44.

23 García (note 18), 53.

24 Joachim (note 14), II, 92.

25 Nicola Vaccai, *Metodo pratico di canto italiano per camera* (London 1832), Lesson xiii.

26 *Caecilia*, vii (1828), 234.

27 *Allgemeine Musikalische Zeitung*, i (1798–99), 461.

28 *Allgemeine Musikalische Zeitung*, xiii (1811), 207.

29 Louis Spohr, *Violinschule* (Vienna 1832), 247.

30 See Louis Adam, *Méthode du piano du Conservatoire*, translated into German as *Pianoforteschule des Conservatoriums der Musik in Paris* (Bonn/Cologne 1802), II, 59; Albert Lavignac and Lionel de La Laurencie, *Encyclopédie de la musique et dictionnaire du Conservatoire*, Part II: 'Technique — Esthétique — Pédagogie' (Paris 1925), 335.

31 Heinrich Christoph Koch, *Musikalisches Lexikon, welches die theoretische und praktische Tonkunst, encyclopädisch bearbeitet, alle alten und neuen Kunstwörter erklärt, und die alten und neuen Instrumente beschrieben, enthält* (Frankfurt am Main 1802), 45; Georg Joseph Vogler, *Kuhrpfälzische Tonschule* (Mannheim 1778), 25; and Justin Heinrich Knecht, *Allgemeiner musikalischer Katechismus* (Biberbach 1803), 48. (A direct connection between Vogler's and Knecht's work is indicated by a review of the latter in *Allgemeine Musikalische Zeitung*, vii (1804–05), 802.)

32 Spohr (note 29).

33 G. F. Kogel, 'Vorbereitung' to full score of Marschner's *Hans Heiling* (Peters: Leipzig 1892).

34 *GS* V, 120 (*Gluck's Ouvertüre zu 'Iphigenia in Aulis'*); *PW* III, 164.

35 *Johannes Brahms Briefwechsel* (Berlin 1906–22), VI, 161–63.

36 *Richard Wagner: Sämtliche Werke*, vol. 30 (Dokumente zur Entstehung und ersten Aufführung des Bühnenweihfestspiels Parsifal), ed. Martin Geck and Egon Voss (Mainz 1970), 174.

37 *GS* X, 299 (*Das Bühnenweihfestspiel in Bayreuth 1882*); *PW* VI, 305.

38 Title-page of autograph of *Lohengrin*: see *WWV* 317.

39 Weimar, March 1856, reprinted in preface to vol. I of Collected Edition of Liszt's works, ed. F. Busoni, P. Raabe, et al. (Leipzig 1907–36).

40 Johann Nepomuk Hummel, *Ausführlich theoretisch-practische Anweisung zum Piano-forte Spiel* (Vienna 1828), III, 65.

41 García (note 18), 51.

42 *Neue Zeitschrift für Musik*, iv (1836), 129.

43 *GS* VIII, 287 (*Über das Dirigieren*); *PW* IV, 316.

44 *GS* VIII, 296; *PW* IV, 325.

45 *The Athenaeum*, xxviii (1855), 329.

46 *The Sunday Times*, 17 June 1855, p. 3.

47 Porges (note 21), 82.

48 *GS* V, 144 (*Über die Aufführung des 'Tannhäuser'*); *PW* III, 190.

49 *GS* I, 169 (*Der Virtuos und der Künstler*); *PW* VII, 111.

50 *GS* X, 96–97 (*Das Publikum in Zeit und Raum*); *PW* VI, 89–90.

Chapter 7   The Reception of Wagner in Vienna, 1860–1900

1 *ML* 755; English trans. 739.

2 *ML* 70; English trans. 62.

3 *GS* III, 172 (*Das Kunstwerk der Zukunft*); *PW* I, 207.

4 *ML* 70–71; English trans. 62–63.

5 *ML* 381; English trans. 367–68.

6 *ML* 657; English trans. 643.

7 *SB* VII, 56, letter to Liszt of 20(?) March 1855; *Correspondence of Wagner and Liszt*, translated by Francis Hueffer, 2d ed. revised by W. Ashton Ellis (New York 1973), II, 70.

8 See Theodor Helm, 'Fünfzig Jahre des Wiener Musiklebens', *Der Merker*, vi (1915), 171 and vii (1916), 685.

9 *Richard Wagners Briefe an Hans von Bülow*, ed. Daniela Thode (Jena 1916), 170–71; letter of 17 Dec. 1861; translation in *Wagner: A Documentary Study*, ed. Herbert Barth, Dietrich Mack, and Egon Voss (London 1975), 198. Wagner first talked of wanting a theatre of his own in a letter to Ernst Benedikt Kietz of 14 Sept. 1850 (*SB* III, 404–05; *Selected Letters of Richard Wagner*, trans. and ed. Stewart Spencer and Barry Millington [London 1987], 216–17).

10 *Friedrich Hebbel Säkular-Ausgabe 1813–1913* (Berlin n.d.), X, 317; translation in *Wagner: A Documentary Study* (note 9), 200.

11 See note 9.

12 *GS* VI, 272–73 and 280–81 (*Vorwort zur Herausgabe der Dichtung des Bühnenfestspieles 'Der Ring des Nibelungen'*); *PW* III, 274–75 and 281.

13 *SS* XVI, 41; translation in *Wagner: A Documentary Study* (note 9), 208.

14 *GS* VI, 273; *PW* III, 274.

15 *Bayreuther Briefe von Richard Wagner (1871–1883)*, ed. Carl Friedrich Glasenapp (Berlin/Leipzig 1907),

78–79, letter to Friedrich Feustel of 12 April 1872; translation in *Selected Letters of Richard Wagner* (note 9), 793.

16   *Richard Wagner an seine Künstler*, ed. Erich Kloss (Berlin/Leipzig 1908), 31, letter to Heinrich Porges of 6 Nov. 1872; translation in *Selected Letters of Richard Wagner* (note 9), 816.

17   Hans von Wolzogen, 'An unsere Leser', *Bayreuther Blätter*, iv (1881), 1.

18   Heinrich Porges, *Die Bühnenproben zu den Bayreuther Festspielen des Jahres 1876* (Chemnitz/Leipzig 1881–96), I, 3–4; translated by Robert L. Jacobs as *Wagner Rehearsing the 'Ring'* (Cambridge 1983), 1–2.

19   See, for example, the articles on Robert Franz's lieder, 'Richard Wagner über deutsche Lyrik und Robert Franz', *Bayreuther Blätter*, xiii (1890), 190–91 and Heinrich Schuster, 'Die Verbindung von Musik und Poesie im Liede: Zu Robert Franz' 75. Geburtstage', *Bayreuther Blätter*, xiii (1890), 192–201. See also the special appendix devoted to Siegfried Wagner's fairy-tale opera *Der Bärenhäuter*, 'Bärenhäuter-Blätter', *Bayreuther Blätter*, xxii (1899).

20   Quoted by Hans von Wolzogen in 'Richard Wagner über die Bayreuther Blätter — Erinnerungen und Mahnungen aus sechs Jahren für das siebente', *Bayreuther Blätter*, vii (1884), 6.

21   *König Ludwig II. und Richard Wagner: Briefwechsel*, ed. Otto Strobel (Karlsruhe 1936–39), III, 97, letter of 21 Oct. 1876; translation in *Wagner: A Documentary Study* (note 9), 238.

22   See Wagner's announcement of the arrangements for the first Bayreuth Festival, *SS* XVI, 131–32; translation in *Wagner: A Documentary Study* (note 9), 219.

23   *ML* 659; English trans. 644.

24   Porges (note 18), I, 4–5; English trans. 2–3.

25   *Der Merker*, vii (1916), 36–37.

26   *Der Merker*, vii (1916), 309.

27   *Der Merker*, vi (1915), 435.

28   *Der Merker*, vii (1916), 308.

29   Albert Gutmann, *Aus dem Wiener Musikleben* (Vienna 1914), I, 121; he referred to Wagner's remarks becoming 'geflügelte Worte' (standard quotations). Their impact was also noted by Helm, *Der Merker*, vii (1916), 309.

30   *Der Merker*, vii (1916), 311.

31   *ML* 659 and 711; English trans. 644 and 694–95.

32   Helm, *Der Merker*, vii (1916), 440 and 767.

33   *Hugo Wolf: Musikalische Kritiken*, ed. Richard Batka and Heinrich Werner (Leipzig 1911), 172; translated by Henry Pleasants as *The Music Criticism of Hugo Wolf* (New York 1978), 132.

34   Helm, *Der Merker*, vii (1916), 646–47.

35   Heinrich Werner, *Hugo Wolf und der Wiener akademische Wagner-Verein* (Regensburg 1926), 9.

36   'Geschichte der selbständigen Wagner-Vereine: Wien', *Bayreuther Blätter*, i (1878), 141–42.

37   Wolzogen, 'Heutiges für Künftiges', *Bayreuther Blätter*, v (1882), 2–3.

38   See Gustav Schur, *Erinnerungen an Hugo Wolf*, ed. Heinrich Werner (Regensburg 1922), 14.

39   Helm, *Der Merker*, vii (1916), 647.

40   'Vereinsnachrichten: Wien', *Bayreuther Blätter*, viii (1885), 160 and 360.

41   Helm, *Der Merker*, vii (1916), 444.

42   See Wolf's report on one of the Vienna Wagner Society's concerts in *Musikalische Kritiken* (note 33), 127–30; English trans. 100–102.

43   Josef Schalk, 'Beiträge zur Charakteristik der Zeit: Lichtblicke aus der Zeitgenossenschaft — Anton Bruckner', *Bayreuther Blätter*, vii (1884), 329–34.

44   Helm, *Der Merker*, vii (1916), 766.

45   Werner (note 35), 9–10.

46   Carl Friedrich Glasenapp, 'Richard Wagner and the "Bayreuther Blaetter",' *The Meister*, i (1888), 13–14.

47   Friedrich Nietzsche, 'Richard Wagner in Bayreuth', *Kritische*

Studienausgabe, ed. Giorgio Colli and Mazzino Montinari (Munich 1988), I, 497; English trans. *Unmodern Observations*, ed. William Arrowsmith, trans. Gary Brown (New Haven/London 1990), 296.

48 See Walter Niemann, *Die Musik seit Richard Wagner* (Berlin 1913), 66.

49 Arthur Seidl, 'Hat Richard Wagner eine Schule hinterlassen?', *Deutsche Schriften für Litteratur*, ed. Eugen Wolff (Kiel/Leipzig 1892), series 2, part 3, p. 3.

50 See the 'literary advertisement' for Seidl's essay at the end of the October–November issue of the *Bayreuther Blätter*, xv (1892). Ernst Decsey (*Hugo Wolf* [Berlin/Leipzig 1904], III, 11) refers to the journal's 'Notizen' (see notes 58 and 59 below) as reviews, coming from Wolzogen himself.

51 Seidl (note 49), 30.

52 Schalk (note 43), 334.

53 See Thomas Leibnitz, 'Josef Schalk: Ein Wagnerianer zwischen Anton Bruckner und Hugo Wolf', *Bruckner-Jahrbuch* (Linz 1980), 124–25.

54 See Josef Schalk, 'Das Musikmachen in Wagner-Vereinen', *Neunzehnter Jahresbericht des Wiener Akademischen Wagnervereins für das Jahr 1891* (Vienna 1892), 21–22.

55 Ibid., 22.

56 See Schur (note 38), 14. According to Schur, Wolf's works were performed in thirty-six of the sixty-four concerts given by the Vienna Wagner Society from 1888 to 1902.

57 See Werner (note 35), 50 and Helm, *Der Merker*, viii (1917), 275.

58 See the 'musical advertisement' for Wolf's *Mörike Lieder* at the end of the December issue of the *Bayreuther Blätter*, xii (1889).

59 See the 'musical advertisement' for Wolf's *Goethe Lieder* at the end of the June issue of the *Bayreuther Blätter*, xiii (1890).

60 In a letter to Oskar Grohe of 26 Aug. 1896, Wolf said that Plüddemann had been greeted as a 'true Messiah' that year in Bayreuth (*Hugo Wolf:*

Briefe an Oskar Grohe, ed. Heinrich Werner [Berlin 1905], 239). To Hugo Faisst, in a letter of 23 April 1897, Wolf complained that Hans von Wolzogen now saw Hans Sommer's songs alone as the 'alpha and omega of modern lieder' (*Hugo Wolf: Briefe an Hugo Faisst* [Stuttgart 1904], 158). Plüddemann had written a *Gedächtnisfeier für Richard Wagner* and a ballad called *Walther von der Vogelweide*, while one of Sommer's songs was entitled *Tannhäuser*.

61 Arthur Seidl, *Moderner Geist in der deutschen Tonkunst* (Berlin 1901), 122–25.

62 Schur (note 38), 17.

63 References to partisan unrest are made in the *Siebzehnter Jahresbericht des Wiener Akademischen Wagnervereins für das Jahr 1889* (Vienna 1890), 8–9. The 'Neuer Wagner-Verein zu Wien' is announced in the *Achtzehnter Jahresbericht des Wiener Akademischen Wagnervereins für das Jahr 1890* (Vienna 1891), 5.

64 Schalk (note 54), 20–21. Schalk quoted from Wagner's *Eine Mitteilung an meine Freunde*, GS IV, 237; PW I, 276.

65 GS IV, 207–08 (*Oper und Drama*); PW II, 354.

66 SB IV, 460, letter to Liszt of 8 Sept. 1852; English trans. *Selected Letters of Richard Wagner* (note 9), 269.

67 Leibnitz (note 53), 125–26. Leibnitz reports in particular that Schalk and Ferdinand Löwe were always pressing Bruckner to make his orchestra sound more like Wagner's.

68 See Friedrich Eckstein, *Alte unnennbare Tage* (Vienna 1936), 180–81.

69 See Werner (note 35), 51–57.

70 *Hugo Wolf: Briefe an Emil Kauffmann*, ed. Edmund Hellmer (Berlin 1903), 114. In this edition some of the text of this letter of 24 Nov. 1893 has been deleted. The missing text is quoted by Werner (note 35), 86–87.

71 See Schur (note 38), 19.

72 Schalk (note 54), 22.

73 From a letter to Felix Mottl of 26 Feb. 1883, quoted in Frank Walker, _Hugo Wolf_ (London 1968), 139.

74 _Hugo Wolf: Briefe an Emil Kauffmann_ (note 70), 104, letter of 5 Aug. 1893.

75 See Max Graf, _Wagner-Probleme_ (Vienna 1900), 75 and 85–86.

76 See Schur (note 38), 18–19.

77 Eckstein (note 68), 180–81.

78 Ibid., 195–96.

79 See Heinrich Werner, 'Hugo Wolf und Richard Wagner', _Österreichische Rundschau_, 10 May 1906, p. 58.

80 Some of Wolf's questioning is revealed in his letters to the writer Rosa Mayreder, a convinced Nietzschean. Wolf persuaded her to attend a performance of _Parsifal_; but in a letter of 7 Sept. 1897 he said he sympathized with her conflict of feelings about the work and had fought hard to gain an objective view of 'the old Wagner' (_Hugo Wolf: Briefe an Rosa Mayreder_, ed. Heinrich Werner [Vienna 1921], 90–91).

81 Eckstein (note 68), 107–10 and 115.

82 Graf (note 75), 5–8.

83 Ibid., 71–74.

Chapter 8   Taking the Waters at Bayreuth

1 _ML_ 487; English trans. 475.

2 _ML_ 485; English trans. 473.

3 See Hans Peter Duerr, _Nacktheit und Scham: Der Mythos vom Zivilisationsprozeß_ (Frankfurt 1988).

4 Max Höfler, _Volksmedizin und Aberglaube in Oberbayerns Gegenwart und Vergangenheit_ (Munich 1888).

5 See Juvenal, _Satires_, VI, 522ff.

6 Prudentius, _Peristephanon_, X, 1111ff; I am grateful to Joseph Vogt for drawing this to my attention.

7 See W. Amelung, 'Zur Geschichte der Bäder- und Klimaheilkunde' in _Grundlagen der Kurortmedizin_, ed. Deutscher Bäderverband e.V. (Bonn 1987), 198.

8 Pindar, _Olympian Odes_, V, 1.

9 Figures from Johannes Steudel, 'Therapeutische und soziologische Funktion der Mineralbäder im 19. Jahrhundert' in _Der Arzt und der Kranke in der Gesellschaft des 19. Jahrhunderts_, ed. Walter Artelt and Walter Rüegg (Stuttgart 1967), 89.

10 _Balneologische Zeitung_, iv (1857), 334; quoted in Steudel (note 9), 96. Steudel believes the author to have been Ernst Kossak.

11 First published in 1813. All references to Kerner's _Wildbad im Königreich Württemberg_ are to Uwe Ziegler's edition (Bad Liebenzell 1985); I am grateful to Franz Groborz for drawing this to my attention.

12 Ibid., 73.

13 Quoted in Amelung (note 7), 197.

14 Quoted in Duerr (note 3), 114.

15 See Max Fehr, _Richard Wagners Schweizer Zeit_ (Aarau/Leipzig [1934]), I, 121.

16 Illustration in Hans Erismann, _Richard Wagner in Zürich_ (Zurich 1987), facing p. 167. The caption to this illustration represents one of the few attempts to draw a parallel between hydropathy and the water imagery in _Das Rheingold_.

17 _SB_ III, 308.

18 Wagner read _Wasser thuts freilich!_ (Zeitz 1839; translated by C. H. Mecker as _The Water-Cure, Applied to Every Known Disease: A Complete Demonstration of the Advantages of the Hydropathic System of Curing Diseases; showing, also, the Fallacy of the Medicinal Method_ [New York 1847]); _Ueber die gewöhnlichsten Missgriffe beim Gebrauch des Wassers als Heilmittel: Nebst einer Abhandlung über die Aufsaugung und Ablagerung der Gifte und Medikamente im lebenden animalischen Körper und einer Kritik der Kurmethode des Vincenz Priessnitz_ (Leipzig 1847; translated by Robert Baikie as _Outlines of a New Theory of Disease, Applied to Hydropathy: With Observations on the Errors Committed in the Practice of Hydropathy, Notes on the Cure of Cholera by Cold Water, and a Critique of Priessnitz's Mode of Treatment_ [London 1849]); and _Anleitung zur Ausübung der Wasserheilkunde für Jedermann, der zu_

lesen versteht (Leipzig 1850). See *SB* IV, 99, where the titles of Rausse's books are typically garbled.

19 Letter to Uhlig of 7–11 March 1852, *SB* IV, 309.

20 Letter to Uhlig of 9 Oct. 1850, *SB* III, 444.

21 Letter to Uhlig of 22 Oct. 1850, *SB* III, 461; translation from *Selected Letters of Richard Wagner*, trans. and ed. Stewart Spencer and Barry Millington (London 1987), 219; on the concept of death and destruction in Wagner's works, see Friedrich Kittler, 'Wagners Untergänge' in *Die Programmhefte der Bayreuther Festspiele 1987: III — 'Tristan und Isolde'*, 1–19; English trans. 67–76.

22 Preface to Richard Wagner, *Mein Denken* (Munich 1982), 11.

23 *SB* III, 457–62; translation from *Selected Letters of Richard Wagner* (note 21), 217–20.

24 *SB* III, 456.

25 *SB* III, 477.

26 *SB* III, 479. (Following the example of Jacob and Wilhelm Grimm, Wagner began to use roman script in December 1848, a practice he continued until the end of his life. His concomitant decision to spell all German nouns with lower-case initial letters was gradually abandoned, however. The correspondence of the early 1850s reflects a transitional phase, when he tended to use upper-case initials for emphasis.)

27 Letter to Uhlig of 20 Jan. 1851, *SB* III, 499.

28 *SB* IV, 99.

29 Letter to Uhlig of 8 Sept. 1851, *SB* IV, 101.

30 Letter to Minna Wagner of 21 Oct. 1851, *SB* IV, 142.

31 Letter to Uhlig of 11 Nov. 1851, *SB* IV, 171; translation from *Selected Letters of Richard Wagner* (note 21), 231.

32 *BB* 120; English trans. 101.

33 *ML* 488; English trans. 476.

34 See, for example, Wagner's letter to Jakob Sulzer of 15 Dec. 1851, *SB* IV, 224.

35 *ML* 486; English trans. 474.

36 See Ulrich Müller and Oswald Panagl (eds.), 'Literatur und Mythologie der Griechen in Richard Wagners "Ring"-Dichtung' in *Die Programmhefte der Bayreuther Festspiele 1990: III — 'Das Rheingold'*, 17–31; English trans. 45–59; *IV — 'Die Walküre'*, 13–18; English trans. 26–31; *V — 'Siegfried'*, 10–30; English trans. 39–63; *VI — 'Götterdämmerung'*, 26–35; English trans. 57–64.

37 *ML* 356; English trans. 342.

38 To what extent elements of mystery cults found their way into Aristotle's concept of catharsis or into the praxis of those performances which may derive from orgiastic mysteries is a complex philological question which is, however, of only limited interest here, not least because, as far as I am aware, there is no evidence that Wagner, adept though he was at making connections between otherwise unconnected concepts, studied mystery cults. This does not, of course, rule out indirect borrowings, as the concept of catharsis shows.

39 *SB* III, 362.

40 Ibid.

41 *ML* 487; English trans. 475.

42 See Jürgen Maehder, 'Studien zur Sprachvertonung in Richard Wagners "Ring des Nibelungen"' in *Die Programmhefte der Bayreuther Festspiele 1983: III — 'Die Walküre'*, 1–26; English trans. 71–94; *IV — 'Siegfried'*, 1–27; English trans. 59–84.

43 *SB* IV, 185; translation from *Selected Letters of Richard Wagner* (note 21), 236.

44 *ML* 487; English trans. 475.

45 *SB* IV, 186–87; translation from *Selected Letters of Richard Wagner* (note 21), 237.

46 *SB* IV, 188; English trans. 239.

47 See *ML* 511–12; English trans. 499; see also John Deathridge and Carl Dahlhaus, *The New Grove Wagner* (London 1984), 39–40; and (for a more cautious approach) Warren

Darcy, *'Creatio ex nihilo:* The Genesis, Structure, and Meaning of the *Rheingold* Prelude' in *19th Century Music*, xiii (1989), 79–100.

48 *SB* III, 404–05; translation from *Selected Letters of Richard Wagner* (note 21), 216–17.

49 *SB* IV, 175–6; translation from *Selected Letters of Richard Wagner* (note 21), 233–34.

50 See Udo Bermbach, 'Die Destruktion der Institutionen: Überlegungen zum politischen Gehalt von Richard Wagners "Der Ring des Nibelungen"' in *Die Programmhefte der Bayreuther Festspiele 1988: III — 'Die Walküre'*, 13–66; English trans. 122–46; also 'Wagner und Lukács' in *Die Programmhefte der Bayreuther Festspiele 1990: II — 'Lohengrin'*, 1–27; English trans. 41–62.

51 It is, perhaps, worth mentioning in passing the link between Klingsor and the cult of Cybele, with its reputed insistence on self-emasculation.

52 *GS* VI, 256.

53 The stage direction contains the words 'in sprachloser Erschütterung' (in speechless consternation) at this point; in the full score this has become 'in höchster Ergriffenheit' (deeply stirred).

54 Kerner (note 11), 73.

55 As Wagner called the orchestra pit in the Festspielhaus: *GS* IX, 337; *PW* V, 335.

Chapter 9   Wagner on Record

1 Ernest Newman, *The Life of Richard Wagner*, IV (New York 1946; repr. Cambridge 1976), 489–90.

2 Ibid., 692.

3 Samuel Lipman, 'New Life from Old Records', *Arguing for Music, Arguing for Culture* (Boston 1990), 290.

4 See, however, David Hamilton's stimulating discussion of the ways in which recorded performances *do* change, in 'The Furtwängler

Centenary Harvest: A "Mysterious Process" Explored', *Opus*, iii (August 1987), no. 5, pp. 24–29.

5 See Roland Graeme's surprisingly justified nostalgia for the Franz Konwitschny *Tannhäuser* in 'Two Recordings of *Tannhäuser*, Richard Wagner', *Opera Quarterly*, vii (Winter 1990–91), no. 4, p. 173.

6 For example, Conrad L. Osborne opined of Helen Traubel that 'at the time she was singing, she was the second-best Wagnerian soprano in the world, and that would be the situation today, too' (*High Fidelity* [February 1968], 105; repr. in *Records in Review, 1969 Edition* [New York 1969], 423). Osborne later solves his scarcely challenging riddle by identifying Kirsten Flagstad and Birgit Nilsson as Traubel's respective superiors.

7 The Deutsche Grammophon version conducted by Rafael Kubelík, with Gundula Janowitz, Gwyneth Jones, James King, Thomas Stewart, and Karl Ridderbusch in the leading roles.

8 First issued on Preiser, this non-commercial live recording, a Berlin performance of 1942, was conducted by Robert Heger and featured Maria Müller, Margarete Klose, Franz Völker, Jaroslav Prohaska, and Ludwig Hoffmann.

9 Conrad L. Osborne, 'Kubelik's *Lohengrin* — The Most Solid Yet Recorded', *High Fidelity* (December 1971), 79; repr. in *Records in Review, 1972 Edition* (New York 1972), 409–10.

10 I have been compiling a discography of acoustical vocal Wagner recordings for future publication. On the basis of the material I have assembled to date, it is safe to assert that more than 3,000 items fall into this category.

11 Not Ortlinde, as listed in Käte Neupert (ed.), 'Die Besetzung der Bayreuther Festspiele 1876–1960', *Internationale Wagner-Bibliographie, 1956–1960*, ed. Henrik Barth

12 Lehmann's complete published recordings have been issued twice on LP, most accessibly on Preiser CO 384/85. The Sieglinde excerpt also appeared (pitched incorrectly) on EMI-Electrola's *Sänger auf dem grünen Hügel* (1C 181-30 669/78 M), as well as in numerous other anthologies. The unique copy of the Liebestod can be found in the Historical Sound Recordings collection at Yale University, and is rumoured to be slated for transfer to CD before long.

13 Two of Brandt's recordings are available on CD (Symposium 1085); the remaining title, Schumann's 'Frühlingsnacht', was transferred to a 78 rpm disc (IRCC 225) which turns up far more frequently than do copies of the original issue!

14 The Berliner recordings do not date from 1902, as reported by Roberto Bauer, *The New Catalogue of Historical Records, 1898–1908/09* (London 1947), 473. In 1902 G&T reused catalogue numbers originally assigned by Berliner in 1900 to a series of Vienna recordings (among them the earliest Winkelmann titles). See Alan Kelly, John F. Perkins, and John Ward, 'Vienna — the First Gramophone Recordings', *Recorded Sound*, no. 69 (January 1978), 758–61. Although Winkelmann's G&T recordings were frequently reissued on 78s and on LP, to the best of my knowledge there was not a complete edition of them until their appearance, in fine transfers, on CD (Symposium 1081). Favorite 1-25077 ('Stets soll nur dir' from *Tannhäuser*) can be added to the list of Winkelmann recordings for that label which Bauer provides. There may possibly be more Winkelmann titles on Favorite.

15 Available most recently on *The Mapleson Cylinders, 1900–1904:*

Complete Edition, Rodgers and Hammerstein Archives of Recorded Sound R&H-100.

16 Also available in R&H-100. The IRCC issues (78 rpm: 100; LP: L-7006, L-7032) of a recording supposedly by von Hübbenet almost certainly represent a misattribution; see the discussion on p. 62 of the booklet included in R&H-100.

17 Winkelmann shares this attribute with other tenors centred in Vienna before and just after him, such as Gustav Walter and Willy Schüller; more recently, this trait could be found in the singing of Jess Thomas.

18 Brandt may, however, have attempted something of the sort, since she seemed too operatic to Wagner in Act I. See Newman (note 1), IV, 690–91.

19 P. G. Hurst, *The Golden Age Recorded* (London 1947), 91–2. In fact, Sucher could boast no direct connection to Wagner.

20 Michael Scott, *The Record of Singing to 1914* (New York 1977), 195. Similarly, in discussing the recorded legacy of the baritone Karl Scheidemantel, Scott writes that 'in Wolfram's "Als du in kühnem Sange" the style is noble, the phrasing shapely, and there survives — at least in intention — in the passage "War's Zauber, war es reine Macht" something of a real *legato*, an echo from that earlier era when the Master himself still reigned' (p. 206). Earlier in the book (pp. 17–18), Scott discusses Wagner's intentions and Bayreuth's perversion of them at greater length; another study based on the same assumption and pursuing similar tactics more diffusely is Jens Malte Fischer, 'Sprachgesang oder Belcanto? Wagners Sänger und die Bayreuther Schule. Ein Beitrag zur Geschichte der Gesangskunst', *Richard Wagner 1883–1983: Die Rezeption im 19. und 20. Jahrhundert. Gesammelte Beiträge des Salzburger Symposions*, ed. Ursula Müller (Stuttgart 1984), 475–90.

21 David Hamilton, 'Echoes from the Shrine', *Opera News*, xlvii (August 1982), no. 2, pp. 12–13.

22 Eduard Hanslick, 'Richard Wagner's Rienzi (Anhang: Niemann, der Wagner-Sänger)', *Die Moderne Oper. Kritiken und Studien* (Berlin 1900), 282–83.

23 W. J. Henderson, 'Flagstad and Other Great Isoldes', *The Art of Singing* (New York 1938), 491, 493. Note that Brandt was Brangäne in this performance—'not a perfect singer, but authoritative in interpretation', according to Henderson (p. 493).

24 *The Music Criticism of Hugo Wolf*, trans. and ed. Henry Pleasants (New York/London 1979), 91.

25 Ibid., 95.

26 Lilli Lehmann, *My Path through Life*, trans. Alice Benedict Seligman (New York/London 1914), 227.

27 Quoted in Robert Hartford (ed.), *Bayreuth: The Early Years* (London 1980), 68.

28 See Lehmann's comments in *My Path through Life* (note 26) on Amalie Materna (p. 228) and Wilma von Voggenhuber, Berlin's first Isolde in 1876 (p. 232), for the intimation that in those early days the 'text, language, style, and the kind of acting' were foreign to the singers, and that the challenge these largest roles represented was staggering. 'Now these three Brünnhildes have turned into flesh and blood, and, through habit and knowledge, have become child's play as compared with those days' (p. 228). Although in general Materna received praise, Julius Stockhausen, who (as has been mentioned) greatly admired Niemann as Siegmund at Bayreuth, did not concur that in the original *Ring* Materna sang well—'Materna, with her colossal figure and her strong, sharp voice, does not please' (Julia Wirth [ed.], *Julius Stockhausen: Der Sänger des deutschen Liedes nach Dokumenten seiner Zeit dargestellt* [Frankfurt am Main 1927], 409–10).

29 'Am Meer' has circulated widely in EMI's *The Record of Singing*, Volume 1 (RLS 724) and its reissue as *A Record of Singers*, Part 2 (RLS 7706), as well as in *Schubert Lieder on Record* (RLS 766). Brahms's 'Feldeinsamkeit' has appeared in the same company's *Schumann and Brahms Lieder on Record* (RLS 1547003), and the third of the singer's G&Ts, an aria from Thomas's *Mignon*, is presented along with the two lieder recordings on Symposium 1085, together with the Brandt recordings mentioned above and many other valuable German recordings. The unaccompanied *Lohengrin* excerpt and a ditty identified as 'O hör' mein Lied, geliebte Maid' by one 'Ed. Walter' were released in 1985 on a 7-inch, 45 rpm record issued by the Österreichische Akademie der Wissenschaften entitled *k. k. Hofopernsänger* (PHA EP 7).

30 The fullest account appears in Angelo Neumann, *Erinnerungen an Richard Wagner* (Berlin 1907), 154–55; translated by Edith Livermore as *Personal Recollections of Wagner* (London 1909), 148.

31 These present Mime's solos 'Zwangvolle Plage' and 'Das ist nun der Liebe schlimmer Lohn! . . . Als zullendes Kind', and a scene from Act I with Ernst Kraus as Siegfried on two sides (from Siegfried's 'Vieles lehrtest du, Mime' up to his '. . . wer Vater und Mutter mir sei!'), all recorded in 1912. Three years later, Lieban and Kraus recorded a scene from Act II (from Mime's 'Er sinnt und erwägt der Beute Wert' up to Siegfried's '. . . dazu durft' ich ihn schmieden'). Only the Act I scene has appeared on LP (an Ernst Kraus recital on Preiser CO 361).

32 See David Hamilton's open letter to Michael Scott in 'Reader-Author Interchange', *Opera Quarterly*, iv (Summer 1986), no. 2, pp. 206–07 for quotations of two separate assertions to this effect, as well as a thorough discussion of the improbabilities which surround them.

33 Gramophone 043196 (2295c), recorded in August 1911. This recording is included in *The Record of Singing*, Volume 2 (EMI RLS 743).
34 Pathé 15623, recorded in 1909 or 1910. To the best of my knowledge, this recording has not been reissued in any modern format.
35 Dietrich Mack (ed.), *Cosima Wagner: Das zweite Leben* (Munich 1980), 150–51.
36 Briesemeister is not named on the label, but the timbre and enunciatory style present in his solo recording made at the same sessions (a shortened account of 'Immer ist Undank Loges Lohn', available on Symposium 1081) are unmistakably characteristic of the Loge on Breuer's record. Alas, the dubbing of the Breuer/Briesemeister record on the same CD is a semitone sharp; to hear it at the correct pitch, consult EMI-Electrola 1C 181-30 669/78 M, *Sänger auf dem grünen Hügel*.
37 For a lengthy discussion of the Bayreuth style and its place amid the stylistic currents prevalent around the turn of the century, see David M. Breckbill, 'The Bayreuth Singing Style around 1900', Ph.D. diss., University of California at Berkeley, 1991.
38 Grammophon 65701 [B22123] (917as), 1921–22. This extraordinary recording has not, to the best of my knowledge, been reissued in a modern format.
39 See Frida Leider, *Playing My Part*, trans. Charles Osborne (London 1966), 57, for Leider's account of her successful attempt to forge this synthesis.

Chapter 10 Anton Seidl and America's Wagner Cult

1 'His eyes dimmed! His heart still! Not the fleeting stirring of breath. Must she now stand before you mourning?'
2 'Forever united'.
3 My account of Seidl's funeral incorporates information from various New York newspapers which copiously described the event.
4 James Huneker, quoted in Henry T. Finck (ed.), *Anton Seidl: A Memorial by His Friends* (New York 1899; repr. 1983), 116; 'another eulogist' is Edgar J. Levey, quoted on p. 88.
5 Ibid., 117.
6 The fullest documentation of artists and repertory for the Met's German seasons may be found in Gerald Fitzgerald (ed.), *Annals of the Metropolitan Opera* (Boston 1989).
7 Seidl's Coney Island repertory celebrated the Music of the Future. His 1895 season, for example, included 156 Wagner performances, 50 of Liszt, and 46 of Saint-Saëns, only 29 of Beethoven, 15 of Schumann, and 6 of Mozart. Compared to Europe, where such programming was unknown, the United States was less circumscribed by history and tradition. Seidl relished his freedom.
8 Highly relevant and suggestive is the hunger for intense emotional experience in Gilded Age America, analyzed in Jackson Lears, *No Place of Grace: Antimodernism and the Transformation of American Culture, 1880–1920* (New York 1981).
9 *The Musical Courier*, 22 June 1922.
10 Huneker quoted in Finck (note 4), 115; description of *Lohengrin* by Albert Steinberg, quoted on p. 106.
11 Ibid., 117.
12 Lehmann quoted in Finck (note 4), 243; Jean and Edouard de Reszke quoted on p. 259.
13 *The New York Evening Post*, 26 Feb. 1886.
14 *The Musical Courier*, 30 March 1898; Krehbiel quoted in Finck (note 4), 135–36.
15 *GS* VIII, 261–337; *PW* IV, 289–364. A more accessible translation of Wagner's essay is Edward Dannreuther's, published under the title of *Wagner on Conducting* (London 1887, repr. 1989).

16 Seidl's 'On Conducting' is reprinted in Finck (note 4), 215–40.

17 *GSV*, 161–63; PW III, 210–12. I by no means suggest that every Dutchman must follow Wagner's directions to the letter. But deviations, empathetic or deconstructive, should proceed from comprehension, not ignorance.

18 Seidl, 'On Conducting' (note 16), 218–19, 234.

19 Huneker quoted in Finck (note 4), 117; Herbert quoted on p. 125; Finck quoted on p. 162; Krehbiel quoted on p. 136; Finck quoted on p. 168.

20 Krehbiel quoted in Finck (note 4), 133.

21 Henry Krehbiel, *Chapters of Opera* (New York 1909, repr. 1980), 129.

22 Unidentified clipping in 'New York Scrapbooks', Music Research Division, Performing Arts Branch, New York Public Library.

23 Krehbiel (note 21), 170–71. To judge from reviews, audiences during the Met's German seasons were about half German. Both Krehbiel and Seidl favoured giving German operas in English in the United States.

24 Ibid., 172–73; the wreath inscription translates: 'Return again, intrepid singer'.

25 Ibid., 168.

26 *The New York Post*, 9 April 1859.

27 Unidentified clipping dated 13 Jan. 1890, 'New York Scrapbooks' (note 22).

28 To date the most notable accounts of America's Wagner cult as an aspect of genteel intellectual culture are Joseph Mussulman, *Music in the Cultured Generation* (Evanston, Ill., 1971), 142–68, and Anne Dzamba Sessa, 'At Wagner's Shrine: British and American Wagnerism', *Wagnerism in European Culture and Politics*, ed. David C. Large and William Weber (Ithaca/London 1984).

29 James Huneker, *Steeplejack* (New York 1920), II, 40–41. For more on New York's first response to Toscanini, see Joseph Horowitz, *Understanding Toscanini: How He Became an American Culture-God and Helped Create a New Audience for Old Music* (New York 1987, Minneapolis 1988), 54–69.

30 In Seidl's day, reverent Wagnerites subdued the gabble of fashionable boxholders. A decade later, the religious ambiance was gone. Here is Carl Burrian, Mahler's and Toscanini's distinguished New York Siegmund, Siegfried, and Tristan, writing in 1908: 'The Wagner performances are the least patronized by the public. The whole business apparently bores the audiences to death . . . There is a constant coming and going; the spectators greet one another, look around them and see who is there . . . The principal thing is the long intermission during which the gentlemen and ladies of society promenade about arm in arm to show their toilets and diamonds' (*The New York Sun*, 27 Dec. 1908).

31 Horowitz (note 29), 69–77.

32 *The New York Tribune*, 21 May 1911.

The Contributors

Mike Ashman studied at Magdalene College, Cambridge, 1968–72, and became a staff producer at Welsh National Opera (1979–84) and the Royal Opera House (1984–6). After making an impressive début with *Parsifal* for the WNO in 1983 (a performance prepared by Sir Reginald Goodall), he was responsible for a series of productions both at home and abroad, including *Der fliegende Holländer* (1986) and *Médée* (1989) at Covent Garden. He is currently working on a *Ring* cycle for Oslo Opera.

David Breckbill holds graduate degrees in musicology from the University of Iowa (MA, 1983) and the University of California at Berkeley (PhD, 1991). His work has centred on the identification, description, and tracing of historical performance styles in 19th-century music (especially Wagner and piano music). His PhD dissertation analyzed the singing style employed at Cosima Wagner's Bayreuth, and he is also preparing a comprehensive critical discography of acoustical vocal Wagner recordings.

Clive Brown was Lecturer in Music at The Queen's College, Oxford, 1981–9, and has conducted productions of rare operas, including the British premieres of Schubert's *Fierrabras* and Mendelssohn's *Camacho*. As a violinist he specializes in late eighteenth– and nineteenth–century repertory and advises several London period-instrument orchestras on playing style. He has designed concerts for the South Bank, Edinburgh Festival, and other venues, in some of which he has also been involved as a performer. His publications include a critical biography of Spohr and he is currently working on a book on Classical and Romantic performing practice.

Patrick Carnegy was on the editorial staff of the *Times Literary Supplement* before becoming Music Books Editor for Faber and Faber. In 1988 he was appointed Dramaturg of the Royal Opera House, the first person to hold such an appointment at that theatre. His publica-

tions include a book on Thomas Mann's *Doktor Faustus* and articles
for various periodicals. He is currently working on a historical study
of the design of Wagner's operas.

Christopher Fifield was a member of the music staff at Glyndebourne
for twelve years, returning to Britain, after a period abroad, to work
freelance. He is Music Director of the Lambeth Orchestra, North-
ampton Symphony Orchestra, Central Festival Opera, the Jubilate
Choir, and Artistic Director of the UK Wagner Society. From 1980 to
1990 he was Director of Music at University College London. He is
the author of the first biography of Max Bruch and has recently
completed the first of Hans Richter.

Amanda Glauert gained a first-class honours degree in Music at Clare
College, Cambridge, in 1977, staying on for postgraduate research
until she was appointed as a music lecturer at Trinity College, Dub-
lin, in 1981. In 1983 she moved to her present post as a lecturer at
Colchester Institute, where she is in charge of Music History and
Aesthetics. Her doctoral thesis '*Wagner of the Lied?' The Artistic Identity
of Hugo Wolf* was passed by London University in 1991. In addition to
writing on Wolf, Dr Glauert has published material on Beethoven
and Wagner and contributed a variety of articles to the *New Grove
Dictionary of Opera.*

Joseph Horowitz was a music critic for the *New York Times* from 1976
to 1980. Since 1981 he has been programme editor for the Kaufmann
Concert Hall of the 92nd Street Y, one of New York's major concert
halls. He also teaches at the Mannes College of Music, and has served
as Visiting Professor at the Institute for Studies in American Music at
Brooklyn College. His books include *Conversations with Arrau, Understanding Toscanini,* and *The Ivory Trade.*

Barry Millington, an acknowledged specialist in Wagner studies, has
written widely on music in many periodicals and newspapers including *The Times, The Observer* and *Opera* magazine. He is the author of
the Master Musicians volume *Wagner,* co-editor of *Selected Letters of
Richard Wagner* and editor of *The Wagner Compendium.*

Jean-Jacques Nattiez has been Professor of Musicology at the University of Montreal since 1972. His books include *Tétralogies, Proust as
Musician, Music and Discourse,* and *Wagner the androgyne.* In addition
to his work on semiology, he has published widely on the music and
writings of Pierre Boulez, while his interest in ethnomusicology has
resulted in a series of studies on Inuit music. He was awarded the
Dent Medal of the Royal Music Association in 1989 and the Molson
Prize in Human Sciences in 1990.

Desmond Shawe-Taylor worked before the Second World War as literary and occasional music critic for various journals, especially *The Spectator* and the *New Statesman*. From 1945 to 1958 he was music critic of the latter and in 1958 became music critic of *The Sunday Times* in succession to Ernest Newman, continuing in the post until 1983. From 1951 to 1973 he contributed to *The Gramophone* a quarterly survey of vocal recordings. He was guest critic of *The New Yorker*, 1973–4.

Stewart Spencer is a writer and translator, editor of *Wagner* magazine and co-editor of *Selected Letters of Richard Wagner*.

Matthias Theodor Vogt was, from 1986 to 1989, press officer of the Bayreuth Festival. Since then he has worked as a freelance director, producing *Rigoletto* at the Narodni Opera Russe and Alexander Knaifel's *Kentervilskoye Prividenie* at the Forum Theatre in Moscow. In 1986 he founded the Allan Pettersson Jahrbuch and has published widely on contemporary music theatre and twentieth-century music, in addition to undertaking many lecture tours in Europe and the Far East.

Index